# Computer Science, Technology and Applications

nova
science publishers
www.novapublishers.com

# Computer Science, Technology and Applications

**Internet of Everything: Smart Sensing Technologies**
T. Kavitha, V. Ajantha Devi, S. Neelavathy Pari
and Sakkaravarthi Ramanathan (Editors)
2022. ISBN: 978-1-68507-865-2 (Hardcover)
2022. ISBN: 978-1-68507-943-7 (eBook)

**A Beginner's Guide to Virtual Reality (VR) Modeling in Healthcare Applications with Blender**
Yuk Ming Tang, Ho Lun Ho, Ka Yin Chau, Yan Wan (Authors)
2022. ISBN: 978-1-68507-811-9 (Softcover)
2022. ISBN: 978-1-68507-945-1 (eBook)

**Applying an Advanced Information Search and Retrieval Model in Organisations: Research and Opportunities**
Maria del Carmen Cruz Gil (Author)
2022. ISBN: 978-1-68507-560-6 (Softcover)
2022. ISBN: 978-1-68507-914-7 (eBook)

**Neural Network Control of Vehicles: Modeling and Simulation**
Igor Astrov (Author)
2022. ISBN: 978-1-68507-757-0 (Hardcover)
2022. ISBN: 978-1-68507-916-1 (eBook)

**Frontiers in Quantum Computing: New Research**
R. Anandan, PhD (Editor)
2022. ISBN: 978-1-68507-816-4 (Hardcover)
2022. ISBN: 978-1-68507-900-0 (eBook)

More information about this series can be found at
https://novapublishers.com/product-category/series/computer-science-technology-and-applications/

**Vasile-Florian Păiș**
Editor

# Speech Recognition Technology and Applications

nova
science publishers
www.novapublishers.com

https://doi.org/10.52305/BKWM8996



## NOTICE TO THE READER



**Library of Congress Cataloging-in-Publication Data**

ISBN: 978-1-68507-929-1

*Published by Nova Science Publishers, Inc. † New York*

# Contents

# Preface

Speech represents the most natural means of communication between humans. By using Automatic Speech Recognition (ASR) and Text-to-Speech (TTS) systems, machines also become able to interact with humans using speech. This technology was made increasingly popular by voice enabled search agents, such as Amazon Alexa, Google, Apple's Siri, and Microsoft Cortana. Furthermore, speech recognition technology can be found in many other applications, including phone voice dialing, voice commands for robots or other equipment, voice controlled home automation, speech-based chatbots, and voice-based information retrieval. In this book we explore modern ASR approaches and applications such as speech-enabled dialogue. Example implementations are given for the Romanian language, which is considered a low-resourced language in regard to speech resources.

Chapter 1 explores several ASR implementations, such as CMUSphinx, DeepSpeech 1 and 2, and Kaldi. Furthermore, it introduces preprocessing and augmentation methods employed to build a robust ASR system when limited training data are available. In addition, language-specific enhancements to the envisaged systems are presented, such as adaptation of the used alphabet to include Romanian diacritics. Finally, the results from each system are given and a comparison between systems is performed, while also considering previously published results.

Chapter 2 is dedicated to a state-of-the-art approach for building ASR systems based on a pre-trained multilingual Wav2Vec2 model. The results indicate a very good performance when applied to a small Romanian speech corpus, surpassing previously reported results using a DeepSpeech 2 variant. Furthermore, this chapter presents the integration of an ASR system into the RELATE platform, dedicated to processing the Romanian language. Integration is performed by first exposing the ASR functionality as a web service which is then invoked from within the platform. This approach can be adapted to any other ASR system, regardless of the language used.

Chapter 3 analyses the performance implications of an ASR component over an entire voice-enabled dialogue system. For exemplification, the authors consider a system resulting from the ROBIN project, based on micro-worlds and intended to be deployed on the Pepper robot. In their analysis, the authors consider both the quality of the transcriptions and the processing time required.

Chapter 4 focuses on the application of ASR technology in the medical domain. Automated digital scribes make use of ASR and other natural language processing techniques to automatically transcribe patient-clinician conversations and medical notes. The authors note that in medical conversations, different linguistic phenomena are present, such as disfluencies, nonlexical pauses, repeated words, restarted sentences, lack of clear juncture for phrases, and complex medical terminology.

Chapter 5 presents punctuation restoration mechanisms and gives an example implementation for the Romanian language. This is particularly important since the vast majority of ASR systems produce transcripts in lower case form and without any punctuation marks. Nevertheless, the proper use of capital letters and punctuation marks influences the way human readers understand text documents. Recent research further emphasizes the importance of punctuation by showing that deaf or hard-of-hearing subjects perceive a larger improvement when punctuation is added compared to regular readers, without hearing difficulties. Apart from human perception, punctuation is also important when performing automated text analysis on the resulting documents.

Chapter 6 addresses applications of linguistic linked data for speech processing. Recent initiatives have worked towards converting several Romanian resources, useful for speech applications, to linked data formats. This allows for unified querying and easy resource exploitation in new ways. The resources are described and several usage scenarios are presented. Among these applications, concept-based retrieval of speech files is considered, by combining the WordNet with the RoLEX lexicon and the RTASC speech corpus.

Chapter 7 concerns the final component of a speech-based machine interaction system, the TTS component. Apart from their use in interactive systems, TTS modules are sometimes used for data augmentation when training ASR systems, particularly in low resource scenarios. The authors provide an introduction to deep neural models for speech synthesis, such as Tacotron 2, Transformer-TTS, FastSpeech 2 and WaveNet. Furthermore, a new male voice dataset, useful for both synthesis and recognition, is introduced. Finally, experiments are performed using both existing resources and the new dataset.

Each book chapter contains introductory descriptions and references to state-of-the-art technologies for speech recognition systems and applications.

Even though experiments are performed using the Romanian language, specific adaptations are described and thus the experiments can be easily replicated in other languages as well. Furthermore, considering the reduced number of speech resources available for Romanian, the authors focused on approaches generally useful in low-resource scenarios.

In: Speech Recognition Technology ... ISBN: 978-1-68507-929-1
Editor: Vasile-Florian Păiş 

Chapter 1

# Building an Automatic Speech Recognition System for a Low-Resource Language

**Dan Ungureanu*** **and Mihai Dascalu**
Computer Science Department,
University Politehnica of Bucharest,
Bucharest, Romania

### Abstract

Many spoken human-computer interactions start with an automatic speech recognition (ASR) system meant to transcribe the user voice and pass it to a natural language processor or to a command module. There are several known solutions built on various technologies, ranging from Hidden Markov Models to complex Deep Neural Networks or hybrid architectures that mix two or more known methods. A common element across all models consists of the large number of transcribed and aligned text fragments required for training. As such, a problem emerges for low-resource languages, where limited training data are available. For example, one such language is Romanian, where all public datasets put together barely surpass 300 hours of recorded utterances, in contrast to a minimum norm of at least 1,000 hours. Our chapter introduces preprocessing and augmentation methods employed to build a robust ASR when limited training data are available. We consider the

*Corresponding Author's Email: dan@ungureanu.me.

best-known open-source ASR projects, namely, CMUSphinx, DeepSpeech, and Kaldi, each being representative of its underlying techniques, as well as audio augmentation before and after feature extraction. This study is a continuation of our previous work, and our best configuration achieves a WER of 3.10%, which is low enough for real-world situations and comparable with models trained on languages where considerably more resources are available, such as English.

**Keywords:** natural language processing, automatic speech recognition, Romanian language, speech augmentation

# 1. Introduction

Spoken human-computer interactions have become a more common way of interaction with surrounding devices, ranging from phones and computers to watches and other home appliances; this process has become possible thanks to recent advancements in domains such as Automatic Speech Recognition (ASR), Natural Language Processing (NLP), and Speech Synthesis. Automatic Speech Recognition, also known as speech-to-text, facilitates interactions by allowing computers to transcribe the users voice into text that can be later processed by the other components of the system, such as a natural language processor.

The process of recognizing words and sentences is a trivial task for a human, but it is a major challenge for computers to recognize and understand verbal communication. This has been a long-standing problem, and over time, various solutions have been proposed, but only in recent years more reliable and accurate solutions have been built. The complexity of the problem stems from several aspects, as people do more than listen to a sequence of spoken words but also consider contextual information and augment previous life experiences and perceptions of the surrounding world. However, part of these aspects is difficult next to impossible to automate and thus cannot serve as inputs to computer systems. This specific issue is not directly related to Automatic Speech Recognition and is a general one related to Natural Language Processing.

## 1.1. Romanian as a Low-Resource Language

Datasets are integral parts of artificial intelligence and machine learning. Major advances in this field resulted from advances in neural network architectures and computer hardware but also thanks to the increasing availability of data. In the recent past, datasets became of higher quality and of larger volumes. For example, datasets of hundreds of hours of labeled speech are now usual. However, high-quality training datasets are difficult and expensive to produce because of the amount of time required to obtain and label the data. To a certain extent, it is possible to make use of unlabeled or lower-quality data through unsupervised learning, but thus far, none of these approaches work better than supervised methods.

Training data shortages have also been one of the biggest limitations in training accurate speech-to-text models for the Romanian language. Romanian is spoken by approximately 22-26 million people, being far from a popular language. The total duration of all available resources is approximately 300 hours, out of which only approximately half can be considered high-quality. As a comparison, much more popular languages such as English, Russian (Asinovsky et al., 2009), or Chinese[1] have over 1,000 hours of available recordings with annotations.

At present, there are various efforts to crowd-source recordings, such as Mozilla Common Voice[2] or Echo[3] the crowdsourcing platform developed by us, but the generated amount of data is still insufficient. Mozilla has a goal of 1,200 hours, but only approximately 1% of the goal has been achieved so far for Romanian.

The end goal of this research is to train an Automatic Speech Recognition model for the Romanian language. However, there are several byproducts that can prove to be useful in other speech-related domains.

In contrast to our previous work (Ungureanu et al., 2021), in this chapter, we have described our models and corresponding methods in more depth while also improving the automated grapheme-to-phoneme model.

The following section describes the two main architectures for automatic speech recognition systems (Hidden Markov Models and neural networks), as well as the hybrid architecture between the two of them. The

[1]MAGICDATA Mandarin Chinese Read Speech Corpus. https://www.openslr.org/68/
[2]https://commonvoice.mozilla.org
[3]https://echo.readerbench.com

Method section describes the corpora used for training and evaluating the models, the grapheme-to-phoneme conversion process, and methods for increasing the volume of training data through data augmentation, together with projects and configuration parameters. Afterwards, we present the results, discussions, conclusions and future work.

# 2. State-of-the-Art Architectures

Two primary architectures for automatic speech recognition systems exist: a) manual handcrafted pipelines consisting of modules for pre-, post-processing, and recognizing speech and b) newer approaches grounded in neural network architectures as integrated end-to-end pipelines. The first method is the traditional approach, which divides the problem of speech recognition into subproblems that are each solved using several algorithms. Optimizing the system and increasing its accuracy and performance implies tweaking each of its components. The main disadvantage of this solution is its complexity; moreover, this greedy approach leads to a local optimum instead of a global optimum. On the other hand, newer approaches use single deep neural networks with many layers, which can handle inputs and outputs of arbitrary length. For example, recurrent neural networks can take advantage of spatial coherence, which makes them a good fit for audio and speech processing. These later models remove the need for complex pipelines but require significantly more data.

## 2.1. HMM-GMM Based Architectures

Hidden Markov Models (HMMs; Rabiner and Juang (1986)) are probabilistic models that can be used for multiple machine learning tasks. HMMs learn about a system by observing another system whose outcomes are influenced by the outcomes of the first unobservable system (with unobservable or hidden states). HMMs are a class of models that predict a sequence of unknown variables from a set of observed variables, which makes them a good fit for wide-range applications with a temporal pattern, including speech analysis. In the case of automatic speech recognition, HMMs are acoustic models that tie acoustic features and phonemes. For every possible phoneme, the distribution of features is modeled with Gaussian Mixture Models. The acoustic model, together with a pronunciation lexicon and a language model, can infer sequences of words from audio recordings.

A common way of extracting acoustic features is from a cepstral representation of the audio recording, known as Mel-Frequency Cepstral Coefficients (MFCC) (Mermelstein, 1976). The pronunciation lexicon is used to describe the entire set of phonemes and to map a word to a sequence of phonemes. Finally, the language model is used to determine the probability of a sequence of words and improves predictions.

CMUSphinx (Lamere et al., 2003) is one of the best known open-source projects that contain multiple speech recognition systems and tools built using Hidden Markov Models.

## 2.2. Deep Neural Networks Architectures

Current state-of-the-art systems are almost exclusively built using Deep Neural Networks. These systems leverage end-to-end architectures to replace traditional processing pipelines that have inefficient components with very complex implementations. Various neural networks have been explored, ranging from simple recurrent neural networks to long short-term memory and attention mechanisms, mixing supervised and unsupervised training for both speech recognition and language modeling. Some of the most renowned projects are based on transformers, such as (Wang et al., 2020), or convolution-augmented transformers, such as (Gulati et al., 2020).

One of the most renowned solutions that argued for the advantages of neural networks is DeepSpeech, a project employing recurrent neural networks to produce text from audio recordings (Hannun et al., 2014).

## 2.3. Hybrid Architectures

Another less common but efficient architecture consists of hybrid architectures. These models combine two or more components from the previous types, often Hidden Markov Models and deep neural networks, to take advantage of the qualities of each system. The former is usually used for bootstrapping the latter, or one model may be included in the internals of the other.

Kaldi is a well-known open-source toolkit for speech recognition that contains the necessary components for building speech recognition systems, including examples and documentation of complete pipelines. In Kaldi, deep neural networks are used to provide posterior probability estimates for the states of the HMM (Veselý et al., 2013).

## 2.4. Language Models

Language modeling refers to the use of statistical models to determine the probability of a sequence of words. In other words, language modeling is the task of predicting what word comes next in a sequence of words or a sentence. These models are trained on large text corpora and are often used in NLP applications, such as text generation or automatic speech recognition. The language model is an essential part of speech recognition, as it is used to restrict word search in the decoding stage. There are two directions of research in terms of language models integrated in speech-to-text pipelines: bag-of-words/N-gram or deep neural models.

N-gram models consider a bag-of-words approach that can store spatial information. These are the simplest language models whose complexity increases only with N, the number of words (or units) in a stored sequence; however, their performance is limited by their intrinsic lack of complexity.

In recent years, the advent of neural networks ensured major advancements in NLP; language modeling also benefited from this. First, recurrent neural networks with long short-term memory (LSTM) or gated recurrent units (GRU) achieved state of the art results for many text tasks. More recently, architectures like Generative Pre-trained Transformer (GPT) (Radford and Narasimhan, 2018) and Bidirectional Encoder Representations from Transformers (BERT) (Devlin et al., 2019) have become ubiquitous baselines in NLP experiments. One of the advantages of using GPT and BERT-based language models for automatically correcting the outputs of automatic speech recognition systems is that prior work already exists (Zheng et al., 2021), including the possibility to perform automated text corrections for Romanian (Cotet et al., 2020).

Another approach to language modeling relies on gated convolutional networks (Dauphin et al., 2017). The primary advantage of such networks is that, unlike their recurrent counterparts, they are more efficient by enabling parallelization over sequential tokens. This architecture reduces the latency of the scoring process for a sentence by an order of magnitude, when compared to a recurrent baseline.

# 3. Method

In this section, we describe our research method, including the corpora used, the split between training and evaluation datasets, how we perform grapheme-to-phoneme translation using a transformer-based model, language models, data augmentation methods and implementations of speech-to-text models.

## 3.1. Corpora

There are several corpora available for Romanian speech, all of them summing up to approximately 300 hours. Out of all these datasets, we selected a subset (see Table 1) that has diverse characteristics, ranging from little to some background noise, with recordings of good quality, where the speakers voice is clear and the transcripts match the recordings.

We selected the SWARA Corpus (Stan et al., 2017) dataset as our clean dataset, which contains little to no background noise, with the highest quality of all datasets recorded in a professional studio. For evaluation, we sampled 20% of the SWARA dataset, in addition to the two dedicated SSC evaluation partitions. All remaining entries from SWARA together with the other datasets were then combined into a single aggregated dataset.

**Table 1. Datasets in our experiments**

| Corpus | Duration (hours) | Recordings | Speakers | Word Count | Unique Word Count |
|---|---|---|---|---|---|
| Integrated Dataset | 29 | 17,646 | 3,372 | 257,449 | 34,999 |
| Read-Speech Corpus | 99 | 136,120 | 164 | 574,562 | 18,485 |
| RoDigits Speech Corpus | 37 | 15,389 | 154 | 184,668 | 10 |
| cdep-eval | 5 | 296 | N/A | 34,333 | 7,084 |
| SSC-eval1 | 3.5 | 3,035 | N/A | 36,409 | 8,922 |
| SSC-eval2 | 1.5 | 100 | N/A | 13,908 | 4,371 |
| SWARA Corpus | 21 | 19,292 | 17 | 201,296 | 6,102 |
| Total (Aggregated Dataset) | 196 | 191,878 | 3,686+ | 1,302,625 | 54,149 |

The Integrated Dataset is a collection of various datasets organized by Ungureanu et al. (2021). Read-Speech Corpus (Georgescu et al., 2020) is a large speech corpus collected by the Speech and Dialogue Research Laboratory recorded under different conditions. The RoDigits Speech Corpus (Georgescu et al., 2018) is a similar corpus but contains only recordings of read digits. Spontaneous Speech Corpus evaluation sets and Chamber Of Deputies Speech Corpus evaluation sets (Georgescu et al., 2021) were exclusively used for evaluation purposes. Finally, the SWARA Corpus (Stan et al., 2017) is a large parallel Romanian read speech dataset recorded by various speakers in a professional recording studio.

### 3.2. Automatic Grapheme-to-Phoneme Conversion

An important requirement of HMM-GMM-based architectures is a method to translate words into their phonetic representation; as such, either a predefined dictionary or a grapheme-to-phoneme model to automatically extract the phonemes can be used. For example, the NaviRo dictionary[4] (Domokos et al., 2012) contains 138,500 unique words. We corrected misspellings and standardized phoneme names, while words with missing characters (for example, -, q, x and w) were added.

This issue of missing phonetic transcriptions was resolved by using a sequence-to-sequence grapheme-to-phoneme transformer model (Yolchuyeva et al., 2019) that was adapted to our needs and trained on the extended NaviRo dictionary. A list of words was compiled from the training data, whereas the words missing from the dictionary were automatically transformed to their phonetic representation with the previous model.

### 3.3. Language Models

In our experiments, we trained multiple language models using all available transcripts. These have been used to compile a 5-gram model using KenLM (Heafield, 2011) (for DeepSpeech 1 and 2) and SRILM (Stolcke, 2002) (for Kaldi and CMUSphinx).

### 3.4. Data Augmentation

Training machine learning models require parameter tuning for a particular task, and state-of-the-art systems often have millions of parameters that

[4]https://users.utcluj.ro/ jdomokos/naviro

are adjusted continuously until reaching a high accuracy. The volume of data required for achieving good performance without overfitting is often proportional to the number of parameters, which, in turn, is dependent on the complexity of the problem.

Data augmentation is a technique employed to increase the amount of existing data by adding modified copies. There are numerous alternatives, for example, modifying existing data or generating new synthetic data and performing augmentation before preprocessing training data (offline augmentation) or before training (online augmentation).

The basic augmentation method for speech recognition systems consists of modifying the audio recording directly by adding noise, shifting time, adjusting pitch, or speed. Another augmentation method for speech recognition systems is SpecAugment (Park et al., 2019), which is applied directly to the feature inputs of a neural network and consists of warping or masking blocks of frequency channels or time steps.

## 3.5. Speech-to-Text Architectures for Romanian

### 3.5.1. CMUSphinx

CMUSphinx (Lamere et al., 2003) is one of the oldest and well-known speech recognition systems implementing HMM-GMM-based speech recognition architectures (see Figure 1). SphinxTrain[5] provides support for training three types of acoustic models: continuous, semicontinuous, and phonetic-tied. Configuration files are automatically generated to train and evaluate these models. Across our experiments, the default system parameters remained unchanged.

CMUSphinx is a stable, well-maintained project with a streamlined training process that consists of several stages: a) splitting data between train and test datasets, b) generating ".fileids" and ".transcripts" files, c) building grapheme-to-phoneme dictionaries for each word in the training dataset, and d) training a language model. ".fileids" and ".transcription" files contain one row for each input recording, and the lines from ".fileids" and ".transcripts" are direct correspondents. ".fileids" files contain the name of each recording and must be equal to the filename of the recording without the extension.".transcription" files have one line for each recording

[5]https://github.com/cmusphinx/sphinxtrain

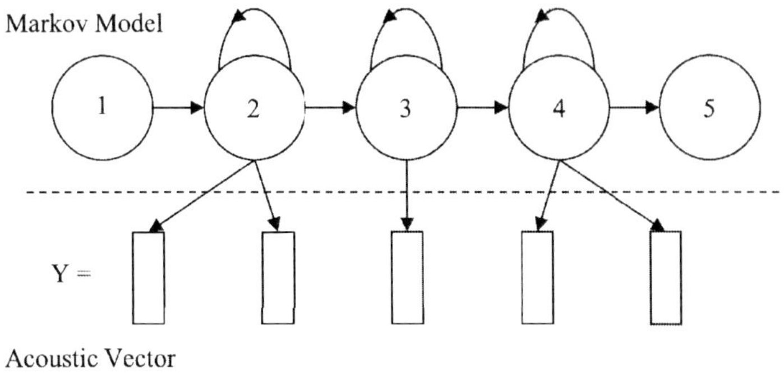


Figure 1. Generic Hidden Markov Model architecture.

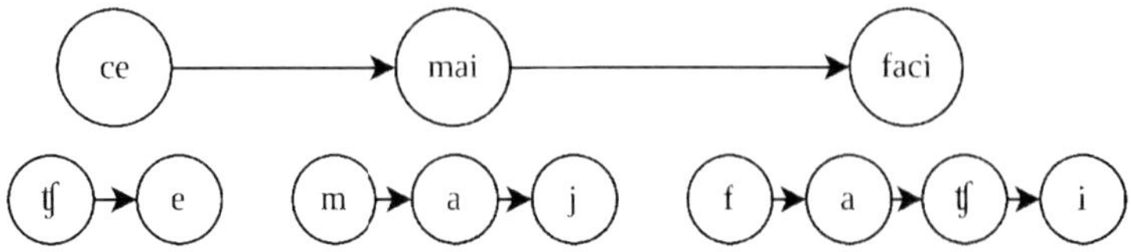


Figure 2. Decomposition of words into phonemes.

in the format "<s>transcript</s>(name)", where "transcript" is the actual text that can be heard in the recording and its name matches the one in ".fileids".

The grapheme-to-phoneme dictionary is essential to building Hidden Markov Models, as the phonemes describe the states of the model (see Figure 2). Each word in the training input is transformed into phonemes, and the resulting sequence of phonemes is used in training the acoustic model.

### 3.5.2. DeepSpeech

DeepSpeech introduces several new concepts and is one of the best-known solutions implementing deep neural networks. DeepSpeech performs well even in real-life situations, with noisy environments or speaker variations (Hannun et al., 2014).

The model (see Figure 3) consists of 5 hidden layers that are composed of Rectified Linear Unit (ReLU) cells (Nair and Hinton, 2010). For each

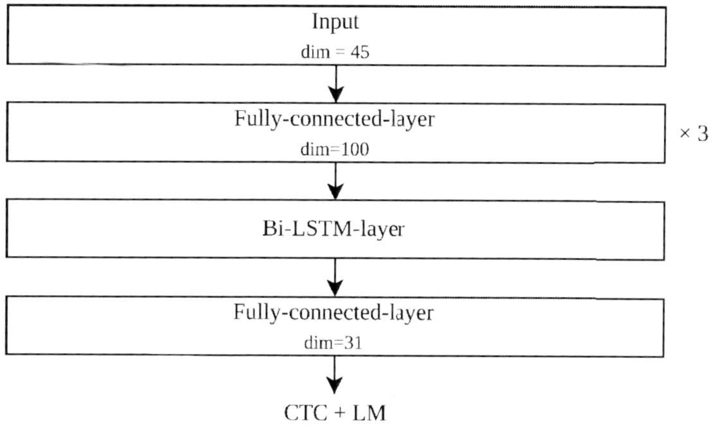


Figure 3. DeepSpeech 1 Model Architecture.

step, the first layer operates on the corresponding MFCC frame, together with a context of 9 frames on each side. The first three layers are fully connected and use independent inputs for each time frame. The fourth layer is a recurrent layer made up of LSTM cells (Hochreiter and Schmidhuber, 1997) that model long-term dependencies. The output layer uses the SoftMax function to compute the character probabilities for each time step. After computing the probability distribution, the error in prediction is measured with the Connectionist Temporal Classification (CTC) decoder (Hannun et al., 2014).

### 3.5.3. DeepSpeech 2

DeepSpeech 1 and 2 are at their core very similar, using a recurrent neural network and having speech spectrograms as inputs and text transcripts as outputs. However, a more complex model was necessary for the system to be trained on large corpora. DeepSpeech 2 (see Figure 4) is a deeper model, alongside several optimizations that reduced training and evaluation times, which achieved a reduction of the word error rate (WER) from 3.77% down to 3.1% and was usable in production.

The most important optimizations applied include a) batch normalization increasing the number of hidden layers, b) SortaGrad (Amodei et al., 2016) sorting minibatches of inputs, c) the usage of Gated Recurrent Units

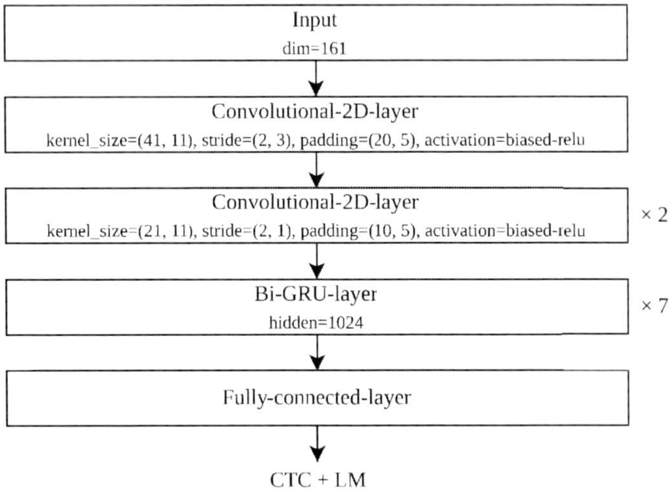


Figure 4. DeepSpeech 2 Model Architecture.

(Cho et al., 2014) instead of Long Short-Term Memory units, and d) a better language model trained on a larger text corpus.

The most important prerequisite for training a DeepSpeech model consists of a large amount of labeled speech data. The language model is another important prerequisite that can significantly impact the performance of the system. Other than these, DeepSpeech has no other prerequisite, such as HMM models, where data require proper alignment or a grapheme-to-phoneme dictionary.

Language-specific setups included updating the alphabet with diacritics for the Romanian language (, , , , ), as well as creating the previously described custom language model. Experiments were performed in multiple configurations to find the optimal hyperparameters: batch size, learning rate, and number of hidden units per layer; default values for the other hyperparameters were used.

### 3.5.4. Kaldi

A Kaldi recipe combines and streamlines the processes of data preparation, training, and evaluation. A Kaldi recipe consists of multiple stages, each of them being a prerequisite of the next one. Some of the most important stages of such a Kaldi recipe represent the training of the Markov Models and of the neural network-based model. Our Kaldi recipe started from the recipe for the Wall Street Journal corpus (Paul and Baker, 1992) present in the official Kaldi repository[6], while most hyperparameters have the default values found in the example scripts.

The first step in training any Kaldi model (Povey et al., 2011) extracts acoustic features from input recordings by computing the Mel Frequency Cepstral Coefficients (MFCC), followed by the Cepstral Mean and Variance Normalization (CMVN) technique. As such, the first trained component is a basic, context-independent monophone system. The second system uses the first one for aligning training data and is a more complex, triphone context-dependent system trained using first (delta) and second derivates (delta-delta) features. The third component enhances the input training data by expanding it with Linear Discriminant Analysis (LDA) and a diagonalizing transformation known as Maximum Likelihood Linear Transform (MLLT). Fourth, a Hidden Markov Model is built on the third model, and features are transformed one more time using a feature space maximum likelihood linear regression (fMLLR), which is known to be a Speaker Adaptive Training (SAT).

The last model trained is a Time Delay Neural Network Factorization (TDNN-F) with 12 layers, and the complete architecture is presented in Figure 5. Mel-Frequency Cepstral Coefficients and the identity vectors (also known as iVectors) representative of speaker characteristics are the inputs. The MFCC are extracted from segments of 25 ms with a stride of 10 ms. The derivates are added to the MFCC and then processed by twelve layers of time-delay neural networks (Peddinti et al., 2015).

The network from Figure 5 contains both neural network layers and other utility layers. One such layer is the "IDCT-layer" which outputs the inverse discrete cosine transform (IDCT) of the input array. In the context of this network, the layer returns the inverse discrete cosine transform of the Mel-frequency cepstrum coefficients, thus outputting filterbank Mel energies, suitable as inputs for the following convolutional layers.

Time Delay Neural Network (TDDN) can classify patterns with shift invariance and learn context at each layer of the network. This type of network has the advantage that it does not require explicit segmentation

[6]https://github.com/kaldi-asr/kaldi/tree/master/egs/wsj

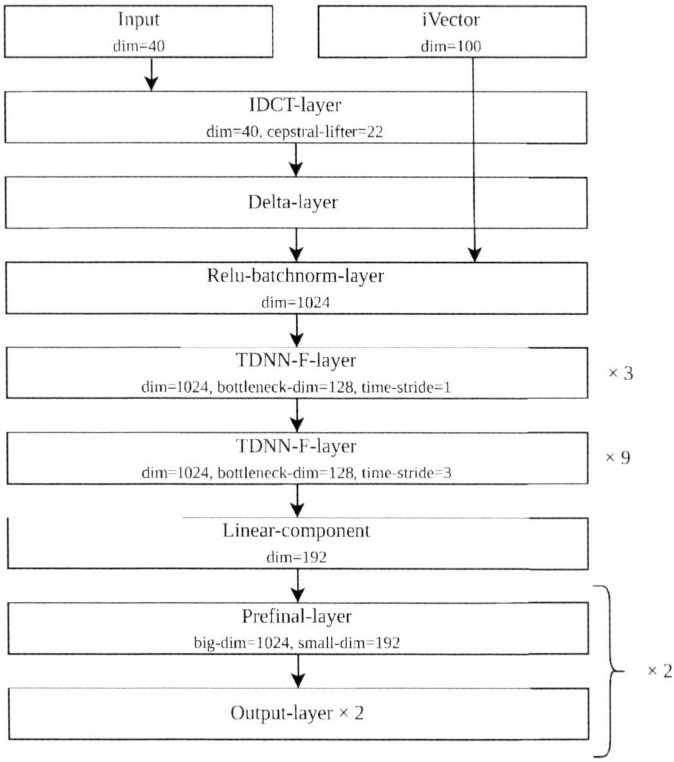


Figure 5. Kaldi DNN Model Architecture.

prior to classification. For each of the more advanced models, the amount of data and its complexity increases; for example, the monophone model was trained using only approximately 20 hours of the aggregated dataset.

In contrast to the previous systems, Kaldi has the most complex training process, as it requires training several HMMs and a Deep Neural Network. Each dataset must consist of the audio recording files and manifest files: wav.scp includes recording names and preprocessing step, text includes recordings names and transcripts, utt2spk associates recording names with speaker names, and last spk2gender associates genders to speakers. The scripts provided by Kaldi (Povey et al., 2011) were used to split the dataset into smaller datasets, extract features from the input files, and generate the SRILM language model.

### 3.6. Replicable Experiments with Containerization

Containerization was considered to perform a fair comparison of all employed architectures and to ensure ease of deployment in production. Essentially, each training environment consisted of a common database (training and evaluation data), tools to transform the data and solution-specific tools. All containers can be provided upon request for research purposes.

## 4. Results

### 4.1. CMUSphinx

The best results for English language [7] on CMUSphinx are 19.4% WER (continuous model) and 30.3% WER (phonetically tied model) when trained on a subset of LibriSpeech (Panayotov et al., 2015) consisting of 100 hours of clean speech.

Table 2 presents the performance of the continuous, semicontinuous, and phonetic-tied models trained on both clean and other datasets for the Romanian language. The best WER for the Romanian language was 3.6% and was obtained on the clean dataset for the phonetically tied model. However, the same performance could not be replicated for the aggregated dataset that is closer to the real world, which scored 23.17%, essentially almost one of four words being misrecognized.

**Table 2. Results for CMUSphinx models**

| | Clean Dataset (SWARA) | Aggregated Dataset |
|---|---|---|
| Continuous | 3.8% | 23.17% |
| Semicontinuous | 3.7% | N/A |
| Phonetically tied | 3.6% | 25.09% |

### 4.2. DeepSpeech

In terms of results, the best accuracy for English (16% WER) in the initial experiments was obtained after training the engine on the Switchboard

[7]https://abuccts.blogspot.com/2017/08/gsoc-2017-with-cmusphinx-post-11.html

dataset (Godfrey et al., 1992), which consists of 300 hours of labeled speech data (Hannun et al., 2014). The second version of DeepSpeech achieved 12.73% WER (Amodei et al., 2016) on LibriSpeech. The most remarkable result, which leverages deep neural networks, was achieved by CAPIO (Han et al., 2018), a model leveraging densely connected LSTMs, which achieved a 7.64% WER on the same dataset.

A DeepSpeech 1 Romanian model was trained by (Panaite et al., 2019) and obtained a 39% WER when trained on SWARA dataset. DeepSpeech 2 Romanian model was trained by (Avram et al., 2020) on a dataset of 230 hours and obtained a 9.9% WER. For our experiments (see Table 3), the best obtained WER was 11.39%, which was for the first version of the model. We did not train a DeepSpeech 2 model on the aggregated dataset because the neural network failed to train due to mislabeled data the loss did not decrease during the training process and the neural network failed to generalize.

**Table 3. Results for DeepSpeech 1 and 2**

| | Clean Dataset (SWARA) | Aggregated Dataset |
|---|---:|---:|
| DeepSpeech 1 | 12.80% | 11.39% |
| DeepSpeech 2 | 17.55% | N/A |

## 4.3. Kaldi

For the Switchboard dataset, the best result obtained with this architecture was 18.6% WER (Veselý et al., 2013). The best result for a hybrid architecture combining HMMs and DNNs (Lüscher et al., 2019) is a 5.0% WER on the LibriSpeech dataset. Among the most recently published results for Kaldi in the Romanian language, Georgescu et al. (2020) trained on RSC and obtained a 3.27% WER, while (Georgescu et al., 2019) obtained a 2.79% WER.

In the context of our experiments, we observed a steady improvement in each successive model, the most accurate being the Neural Network one which obtained word error rates of 2.73% and 3.77% on the clean dataset and the aggregated dataset, respectively.

**Table 4. Results for Kaldi's models**

| Configuration | Clean Dataset (SWARA) | Aggregated Dataset |
|---|---|---|
| Monophone | 12.54% | 22.42% |
| Triphone | 8.43% | 13.58% |
| LDA + MLLT | 8.38% | 12.13% |
| LDA + MLLT + SAT | 4.94% | 6.46% |
| Neural Network | 2.73% | 3.77% |

Long sentences made up of several phrases are frequently encountered in real-world situations, often with short pauses in-between. We decided to evaluate the best Kaldi configuration capabilities of decoding such long recordings and extracted the cdep evaluation dataset from the integral evaluation dataset. The recordings from this dataset are one minute long, and the average word count per recording is 115. The system scored a WER of 8.44%. suggesting that long recordings are more difficult to decode; however, a WER below 10% also makes it usable on such recordings.

## 4.4. Data Augmentation and SpecAugment

Starting from the Kaldi hybrid model, the most promising architecture thus far, we experimented with multiple data augmentation techniques. Offline techniques, such as adding noise or speeding up the recordings, brough insignificant improvements in WER. We noticed that the system could learn the synthetic noise added to the recordings; thus, the model learned from the same amount of data ignoring the added noise, making augmentation ineffective; the same was noticed while training DeepSpeech models.

The technique that succeeded in decreasing from 3.77% down to 3.10%, is SpecAugment. It was implemented as a Kaldi layer in the neural network and inserted before the layer that computes and appends the delta features.

# 5. Discussion

## 5.1. CMUSphinx

Previous research[8] shows that continuous models have a lower WER, between 10.9% and 11.1%, than phonetically tied models. In this situation, it is surprising that the continuous model performs better than the phonetically tied model on the clean dataset; however, the improvement is insignificant (3.8% vs 3.6%).

An unsurprising result is the difference between the clean and aggregated datasets. We obtained good results when training on the clean dataset due to clear recordings, with perfect annotations and no background noise. However, HMM-based models did not generalize well and were considerably less accurate in real-world situations; a large portion of the aggregated dataset consists of such recordings.

## 5.2. DeepSpeech

In comparison with the previously trained system, DeepSpeech scored far more consistent results and managed to have a good WER even on the aggregated dataset, being approximately 3 times more accurate. This strengthens our previous observation that neural networks generalize and learn even from noisy data. Our experiments with DeepSpeech 2 did not provide any results due to its sensitivity to bad data. We also observed that DeepSpeech 1 offers better results when trained with a smaller amount of data, probably due to its simpler internal structure.

## 5.3. Kaldi

The Kaldi results for Hidden Markov Models (monophone, triphone and LDA + MLLT + SAT) resemble the results of CMUSphinx, thus denoting that WER is a limitation of Hidden Markov Models rather than due to the model architecture or the underlying implementation. In contrast, the Neural Network Model implementation from Kaldi offered far better results than the DeepSpeech architectures. We believe that the alignment of preprocessing steps that use previously trained models makes the model more resilient to noisy or mislabeled data.

---

[8] https://abuccts.blogspot.com/2017/08/gsoc-2017-with-cmusphinx-post-11.html

## Conclusion and Future Work

In this chapter, we presented and evaluated three of the most popular architectures of automatic speech recognition tailored for the Romanian language. We built an automatic grapheme-to-phoneme converter, trained language models, and compiled a diverse Romanian speech corpus. Along the process, we emphasized the replicability of the experiments and built an experimental infrastructure and tools to ensure a fair comparison.

The best result of all systems obtained a WER of 3.1% on the test set, which is comparable to the 5.8% WER humans have for English language (Amodei et al., 2016). Assuming that the word error rates are constant between languages, our trained model could be used in real-world situations.

One aspect difficult to replicate in experiments is the real-world factor. This can be simulated to a certain extent using recordings from humans having a casual conversation (e.g., talking over the phone); nevertheless, the current training and evaluation data are not diverse enough. This is visible as models seem to be better handling contexts like the ones on which they were trained. In our experiments, this difference is visible between the results on the clean dataset and the aggregated dataset. Nevertheless, humans observe and consider contextual information, which improves their perception and makes it less influenceable due to differences in the environment.

Between older architectures based on Hidden Markov Models and newer neural network-based approaches, we found the latter architectures to be simpler, have a simpler tuning process and be capable of inferring information from the entire training dataset. Based on our observations, we think that end-to-end approaches are more suitable for future research. Hidden Markov Models excel when the training data are scarce or for fulfilling prerequisites such as alignment, enabling hybrid architectures to score the best.

All trained models described in this chapter are accessible through a web interface[9] where users can upload voice recordings and automatically transform them to text.

The largest constraint in building more accurate Romanian speech-to-text models is the insufficient training data that is currently available. Romanian is far from being a popular language, and the total resources are

[9]https://readerbench.com/stt

not enough for building robust deep neural networks. Nevertheless, newer models are becoming better with the current amount of data, and the situation improves when considering unsupervised learning algorithms.

In addition, we foresee several future research directions in the domain of Automatic Speech Recognition tailored for Romanian language. The first one is to leverage new deep learning architectures, such as Transformers (Vaswani et al., 2017), that have changed the NLP landscape for most tasks centered on text analysis. Second, we consider using unsupervised, semi-supervised or self-supervised algorithms for considering additional unlabeled or potentially mislabeled data. Third, there is room for improvement on post-corrections. To a certain extent, language models represent a post-correction that selects the most probable word among a set of words with similar pronunciations. We can further expand to automatically capitalize names, proper nouns, or adding punctuation, using any of the methods described by Păiș and Tufiș (2021). For example, Bidirectional Encoder Representations from Transformers (BERT) can solve all tasks at once with a token classification head for each task (e.g., one classification head for punctuation, one for capitalization).

## Acknowledgment

This work was supported by a grant of the Ministry of Research, Innovation and Digitization, CNCS/CCCDI - UEFISCDI, project number PN-III-P2-2.1-SOL-2021-2-0223, within PNCDI III.

## References

Amodei, D., Ananthanarayanan, S., Anubhai, R., Bai, J., Battenberg, E., Case, C., Casper, J., Catanzaro, B., Cheng, Q., Chen, G., Chen, J., Chen, J., Chen, Z., Chrzanowski, M., Coates, A., Diamos, G., Ding, K., Du, N., Elsen, E., Engel, J., Fang, W., Fan, L., Fougner, C., Gao, L., Gong, C., Hannun, A., Han, T., Johannes, L., Jiang, B., Ju, C., Jun, B., LeGresley, P., Lin, L., Liu, J., Liu, Y., Li, W., Li, X., Ma, D., Narang, S., Ng, A., Ozair, S., Peng, Y., Prenger, R., Qian, S., Quan, Z., Raiman, J., Rao, V., Satheesh, S., Seetapun, D., Sengupta, S., Srinet, K., Sriram, A., Tang, H., Tang, L., Wang, C., Wang, J., Wang, K., Wang, Y., Wang, Z., Wang,

Z., Wu, S., Wei, L., Xiao, B., Xie, W., Xie, Y., Yogatama, D., Yuan, B., Zhan, J., and Zhu, Z. (2016). Deep speech 2 : End-to-end speech recognition in english and mandarin. In Balcan, M. F. and Weinberger, K. Q., editors, *Proceedings of The 33rd International Conference on Machine Learning*, volume 48 of *Proceedings of Machine Learning Research*, pages 173–182, New York, New York, USA. PMLR.

Asinovsky, A., Bogdanova, N., Rusakova, M., Ryko, A., Stepanova, S., and Sherstinova, T. (2009). The ORD speech corpus of Russian everyday communication "one speaker's day": Creation principles and annotation. In Matoušek, V. and Mautner, P., editors, *Text, Speech and Dialogue*, pages 250–257, Berlin, Heidelberg. Springer Berlin Heidelberg.

Avram, A.-M., Păiș, V., and Tufiș, D. (2020). Towards a Romanian end-to-end automatic speech recognition based on DeepSpeech2. In *Proc. Rom. Acad. Ser. A*, volume 21, pages 395–402.

Cho, K., van Merriënboer, B., Gulcehre, C., Bahdanau, D., Bougares, F., Schwenk, H., and Bengio, Y. (2014). Learning phrase representations using RNN encoder–decoder for statistical machine translation. In *Proceedings of the 2014 Conference on Empirical Methods in Natural Language Processing (EMNLP)*, pages 1724–1734, Doha, Qatar. Association for Computational Linguistics.

Cotet, T.-M., Ruseti, S., and Dascalu, M. (2020). Neural grammatical error correction for Romanian. In *2020 IEEE 32nd International Conference on Tools with Artificial Intelligence (ICTAI)*, pages 625–631.

Dauphin, Y. N., Fan, A., Auli, M., and Grangier, D. (2017). Language modeling with gated convolutional networks. In *Proceedings of the 34th International Conference on Machine Learning - Volume 70*, ICML'17, page 933941. JMLR.org.

Devlin, J., Chang, M.-W., Lee, K., and Toutanova, K. (2019). BERT: Pre-training of deep bidirectional transformers for language understanding. In *Proceedings of the 2019 Conference of the North American Chapter of the Association for Computational Linguistics: Human Language Technologies, Volume 1 (Long and Short Papers)*, pages 4171–4186, Minneapolis, Minnesota. Association for Computational Linguistics.

Domokos, J., Buza, O., and Toderean, G. (2012). 100k+ words, machine-readable, pronunciation dictionary for the Romanian language. In *2012 Proceedings of the 20th European Signal Processing Conference (EUSIPCO)*, pages 320–324.

Georgescu, A., Caranica, A., Cucu, H., and Burileanu, C. (2018). RoDigits - a Romanian connected-digits speech corpus for automatic speech and speaker recognition. *UPB Scientific Bulletin, Series C: Electrical Engineering and Computer Science*, 80:45–62.

Georgescu, A.-L., Cucu, H., and Burileanu, C. (2019). Kaldi-based DNN architectures for speech recognition in Romanian. In *2019 International Conference on Speech Technology and Human-Computer Dialogue (SpeD)*, pages 1–6.

Georgescu, A.-L., Cucu, H., and Burileanu, C. (2021). Improvements of SpeeD's Romanian asr system during reterom project. In *2021 International Conference on Speech Technology and Human-Computer Dialogue (SpeD)*, pages 177–182.

Georgescu, A.-L., Cucu, H., Buzo, A., and Burileanu, C. (2020). RSC: A Romanian read speech corpus for automatic speech recognition. In *Proceedings of the 12th Language Resources and Evaluation Conference*, pages 6606–6612, Marseille, France. European Language Resources Association.

Godfrey, J., Holliman, E., and McDaniel, J. (1992). SWITCHBOARD: telephone speech corpus for research and development. In *Proceedings ICASSP-92: 1992 IEEE International Conference on Acoustics, Speech, and Signal Processing*, volume 1, pages 517–520 vol.1.

Gulati, A., Qin, J., Chiu, C.-C., Parmar, N., Zhang, Y., Yu, J., Han, W., Wang, S., Zhang, Z., Wu, Y., and Pang, R. (2020). Conformer: Convolution-augmented Transformer for Speech Recognition. In *Proc. Interspeech 2020*, pages 5036–5040.

Han, K. J., Chandrashekaran, A., Kim, J., and Lane, I. (2018). The capio 2017 conversational speech recognition system.

Hannun, A., Case, C., Casper, J., Catanzaro, B., Diamos, G., Elsen, E., Prenger, R., Satheesh, S., Sengupta, S., Coates, A., and Ng, A. Y. (2014). *Deep speech: Scaling up end-to-end speech recognition.*

Heafield, K. (2011). KenLM: Faster and smaller language model queries. In *Proceedings of the Sixth Workshop on Statistical Machine Translation*, pages 187–197, Edinburgh, Scotland. Association for Computational Linguistics.

Hochreiter, S. and Schmidhuber, J. (1997). Long short-term memory. *Neural Comput.*, 9(8):1735–1780.

Lamere, P., Kwok, P., Walker, W., Gouvêa, E. B., Singh, R., Raj, B., and Wolf, P. (2003). Design of the CMU sphinx-4 decoder. In *INTERSPEECH*. ISCA.

Lüscher, C., Beck, E., Irie, K., Kitza, M., Michel, W., Zeyer, A., Schlüter, R., and Ney, H. (2019). RWTH ASR Systems for LibriSpeech: Hybrid vs Attention. In *Proc. Interspeech 2019*, pages 231–235.

Mermelstein, P. (1976). Distance measures for speech recognition, psychological and instrumental. *Pattern Recognition and Artificial Intelligence*, pages 374–388.

Nair, V. and Hinton, G. E. (2010). Rectified linear units improve restricted Boltzmann machines. In *Proceedings of the 27th International Conference on International Conference on Machine Learning*, ICML'10, page 807814, Madison, WI, USA. Omnipress.

Panaite, M., Ruseti, S., Dascalu, M., and Trausan-Matu, S. (2019). Towards a deep speech model for Romanian language. In *2019 22nd International Conference on Control Systems and Computer Science (CSCS)*, pages 416–419.

Panayotov, V., Chen, G., Povey, D., and Khudanpur, S. (2015). Librispeech: An asr corpus based on public domain audio books. In *2015 IEEE International Conference on Acoustics, Speech and Signal Processing (ICASSP)*, pages 5206–5210.

Park, D. S., Chan, W., Zhang, Y., Chiu, C.-C., Zoph, B., Cubuk, E. D., and Le, Q. V. (2019). SpecAugment: A Simple Data Augmentation Method for Automatic Speech Recognition. In *Proc. Interspeech 2019*, pages 2613–2617.

Paul, D. B. and Baker, J. (1992). The design for the Wall Street journal-based CSR corpus. In *Speech and Natural Language: Proceedings of a Workshop Held at Harriman, New York*, February 23-26, 1992.

Peddinti, V., Povey, D., and Khudanpur, S. (2015). A time delay neural network architecture for efficient modeling of long temporal contexts. In *Proc. Interspeech 2015*, pages 3214–3218.

Povey, D., Ghoshal, A., Boulianne, G., Burget, L., Glembek, O., Goel, N., Hannemann, M., Motlicek, P., Qian, Y., Schwarz, P., Silovsky, J., Stemmer, G., and Vesely, K. (2011). The Kaldi speech recognition toolkit. IEEE Signal Processing Society. IEEE Catalog No.: CFP11SRW-USB.

Păiș, V. and Tufiș, D. (2021). Capitalization and punctuation restoration: a survey. *Artificial Intelligence Review*.

Rabiner, L. and Juang, B. (1986). An introduction to hidden markov models. *IEEE ASSP Magazine*, 3(1):4–16.

Radford, A. and Narasimhan, K. (2018). Improving language understanding by generative pre-training.

Stan, A., Dinescu, F., Tiple, C., Meza, S., Orza, B., Chirila, M., and Giurgiu, M. (2017). The SWARA Speech Corpus: A Large Parallel Romanian Read Speech Dataset. In *Proceedings of the 9th Conference on Speech Technology and Human-Computer Dialogue (SpeD)*, Bucharest, Romania.

Stolcke, A. (2002). SRILM - an extensible language modeling toolkit. In Hansen, J. H. L. and Pellom, B. L., editors, *7th International Conference on Spoken Language Processing, ICSLP2002 - INTERSPEECH 2002*, Denver, Colorado, USA, September 16-20, 2002. ISCA.

Ungureanu, D., Badeanu, M., Marica, G.-C., Dascalu, M., and Tufiș, D. (2021). Establishing a baseline of Romanian speech-to-text models. In *2021 International Conference on Speech Technology and Human-Computer Dialogue (SpeD)*, pages 132–138. IEEE.

Vaswani, A., Shazeer, N., Parmar, N., Uszkoreit, J., Jones, L., Gomez, A. N., Kaiser, L. u., and Polosukhin, I. (2017). Attention is all you need. In Guyon, I., Luxburg, U. V., Bengio, S., Wallach, H., Fergus, R., Vishwanathan, S., and Garnett, R., editors, *Advances in Neural Information Processing Systems*, volume 30. Curran Associates, Inc.

Veselý, K., Ghoshal, A., Burget, L., and Povey, D. (2013). Sequence-discriminative training of deep neural networks. In *Proc. Interspeech 2013*, pages 2345–2349.

Wang, Y., Mohamed, A., Le, D., Liu, C., Xiao, A., Mahadeokar, J., Huang, H., Tjandra, A., Zhang, X., Zhang, F., Fuegen, C., Zweig, G., and Seltzer, M. L. (2020). Transformer-based acoustic modeling for hybrid speech recognition. *ICASSP 2020 - 2020 IEEE International Conference on Acoustics, Speech and Signal Processing (ICASSP)*, pages 6874–6878.

Yolchuyeva, S., Németh, G., and Gyires-Tóth, B. (2019). Transformer Based Grapheme-to-Phoneme Conversion. In *Proc. Interspeech 2019*, pages 2095–2099.

Zheng, X., Zhang, C., and Woodland, P. C. (2021). *Adapting GPT, GPT-2 and BERT language models for speech recognition.*

In: Speech Recognition Technology ... ISBN: 978-1-68507-929-1
Editor: Vasile-Florian Păiş 

**Chapter 2**

# Self-Supervised Pre-Training in Speech Recognition Systems

**Andrei-Marius Avram***, **Vasile-Florian Păiş and Dan Tufiş**
Research Institute for Artificial Intelligence
"Mihai Drgnescu", Romanian Academy, Bucharest, Romania

**Abstract**

Supervised learning is a bottleneck for developing more powerful machine learning systems due to the massive amounts of labeled data required to train high-performance models. Self-supervised learning is one of the most common approaches used to mitigate this problem by first training models on large amounts of unlabeled data with artificially created objectives and then transferring the acquired knowledge on a downstream task. This methodology has obtained exceptional results in natural language processing with architectures such as BERT, but it has been struggling to achieve the same performance in domains like computer vision or speech processing because, in comparison with the former, the two operate in a much higher dimensionality. This issue has been recently mitigated by using self-supervised learning on a contrastive objective, allowing such models to be pre-trained on highly dimensional data. Concretely, in automatic speech recognition, Wav2Vec2, a model that was pre-trained on more than 50k hours of audio, managed to obtain competitive performance while using as little as 10 minutes

*Corresponding Author's Email: andrei.avram@racai.ro.

of transcribed speech for fine-tuning in English. These results have led us to investigate the capabilities of this model on the Romanian language and fine-tune several Wav2Vec2 variants on the recently released ROBIN Technical Acquisition Speech Corpus. Our results showed that Wav2Vec2 significantly improved the word error rates obtained by the original DeepSpeech2 baselines, with the best variant boosting the performance by more than three times. Furthermore, the best Wav2Vec2 variant was also intergrated into the RELATE platform and its functionality exposed in the form of a webservice.

**Keywords:** self-supervised learning, automatic speech recognition, contrastive learning, Romanian

# 1. Introduction

Automatic speech recognition (ASR) stands at the forefront of digitalization and is one of the technologies that enables a more natural interaction between humans and computers. With the recent rise of deep learning (LeCun et al., 2015), its performance has greatly improved algorithms, and certain neural network architectures have been able to outperform human level on several speech recognition benchmarks (Amodei et al., 2016; Schneider et al., 2019). However, to attain these results, a large dataset of transcribed audio is usually required, which might be hard to obtain, especially for low-resource languages. In addition, learning only from labeled data is not how humans acquire language. Infants gain knowledge of the specific language by listening to adults around them, a process that allows them to create for themselves good speech representations for themselves.

Unsupervised methods propose a solution to this issue by first training a model on unlabeled data such as plain audio and then transferring the acquired knowledge to a downstream task. Self-supervised methods are a subdomain of unsupervised learning that assign artificially created labels to the samples in a dataset and trains a model on them in a supervised fashion. Masking certain parts of the data samples and making the model predict them, is one of the most common ways of producing pseudolabels and it has been applied with great success in pre-training Transformer-based (Vaswani et al., 2017) models for natural language processing (NLP) (Devlin et al., 2019; Liu et al., 2019). Auto-regressive objectives where a model must learn to predict a future step given the previous context have also been successfully applied in various domains including NLP (Radford et al., 2019; Brown et al., 2020), computer vision (van den Oord et al., 2016) and speech processing (Schneider et al., 2019).

However, although it has been successfully applied in NLP, directly applying masked self-supervised learning to high dimensional data such as audio or images is problematic due to the large number of possibilities that can fit in a masked area. This issue is usually solved by using contrastive learning where, instead of recreating the masked area in the input, a model must generate a hidden representation of the masked area that contains similar samples close to each other and dissimilar samples far from each other. Wav2Vec2 (Baevski et al., 2020) is a model that combines both self-supervised and contrastive learning to produce hidden representation directly from raw audio inputs, obtaining competitive results with as little as 5 minutes of transcribed speech, as the authors mention.

The success of this model made us investigate the performance of several multilingual variations in the Romanian language using the recently released ROBIN Technical Acquisition Speech Corpus (RTASC) (Păiș et al., 2021) as reference. Our results showed that the model significantly outperformed the DeepSpeech2 (Amodei et al., 2016) baselines introduced in the paper, with the best Wav2Vec2 variant improving the word error rate (WER) more than three times and the character error rate (CER) more than twice. In addition, our experiments showed that the size of the model and the proportion of Romanian language in the pre-training corpus plays a critical role in the final accuracy when fine-tuning on RTASC.

In recent years, several models have been proposed as solutions to Romanian speech recognition, including DeepSpeech (Ungureanu et al., 2021), DeepSpeech2 (Avram et al., 2020) and Kaldi (Georgescu et al., 2019; Ungureanu et al., 2021), all of which offer competitive results on various benchmarks and configurations. The publicly available training and evaluation corpora for the Romanian language have also increased with the introduction of datasets such as RTASC, Romanian Digits (RoDigits) (Georgescu et al., 2018), Romanian Speech Corpus (RSC) (Georgescu et al., 2020), SWARA (Stan et al., 2017), or the Romanian parts of Common Voice (Ardila et al., 2020) and VoxPopuli (Wang et al., 2021).

The rest of the chapter is organised as follows. Section 2 presents an in-depth review of contrastive representation learning objectives, together with several key ingredients that are necessary to obtain good and generalizable embeddings. Section 3 outlines the architectural design of two models that were pre-trained on audio data with self-supervision. Section 4 presents a comparison with non-pretrained models, the dataset used for this comparison and the experimental setup. Finally, the work is concluded in the last section, offering also several possibilities for future wofrk.

## 2. Contrastive Representation Learning

Contrastive representation learning is an optimization technique that creates an embedding space where samples that are similar must be positioned close to each other, while dissimilar samples must be positioned far apart. Due to its simplicity and open-endedness, it has become a prominent method in both supervised and unsupervised deep learning, tackling various tasks in speech processing, computer vision or NLP.

### 2.1. Training Objectives

The first contrastive training objective was proposed by Chopra et al. (2005) and it was used to model a function $f_\theta$ with parameters $\theta$ such that it encodes samples $x_i$ with the same class labels into similar vectors and samples from different classes into vectors that are extremely unalike. It takes as input a pair of samples $(x_i, x_j)$, each with its own labels $y_i$ and $y_j$, and tries to minimize the distance between their embeddings when the labels are equal or maximize the distance otherwise. Mathematically, the contrastive loss $\mathcal{L}_{contrast}$ was defined as:

$$\mathcal{L}_{contrast}(x_i, x_j|\theta) = \begin{cases} \xi_{ij} & y_i = y_j \\ \max(0, \epsilon - \xi_{ij}) & y_i \neq y_j \end{cases} \tag{1}$$

where $\xi_{ij}$ is the Euclidean distance between the embeddings defined as $||f_\theta(x_i) - f_\theta(x_J)||_2)^2$, and $\epsilon$ is a lower bound that controls the maximum possible distance between the embeddings.

The *triplet loss* (Schroff et al., 2015) is another contrastive training objective that was first used for face recognition and then in other speech recognition related tasks such as speaker diarization (Bredin, 2017) or speech emotion detection (Huang et al., 2018). It takes an input a triplet

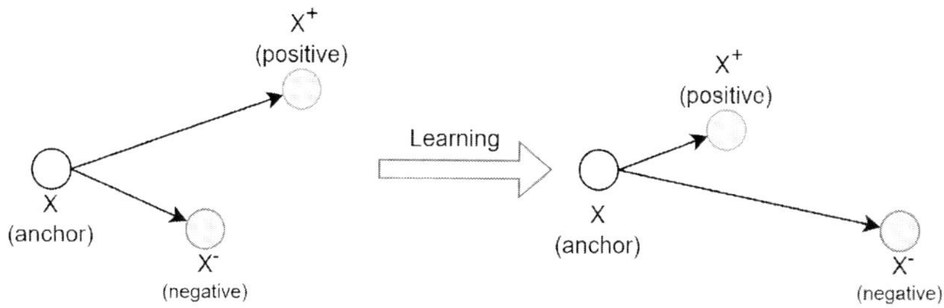


Figure 1. Triplet loss with one anchor, one positive sample and one negative sample.

$(x, x^+, x^-)$ where $x$ is an anchor sample, $x^+$ is a positive sample belonging to the same class and $x^-$ is a negative sample that comes from a different class. Similar to the classical contrastive loss, the triplet loss tries to minimize at the same time the distance between the anchor and the positive sample, and maximize the distance between the anchor and the negative sample (see Figure 1). Using the same function $f_\theta$ that is learned by the model, the triplet loss $\mathcal{L}_{triplet}$ is expressed as:

$$\mathcal{L}_{triplet}(x, x^+, x^-) = \max(0, \xi_+ - \xi_- + \epsilon) \tag{2}$$

where $\xi_+$ and $\xi_-$ are the Euclidean distances between the anchor and the positive sample, and between the anchor and the negative sample, respectively, and $\epsilon$ is a hyperparameter that sets the minimum distance between the positive sample and the negative sample.

The *lifted structured loss* (Oh Song et al., 2016) utilizes both the contrastive loss and the triplet loss by averaging over all the possible losses resulting from combining the samples within one batch. Thus, given a batch of samples $x$ that contains a set of positive samples $\mathcal{P}$ and a set of negative samples $\mathcal{N}$, the lifted structured loss $\mathcal{L}_{struct}$ is computed as:

$$\mathcal{L}_{struct} = \frac{1}{2|\mathcal{P}|} \sum_{(i,j)\in\mathcal{P}} \max(0, \xi_{ij} + \max(\max_{(i,k)\in\mathcal{N}} \epsilon - \xi_{ik}, \max_{(j,l)\in\mathcal{N}} \epsilon - \xi_{jl})) \tag{3}$$

where $\epsilon$ is a hyperparameter that plays the same role as in the classical contrastive loss - limits the maximum distance between samples. It is important to note that the second maximum in the equation is used to identify the nearest negative sample for either of the positive samples in the batch,a technique that has been shown to improve the quality of the embeddings (Robinson et al., 2020). However, because the function is not smooth, the discrete version $\mathcal{L}_{negative}^{ij}$ usually has convergence issues and is usually relaxed as:

$$\mathcal{L}_{negative}^{ij} = \log(\sum_{(i,k)\in\mathcal{N}} e^{\epsilon-\xi_{ik}} + \sum_{(j,l)\in\mathcal{N}} e^{\epsilon-\xi_{jl}}) \tag{4}$$

Another generalization of the triplet loss is the *multi-class N-pair loss* that uses several negative samples for a single positive sample. Thus, given an input tuple $\{x, x^+, x_1^-, x_2^-, ..., x_N^-\}$ that includes the anchor $x$, the positive sample $x^+$ and $N$ negative samples $\{x^-\}_{i=1}^N$, the multi-class N-pair loss is defined as:

$$\mathcal{L}_{N-pair}(x, x^+, \{x^-\}_{i=1}^N) = -\log\frac{e^{\xi_+}}{e^{\xi_+} + \sum_{i=1}^N e^{\xi_-^i}} \tag{5}$$

## 2.2. Essential Components

The first key component for learning good and generalizable embeddings in any self-supervised task, including speech processing, is data augmentation. This step is crucial because it introduces variations to the data that do not modify the semantic meaning and thus makes the model focus on the essential information within the data when learning to produce the embeddings. For instance, in a simple framework for contrastive learning of visual representations (SimCLR) (Chen et al., 2020) the authors showed that combining both random color distortion and random cropping was critical for obtaining image embedding that generalized well.

Another important ingredient is using large batches, especially when in-batch negative samples are required to compute the contrastive loss. A large batch size allows the loss function to cover a diverse range of negative samples and thus forces the model to learn more significant embeddings in order to differentiate between data points. An example of large batch training is presented in Contrastive Language-Image Pre-training (CLIP) (Radford et al., 2021) where a batch size of 32,768 is used.

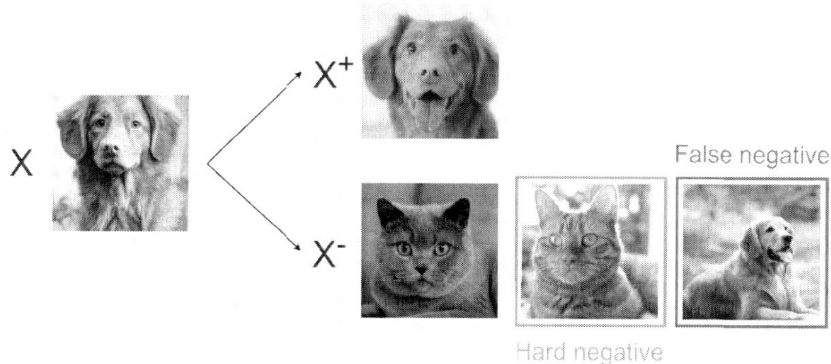


Figure 2. An example of a hard negative sample and of a false negative sample for a given anchor.

Finding good negative samples is also important for contrastive learning. Usually this involves finding samples that have a different class than the anchor, but that are close to its embedding, known as hard negative samples, thus forcing the model to rely on semantically meaningful information rather than on non-essential variations that maximize the distance. However, although it is easy to select such samples in a labeled dataset, finding them in an unlabeled dataset is a difficult task that might produce a high number of false negative samples and in turn result in a model with a poor performance. An example of hard and false negative samples is depicted in Figure 2[1].

Chuang et al. (2020) proposed one influential debiasing technique for contrastive losses in unsupervised settings. Suppose that the true probability of the anchor class is $\eta_+$ and the true probability of the other classes is $\eta_- = 1 - \eta_+$. Given an anchor $x$, then we can observe a positive sample $\hat{x}$ with probability $p_x^+(\hat{x})$ and a negative sample with probability $p_x^-(\hat{x})$. However, when we observe a negative sample $x^-$, because $p_x^-(x^-)$ is unknown, we may sample from the anchor class with probability $\eta_+$. Thus, the actual distribution becomes for selecting a sample $\hat{x}$ for an anchor $x$:

[1]These techniques also apply for contrastive learning in speech processing, either directly from the raw audio or from the spectrograms, but we choose to use images instead in order to better illustrate the algorithm.

$$p(\hat{x}) = \eta_{+}p_x^{+}(\hat{x}) + \eta_{-}p_x^{-}(\hat{x}) \tag{6}$$

We can further debias the loss by sampling $x^-$ with $p^-(\hat{x}) = (p_x(\hat{x}) - \eta_+ p_x^+(\hat{x}))/\eta_-$. This probability can be estimated by using $N$ samples $\{u\}_{i=1}^N$ from $p$ and $M$ samples $\{v\}_{i=1}^M$ from $p_x^+$ as:

$$g(x, \{u\}_{i=1}^N, \{v\}_{i=1}^M) = \max(\epsilon, \frac{1}{\eta_-}(\frac{1}{N}\sum_{i=1}^{N} e^{\xi_u^i} - \frac{\eta_+}{M}\sum_{i=1}^{M} e^{\xi_v^i})) \tag{7}$$

where $\epsilon$ is a hyperparameter that sets the maximum distance between the anchor and the negative samples, $\xi_u^i$ is the Euclidean distance between the anchor and the sample $u_i$ and $\xi_v^i$ is the Euclidean distance between the anchor and the sample $v_i$. By replacing the second term in the denominator of equation 5, we obtain the debiased contrastive loss:

$$\mathcal{L}_{debias}(x, x^+, \{u\}_{i=1}^N, \{v\}_{i=1}^M) = -\log \frac{e^{\xi_+}}{e^{\xi_-} + Ng(x, \{u\}_{i=1}^N, \{v\}_{i=1}^M)} \tag{8}$$

# 3. Pre-Trained ASR Architectures

## 3.1. Wav2Vec

Pre-training models on large amounts of audio audio data using various self-supervised objectives is slowly starting to become the main way of creating modern ASR systems. One of the first models that obtained promising results with this technique is Wav2Vec (Schneider et al., 2019), obtaining a 2.43 (WER) on the Nov92 test set [2] and thus outperforming the previous state-of-the-art by using two orders of magnitude less data. The model is composed of two neural networks: (1) an encoder network and (2) a context network.

The role of the encoder network is to take the input audio data $x_i \in \mathcal{X}$ and to transform it into a latent representation $z_i$ using a function $f : \mathcal{X} \rightarrow \mathcal{Z}$ that is composed of five convolutional layers (LeCun et al., 1998). All

[2]https://catalog.ldc.upenn.edu/docs/LDC93S6A/csrnov92.htm

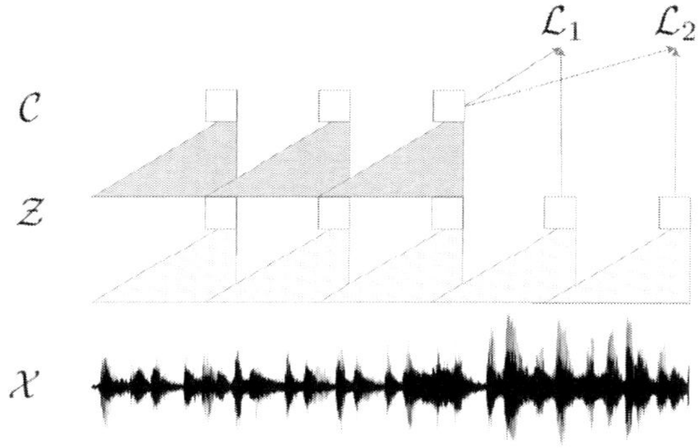


Figure 3. Wav2Vec pre-training algorithm. $\mathcal{X}$ is the input audio data, $\mathcal{Z}$ is the latent representation space, $\mathcal{C}$ is the context representation space and $\mathcal{L}_k$ is the contrastive auto-regressive loss $k$ steps into the future.

the audio samples used for pre-training were standardized to have a 16 kHz sample rate with each $z_i$ in the output encoding approximately 30ms of audio. The context network is defined as a learnable function $g : \mathcal{Z} \rightarrow \mathcal{C}$ that takes as input several latent representations $z_i, ..., z_{i-j}$ that were produced by the encoder and mix them into a contextualized embedding $c = g(v_i...v_{i-j})$. The context network is composed of nine convolutional layers and has a receptive field of approximately 210 ms.

The pre-training objective of Wav2Vec is, using the previous $T$ steps, to differentiate a sample $z_{T+k}$ that is $k$ steps in the future from a noise sample $\tilde{z}$ drawn from a distribution $p_n$ in a contrastive fashion:

$$\mathcal{L}_k = -\sum_{i=1}^{T-k} (\log \sigma(z_{i+k}^{\mathsf{T}} h_k(c_i)) + \lambda \mathbb{E}_{\tilde{z}\ p_n} \log \sigma(-\tilde{z}^{\mathsf{T}} h_k(c_i))) \quad (9)$$

where $\sigma$ is the sigmoid function $\sigma(x) = 1/(1 + e^{-x})$, $h_k$ is a step-specific feed-forward neural network applied to the contextual representation $c_i$ and $\lambda$ is the number of negative samples (i.e the authors use $\lambda = 10$ for pre-training the model). The left part of the sum represents the probability of $z_i + k$ being the true sample, while the right part represents the probability of the noise $\tilde{z}$ being the true sample. The noise $\tilde{z}$ is uniformly sampled from the other steps $z_{j \neq i+k}$ of the same audio sequence. The overall pre-training

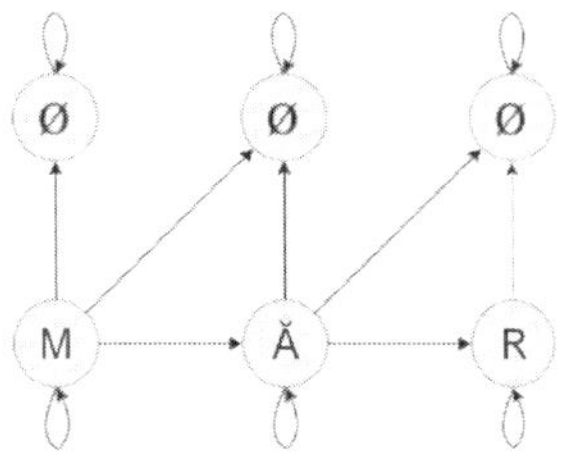


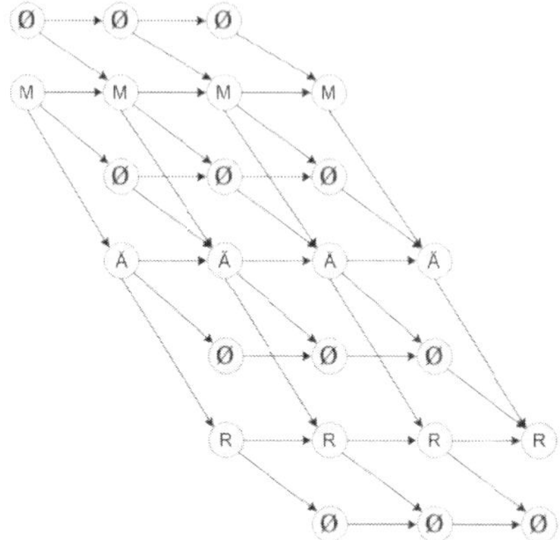


Figure 4. (a) The CTC graph for the "MR" (English: "APPLE") transcription. (b) Unfolded CTC graph for the same transcription. Blank state is denoted by .

architecture and objective of Wav2Vec are further depicted in Figure 3.

Once Wav2Vec has been pre-trained on audio data using the above-mentioned objective, it has to be fine-tuned on transcribed audios to be able to perform speech recognition. The training of ASR models such as Wav2Vec that predict a character for a brief time frame (e.g. 30 ms) is usually done using the Connectionist Temporal Classification (CTC) criterion (Graves et al., 2006). The objective takes into consideration all the possible sequences of letters that can lead to a given transcription while also allowing a special "blank" token in order to (1) remove the unnecessary frames between true letters and (2) keep two identical consecutive letters in the transcription. An example of a graph that is accepted by CTC with the transcription "MR" (English: "APPLE") is depicted in Figure 4a. However, computing all the possibilities in the loss function for a transcription is extremely expensive. This issue is usually solved in practice by taking advantage of the sequences that have reached the same output at the same step and employing a dynamic programming algorithm (Hannun, 2017), the graph being usually unfolded as shown in Figure 4b.

The authors use an improved version of CTC to fine-tune the model - the Auto Segmentation Criterion (ASG) loss (Collobert et al., 2016). This objective offers three new advantages:

1. *No blank labels* - letter repetitions are replaced by a digit that denotes how many times the character has been repeated (e.g. "copii" (English: "children") is represented as "copi2", "cooperare" (English: "cooperation") is represented as "co2perare"). Additionally, by removing the blank token, "garbage" frame modeling is ignored and these frames are replaced with another label. Overall, this methodology creates a simpler graph.

2. *Un-normalized scores on the nodes* - Transition scores between nodes are learned together with the model in contrast to CTC where usually a language model is employed for this.

3. *Global normalization* - this normalization is necessary to ensure that incorrect transcriptions have low confidence.

## 3.2. VQ-Wav2Vec

VQ-Wav2Vec (Baevski et al., 2019) integrates a discretizing function $q$ that maps the latent representations $\mathcal{Z}$ into a quantized latent space $\hat{\mathcal{Z}}$ on which classical NLP algorithms can be used (see Figure 5). It replaces the original representation $z$ by $\hat{z} = e_i$ from a fixed codebook that contains $M$ representations of size $d$. The authors of the paper explore two variants for the quantization module: (1) Gumbel-Softmax function (Jang et al., 2016) and (2) online k-means clustering as in VQ-VAE (van den Oord et al., 2017).

Gumbel-Softmax allows the creation of discrete variables from dense representations in a fully differentiable way by applying two fully-connected layers with a ReLU function between them, outputing $l \in R^N$ logits. During training the probabilities for choosing the $j$th index are:

$$p_j = \frac{(e^{l_i+v_i})/T}{\sum_{j=1}^{M}(e^{l_j+v_j})/T} \tag{10}$$

where $v = -\log(-\log(u))$, with $u$ chosen from a random uniform distribution, $T$ is the temperature and $M$ is the codebook size. In the forward pass the index is chosen as the one with the highest probability and, during the backward pass, the true gradients of the Gumbel-Softmax function are used.

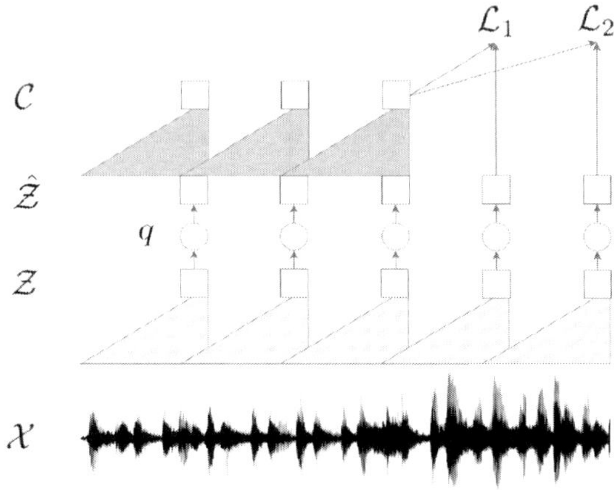


Figure 5. VQ-Wav2Vec pre-training algorithm. Latent representations $\mathcal{Z}$ are quantized into the discrete space $\hat{\mathcal{Z}}$ using function $q$ and then NLP methods are used for fine-tuning acoustic models.

The second approach used in the paper to create a differentiable index selection function focuses on choosing the closest codebook variable $e$ to the latent representation $z$, based on the Euclidean distance. During the backward pass, the gradients are obtained by backpropagating the derivative of the Wav2Vec loss in Equation 9 with respect to $\hat{z}$ (van den Oord et al., 2017). In addition, the final loss of this method adds two other terms: (1) $||sg(z) - \hat{z}||_2^2$ which moves the codebook closer to the model's outputs and (2) $\gamma||z - sg(\hat{z})||_2^2$ which moves the model's outputs around a centroid, where $sg$ is the gradient stop operator $sg(x) = x$, $\frac{d}{dx}sg(x) = 0$.

Once that the VQ-Wav2Vec model has been pre-trained, one can apply classical NLP algorithms that use the discretized audio data as input. The authors of the paper use the BERT model for this task and its pre-training masked language modeling (MLM)[3] algorithm to learn contextualized speech representations. Then, the BERT model can be fine-tuned to a downstream task such as speech recognition.

The authors pre-trained the VQ-Wav2Vec and the BERT models on LibriSpeech (Panayotov et al., 2015), evaluating the system on two bench-

[3]The authors make the MLM pre-training harder by masking a span of 10 consecutive discretized speech tokens, improving the overall performance of the model.

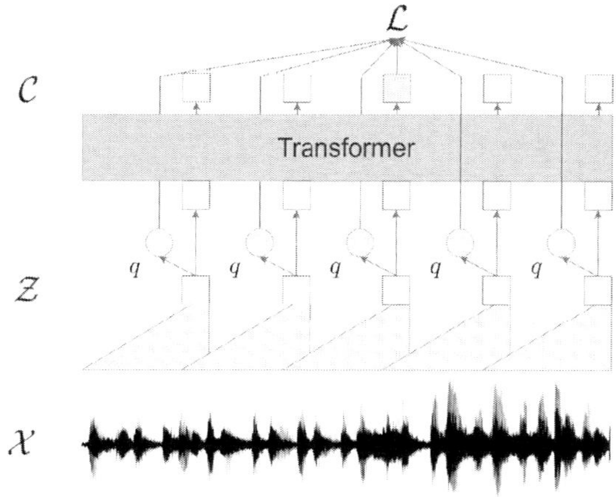


Figure 6. Wav2Vec2 pre-training algorithm.

marks: TIMIT (Garofolo et al., 1993) - a 5 hours dataset with phoneme labeling and Wall Street Journal (Paul and Baker, 1992) - a 81 hours grapheme speech recognition dataset, obtaining state-of-the-art results on both of them.

### 3.3. Wav2Vec2

Wav2vec2 builds speech representations $\mathcal{Z}$ directly from the raw audio data using convolutional layers and feeds them into a transformer that creates contextualized speech representations $\mathcal{C}$, capturing information from the entire utterance. The model is pre-trained in an end-to-end fashion by discretizing the features $z$ into the quantized space $Q$ using the Gumbel-Softmax function and then employing a masking self-supervised objective on these quantized representations. The model architecture and the training algorithm are depicted in Figure 6.

The speech representations are learned using a contrastive loss $\mathcal{L}_m$ that requires recognizing the real quantized speech embedding for a certain time step from a set of distractors. This contrastive loss was further augmented with a codebook diversity loss $\mathcal{L}_d$ that guides the model to also use codebook embeddings. Thus, the final pre-training loss is defined as:

$$\mathcal{L} = \mathcal{L}_m + \alpha \mathcal{L}_d \tag{11}$$

where $alpha$ is a hyperparameter that controls the influence of the codebook entries and was set to 0.1 in their experiments.

The fine-tuning of the Wav2Vec2 model was done by adding a fully-connected layer on the top of the contextual representations $C$ that project them into $C$ classes (e.g. the vocabulary used in the transcripts). Then, the CTC was employed to compute the loss, together with the Spectral Augmentation algorithm (SpecAugment) (Park et al., 2019) that significantly improved the final performance, especially when fewer samples were used.

For pre-training the model, the authors used the spoken part of LibriSpeech that contained 960 hours of speech or the preprocessed audio data from LibriVox that contained in 53k hours of audio (Kahn et al., 2020). Once pre-trained, the pre-trained Wav2Vec2 model was fine-tuned on five labeled speech sets from LibriSpeech: (1) the full 960-hour dataset, (2) the clean 100-hour split of the corpus, together with three limited resource subsets originally extracted from LibriSpeech - (3) a 10-hour subset, a 1-hour subset and a 10-minute subset[4]. The authors also fine-tuned and evaluated the model on TIMIT.

The performance of the Wav2Vec2 model ranged from 1.8%/3.3% WER on LibriSpeech clean/other test sets when the full corpus was employed to 4.8/8.2 when only the 10-minute subset was used. These results demonstrated that competitive results can be obtained in ultra-low resource scenarios when self-supervision on unlabeled data is employed. On the TIMIT dataset, the model obtained an 8.3 phoneme error rate (PER), outperforming the previous state-of-the-art methods by more than 3 PER.

# 4. Comparison with Non-Pre-Trained Models

## 4.1. Dataset

The dataset used in our experiments is the recently released RTASC dataset. The corpus was created in the context of the ROBIN project[5] where 711 sentences were selected for the micro-world scenarios of the dialogue management system (e.g., buying hardware from electronic shops). The dataset has 6 speakers - 3 women and 3 men - of various age groups,

[4]The 10 minutes split corresponds to only 48 of transcribed audio files that have an average length of 12.5 seconds.

[5]https://aimas.cs.pub.ro/robin/en/

and each speaker recorded an approximately equal portion of the total sentences, resulting in a corpus that contains 3,786 of transcribed audio files with a total duration of 6 hours and 25 minutes. The recording of audio files was done using an in-house developed web component that was integrated into the RELATE platform (Păiș et al., 2020) for future usage.

RTASC has a separated test set with 50 new sentences and each of them was recorded by two of the speakers who also recorded a part of the train audio samples (e.g., male-1 and female-5), as well as a new male voice to further test the generalization capabilities of an ASR trained on this speech corpus. In addition, the transcriptions found in the dataset were processed using the Universal Dependencies Pipe (UDPipe) (Straka et al., 2016) and they were further annotated with lemmas, part-of-speech tags and dependencies. Therefore, RTASC also has a *.conllu* file for each *.txt* file that contains a tokenized version of the transcription in the CoNLL-U format[6].

## 4.2. Baseline Models

We compare the results of our WavVec2 variants with the Romanian DeepSpeech2 (DeepSpeech2-Ro) (Avram et al., 2020, 2021a), an open-sourced model[7] that was trained on a corpus composed of 230 hours of transcribed speech. The main audio resource that was used in the training corpus comes from the representative corpus of contemporary Romanian language (CoRoLa) (Mititelu et al., 2018). CoRoLa was jontly developed by two institutions of the Romanian Academy: the Research Institute for Artificial Intelligence Mihai Drgnescu of Bucharest and the Institute of Computer Science in Iai.

The spoken part of CoRoLa comes mainly from professional recordings in various settings (e.g., radio stations or recording studios) that were transcribed by their authors or created by the project partners. The other part of the spoken corpus comes from text reads: news in radio stations, professional speakers in recording studio or extracts from Romanian Wikipedia that were read by volunteers and recorded in non-professional environments. The spoken component of CoRoLa can be interrogated us-

---

[6]https://universaldependencies.org/format.html
[7]https://github.com/racai-ai/RobinASR

ing the Oral Corpus Query Platform (OCQP)[8] which allows searching for words and listening to their pronunciation (Tufiș et al., 2019).

The CoBiLiRo platform (Cristea et al., 2020) was built in the RETEROM project[9] to allow the collection of new bimodal data, with one of the final goals being to enrich the CoRoLa corpus. Thus, additional corpora with transcribed speech were considered for training the Romanian DeepSpeech2 model:

- *RoDigits* - contains approximately 38 hours of spoken digits that were recorded by 154 speakers. Each speaker read 100 sentences that contained 12 randomly generated digits. A semi-automated validation was employed to ensure high quality in the generated data, and the final corpus contained 15,389 of samples.

- *Romanian Commmon Voice* - Common Voice is a dataset that contains transcribed speech in multiple languages. At the time the Romanian DeepSpeech2 paper was written, the corpus had over 7,200 hours of audio in 54 languages from over 50,000 speakers. The Romanian part of the corpus contained 7 hours of transcribed speech that was recorded by 79 speakers, out of which only 5 hours were validated and could be integrated in the overall training set.

- *Romanian Speech Synthesis (RSS)* (Stan et al., 2011) - the corpus was designed for text-to-speech tasks and it contains 4 hours of spoken utterances from a female speaker that used multiple microphones for recording. RSS has 4,000 of read sentences that were extracted from novels, newspapers and fairy-tales. The corpus was further extended with over 1,700 read sentences of two new female speakers, comprising 1.5 hours of new transcribed audio.

- *RSC* - contains 100 hours that were collected from 164 Romanian native speakers, most of them being either students or staff of the University Politehnica of Bucharest, the average of the age being 24 years. The corpus has 133,616 files, out of which approximately 100k audio files are isolated word utterances with a duration of under 2.5 seconds and only less than 200 audio files have a duration of

[8]http://corolaws.racai.ro/corola_sound_search/index.php
[9]http://www.racai.ro/p/reterom/

more than 15 seconds. The authors selected sentences from novels, news and from a list of words specially created to covered all the possible syllables in Romanian.

In addition to the speech dataset that was collected to train the DeepSpeech2 model, a textual corpus was created to train a KenLM language model (Heafield, 2011) in order to better align the words produced by the model with the words in the Romanian language. This corpus was composed of two datasets: (1) the textual part of CoRoLa which accounted for 940 million tokens and (2) the Romanian part of OSCAR which was obtained by filtering the Common Crawl[10] and accounted for over one billion tokens. Together with the language model, the Romanian DeepSpeech2 obtained a 9.9% WER on a test set that was formed of 5,000 randomly selected samples from the speech corpus that were removed during training.

DeepSpeech2-Ro was evaluated on the RTASC test set and obtained an average of 59.71% WER and 28.03% CER. This version was further fine-tuned on the RTASC training set (DeepSpeech2-Ro-FT) and improved the results of the original model, achieving 43.44% WER and 20.21% CER. This fine-tuned version is also considered for comparison in our experiments.

## 4.3. Pre-Trained Wav2Vec2 Models

We evaluated several large Wav2Vec2 variants that were pre-trained on either VoxPopuli (Wang et al., 2021) or on a joint multilingual speech corpus - XLRS (Conneau et al., 2020).

Voxpopuli is a large-scale multilingual corpus that contains approximately 100k hours of unlabeled speech from 23 languages, taken from European Parliament conversations. Out of the 100k hours of audio, 17.9k are in Romanian, making any model pre-trained on the whole corpus a good candidate for fine-tuning an ASR with RTASC. It also contains approximately 1.8k hours of transcribed audio in 16 languages which can be used for supervised training of ASR models, together with 5.1k of their aligned oral interpretations in five other languages that are suitable for speech-to-speech translation systems. The dataset is available under an open license[11].

[10]https://commoncrawl.org/

[11]https://github.com/facebookresearch/voxpopuli

The XLRS corpus contains the audio files found in three subcorpora: (1) CommonVoice (Ardila et al., 2020) - composed of more than 2k hours of read speech data in 38 languages at the time of pre-training the model, (2) BABEL (Gales et al., 2014) - a multilingual speech dataset of telephone conversations covering 17 languages and 1.7k hours of speech, and (3) Multilingual LibriSpeech (MLS) (Pratap et al., 2020) - containing 50k hours of audio derived from audio books in 8 languages. Overall, the corpus is composed of 53 languages and 56k hours of speech data, out of which only the ones found in CommonVoice are in Romanian - approximately 7 hours of audio.

We used the HuggingFace Transformer library[12] to fine-tune the Wav2Vec2 variants due to the reduced overhead it offers for developing such models. The library also makes easily accessible the following pre-trained models that we used in our experiments:

- **Wav2Vec2BASE-V10k**[13] - the base version of Wav2Vec2 pre-trained on the 10k subset of Voxpopuli corpus.
- **Wav2Vec2BASE-V100k**[14] - the base version of Wav2Vec2 pre-trained on the full Voxpopuli corpus.
- **Wav2Vec2LARGE-V10k**[15] - the large version of Wav2Vec2 pre-trained on the 10k subset of Voxpopuli corpus.
- **Wav2Vec2LARGE-V100k**[16] - the large version of Wav2Vec2 pre-trained on the full Voxpopuli corpus.
- **Wav2Vec2LARGE-XLRS**[17] - the large version of Wav2Vec2 pre-trained on the XLRS corpus.

A summary of the BASE and LARGE architecture designs is outlined in Table 1. All BASE variants have 12 layers with a unit size of 768, 8 attention heads, an inner dimension of 3,072, totaling 94.4 million parameters and occupying 363 MB of memory. On the other hand, the LARGE

[12] https://github.com/huggingface/transformers
[13] https://huggingface.co/facebook/wav2vec2-base-10k-voxpopuli
[14] https://huggingface.co/facebook/wav2vec2-base-100k-voxpopuli
[15] https://huggingface.co/facebook/wav2vec2-large-10k-voxpopuli
[16] https://huggingface.co/facebook/wav2vec2-large-100k-voxpopuli
[17] https://huggingface.co/facebook/wav2vec2-large-xlsr-53

**Table 1. Model size comparison between the BASE and LARGE variants of Wav2Vec2**

| Model | Layers | Hidden | Heads | Inner | Size | Params |
|---|---|---|---|---|---|---|
| Wav2Vec2BASE | 12 | 768 | 8 | 3,072 | 363 MB | 94.4M |
| Wav2Vec2LARGE | 24 | 1,024 | 16 | 4,096 | 1.18 GB | 315.5M |

**Table 2. Speech corpora used for pre-training the the Wav2Vec2 variants**

| Corpus | Domain | Hours | Languages | Romanian |
|---|---|---|---|---|
| V10k | Legal | 10k | 23 | 1.8k |
| V100k | Legal | 100k | 23 | 17.9k |
| CommonVoice | Wikipedia | 2k | 38 | 7 |
| BABEL | Conversations | 1.7k | 17 | 0 |
| MLS | Books | 53k | 8 | 0 |
| XLSR (Total) | Diverse | 56k | 53 | 7 |

variants have double the number of layers and attention heads, a hidden unit size of 1,024 and more than trice the number of parameters and size compared to the BASE variants, occupying 1.18 GB of memory with 315.5 million parameters. In addition, we also depict a summary of the pre-training corpora in Table 2, containing the domain of the speech, the number of hours and languages, together with the number of hours in Romanian.

## 4.4. Experimental Setup

We trained each of the Wav2Vec2 variants for 100 epochs with a batch sizes of 32 and 16 for the base and large variants, respectively. We used a learning rate of 5e-5, a weight decay of 5e-3 and clipped all gradients to have values between -2 and 2 to stabilize the training (Pascanu et al., 2013). The training was distributed on two Nvidia 1080 Ti and the whole fine-tuning process took approximately 24 hours for the base variants and 72 hours for the large variants. We fine-tuned the models using the CTC loss and kept the feature extraction convolutional layers frozen to increase the generalization capabilities, as suggested in the original paper (Baevski et al., 2020).

The sample rate of the audio files was set to 16 kHz and each sample was encoded to a 16 bits integer. To improve generalization, we also employed an augmentation pipeline that consisted of modifying the volume of the audio with a gain selected uniformly from the $(-6, 8)$ interval and the speed of speech with a tempo selected uniformly from the $(0.85, 1.15)$ interval.

During evaluation, we used a KenLM language model to better align the words in the predicted transcription with words from the Romanian language. We chose this model because it implements two data structures for effective queries: (1) linear probing hash maps for speed and (2) a trie with interpolation search, packing at the level of bits and sorted records designed for optimized memory consumption. The language model was trained on 3-grams taken from the RTASC train transcripts. A grid search on the development set[18] was also employed to find the best hyperparameters: $\alpha$ (mediates the influence of the language model) and $\beta$ (which controls the probability of inserting a space character). The results of the grid search indicated that $\alpha = 2.8$ and $\beta = 4.9$ are the best values for each Wav2Vec2 variant. In addition, we employed a beam search of 256 during decoding to allow the model not to rely on immediate greedy predictions, but to have a more global view of the possible transcriptions and thus improve its overall performance.

## 4.5. Results

The experimental results of the Wav2Vec2 variants on the RTASC test set are depicted in Table 3. The best average performance was obtained by the large variant that was pre-trained on the full VoxPopuli speech corpus - Wav2Vec2LARGE-V100k. It achieved an average WER of 13.93% and a CER of 9.83%, improving the WER of the DeepSpeech2 baseline by more than three times and the CER by more than twice. This variant also obtained the best individual WER score on the male and female voices from the training set, but was outperformed by Wav2Vec2LARGE-V10k on the new male voice.

The results of the experiments also outline that the LARGE variants

[18]The development set was created by randomly selecting and separating 250 samples from the training set.

**Table 3. Wav2Vec2 results on RTASC test set**

| Model | Male-1 | | Female-5 | | Male-New | | Average | |
|---|---|---|---|---|---|---|---|---|
| | WER | CER | WER | CER | WER | CER | WER | CER |
| *DeepSpeech2-Ro* | 38.71 | 9.42 | 81.23 | 48.41 | 59.21 | 26.28 | 59.71 | 28.03 |
| *DeepSpeech2-Ro-FT* | 28.37 | 9.09 | 57.07 | 29.71 | 44.88 | 21.83 | 43.44 | 20.21 |
| Wav2Vec2BASE-V10k | 9.30 | **5.60** | 22.64 | 14.52 | 24.43 | 15.76 | 18.79 | 11.96 |
| Wav2Vec2BASE-V100k | 12.34 | 6.65 | 20.43 | 14.17 | 21.08 | 13.50 | 17.95 | 11.44 |
| Wav2Vec2LARGE-V10k | 10.10 | 7.13 | 17.39 | **11.23** | **16.24** | 11.61 | 14.58 | 9.99 |
| Wav2Vec2LARGE-V100k | **8.12** | 6.14 | **16.71** | 12.46 | 16.95 | **10.91** | **13.93** | **9.83** |
| Wav2Vec2LARGE-XLSR | 11.60 | 7.05 | 22.61 | 14.41 | 18.31 | 11.32 | 17.51 | 10.93 |

mostly outperformed the BASE variants by approximately 4% WER for both the V10k and V100k pre-training datasets. In addition, it can be observed that there is a clear difference of approximately 3.5% WER between pre-training the Wav2Vec2 model on VoxPopuli and XLSR. This variation might have been caused by the disproportionality in Romanian pre-training hours that is contained in the two corpora. VoxPopuli has vastly more Romanian hours than XLSR and thus the Wav2Vec2 models that were pre-trained on it obtained a significant improvement when fine-tuned on RTASC.

# 5. RELATE Integration

The best Wav2Vec2 variant (i.e., fine-tuned from Wav2Vec2LARGE-V100k) was embedded into a web server, with its functionality exposed in the form of an HTTP REST API web service. The API allows for a wav file to be sent via a standard HTTP request, executes the ASR process and returns the result in JSON format. The returned JSON contains two fields: "transcription" which is the actual text recognized by the ASR process, and "status" which indicates the successful execution of the request or an error. Listing 1 contains an example JSON returned by the ASR web service.

Listing 1. Example JSON result for the ASR web service

```
{
    ‘‘transcription”:‘‘a\u0219 dori s\u0103 aib\u0103
        ecranul mare”,
    ‘‘status”:‘‘OK”
}
```

To allow easy interaction of a human user with the ASR web service, it was further integrated in the RELATE platform as a web component[19]. This component offers the possibility of recording a new audio file directly in the platform or uploading an existing recording. Then, the platform will invoke the web service and present the result on the web page. Finally, the user may employ other platform components to perform analysis of the recognized text, including tokenization, lemmatization, part-of-speech tagging, dependency parsing or named entity recognition. The web user interface of the ASR web services is depicted in Figure 7.

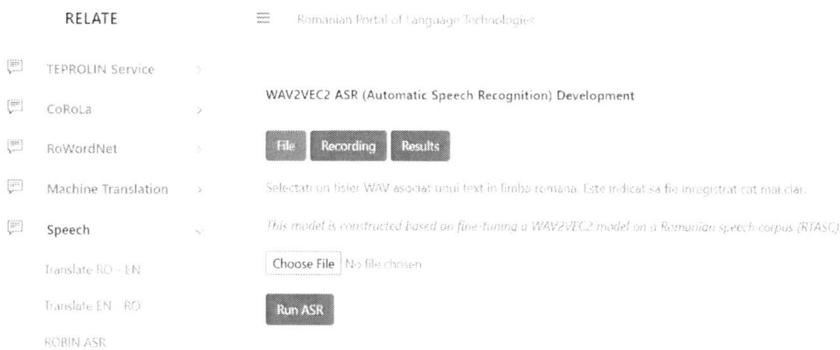


Figure 7. The Wav2Vec2 ASR web component interface in the RELATE platform.

In a previous work (Avram et al., 2021b), we described a modular approach for Romanian-English and English-Romanian speech-to-speech translation. This worked by combining multiple web services that were already integrated in the RELATE platform. They were assembled in a pipeline comprised of four components: ASR, transcription post-processing, translation and text-to-speech (TTS). For each of the pipeline's components, multiple options were available based on the functionalities available within RELATE. This approach allowed us to easily extend the speech translation pipeline and integrate the new Wav2Vec2 model[20]. Similar to the simple ASR web component described previously, the speech-to-speech translation component allows a user to either record or upload an

[19]https://relate.racai.ro/index.php?path=speech/wav2vec2
[20]https://relate.racai.ro/index.php?path=translate/speech_ro_en

audio file in Romanian and have it translated into a corresponding English audio file (or conversely, the process can start with an English audio and have it translated into Romanian). The speech translation web interface is depicted in Figure 8. By using already available modules within the platform, such as punctuation restoration, as described in Chapter 5 and in Păiș and Tufiș (2021), the translation quality is improved.

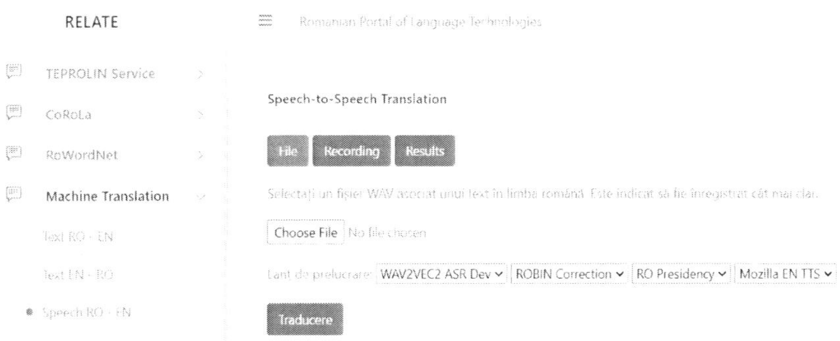


Figure 8. The speech-to-speech translation interface and the component that contains the Wav2Vec2 model.

## Conclusion

Obtaining competitive results with neural networks on speech recognition requires large amounts of labeled data. However, in many settings, labeled audio is hard to obtain. Considering the nearly 7,000 languages spoken worldwide, the thousands of hours of transcribed speech necessary to train such systems are not available for the majority of these languages. To solve this issue, self-supervised algorithms have been developed as a paradigm that allows a model to learn general representations from unlabeled data and then use these representations to fine-tune it on a downstream task. This methodology of developing models has had exceptional results in natural language processing tasks with transformer-based neural networks.

As a result of this success, this technique has become an active area of research in speech recognition. One of the latest models that has obtained competitive results for this task is Wav2Vec2, which managed to attain a 4.8% WER on the test set of LibriSpeech with as little as 10 minutes of fine-tuning data, being the first model to achieve such results in an ultra-low resource scenario. This accomplishment determined us to experiment with several multilingual versions of Wav2Vec2 on a recently released dataset in Romanian that was developed during the ROBIN project - RTASC. The corpus contains 5 hours of transcribed speech from the technical domain and the baseline neural networks that were based on DeepSpeech2 struggled to achieve good performance due to the low amount of data found in the training set.

Our best multilingual Wav2Vec2 variant managed to achieve a 13.93% WER and a 9.83% CER on the test set, reducing the WER of the fine-tuned version of DeepSpeech2 by more than three times and the CER by more than twice. In addition, our experiments outlined the importance of having a high volume of data for the target language in the multilingual speech corpus used for pre-training. There was an approximately 4.5% WER difference when the model was pre-trained on XLSR (containing 7 hours of Romanian audio) and when it was pre-trained on VoxPopuli (containing 17.9k hours of Romanian spoken data).

The model was further integrated into the RELATE platform, allowing a human user to easily interact with the ASR system through a simple web interface in order to transcribe speech or to access a speech-to-speech translation component. Both work with speech either directly recorded in the platform or uploaded as a pre-recorded file. Finally, the advanced text analysis functions available in RELATE can be applied to the transcriptions.

Future work considers fine-tuning the multilingual Wav2Vec2 variants on a larger speech corpus for the Romanian language and evaluate its performance with the previously released models for Romanian language. In addition, we also intend to create a Wav2Vec2 version that is pre-trained only on Romanian audio data. All these models will be open-sourced for public usage and integrated into the RELATE platform.

## References

Amodei, D., Ananthanarayanan, S., Anubhai, R., Bai, J., Battenberg, E., Case, C., Casper, J., Catanzaro, B., Cheng, Q., Chen, G., et al. (2016). Deep speech 2: End-to-end speech recognition in english and mandarin. In *International conference on machine learning*, pages 173–182. PMLR.

Ardila, R., Branson, M., Davis, K., Kohler, M., Meyer, J., Henretty, M., Morais, R., Saunders, L., Tyers, F., and Weber, G. (2020). Common voice: A massively-multilingual speech corpus. In *Proceedings of the 12th Language Resources and Evaluation Conference*, pages 4218–4222.

Avram, A.-M., Păiş, V., and Tufiş, D. (2021a). Romanian speech recognition experiments from the robin project. *arXiv preprint arXiv:2111.12028.*

Avram, A.-M., Păiș, V., and Tufiș, D. (2020). Towards a Romanian end-to-end automatic speech recognition based on DeepSpeech2. *Proceedings of the Romanian Academy Series A*, 21:395–402.

Avram, A.-M., Păiș, V., and Tufiș, D. (2021b). A modular approach for romanian-english speech translation. In Métais, E., Meziane, F., Horacek, H., and Kapetanios, E., editors, *Natural Language Processing and Information Systems*, pages 57–63, Cham. Springer International Publishing.

Baevski, A., Schneider, S., and Auli, M. (2019). vq-wav2vec: Self-supervised learning of discrete speech representations. *arXiv preprint arXiv:1910.05453.*

Baevski, A., Zhou, Y., Mohamed, A., and Auli, M. (2020). wav2vec 2.0: A framework for self-supervised learning of speech representations. *Advances in Neural Information Processing Systems*, 33.

Bredin, H. (2017). Tristounet: triplet loss for speaker turn embedding. In *2017 IEEE international conference on acoustics, speech and signal processing (ICASSP)*, pages 5430–5434. IEEE.

Brown, T. B., Mann, B., Ryder, N., Subbiah, M., Kaplan, J., Dhariwal, P., Neelakantan, A., Shyam, P., Sastry, G., Askell, A., et al. (2020). Language models are few-shot learners. *arXiv preprint arXiv:2005.14165.*

Chen, T., Kornblith, S., Norouzi, M., and Hinton, G. (2020). A simple framework for contrastive learning of visual representations. In *International conference on machine learning*, pages 1597–1607. PMLR.

Chopra, S., Hadsell, R., and LeCun, Y. (2005). Learning a similarity metric discriminatively, with application to face verification. In *2005 IEEE Computer Society Conference on Computer Vision and Pattern Recognition (CVPR'05)*, volume 1, pages 539–546. IEEE.

Chuang, C.-Y., Robinson, J., Yen-Chen, L., Torralba, A., and Jegelka, S. (2020). Debiased contrastive learning. *arXiv preprint arXiv:2007.00224*.

Collobert, R., Puhrsch, C., and Synnaeve, G. (2016). Wav2letter: an end-to-end convnet-based speech recognition system. *arXiv preprint arXiv:1609.03193*.

Conneau, A., Baevski, A., Collobert, R., Mohamed, A., and Auli, M. (2020). Unsupervised cross-lingual representation learning for speech recognition. *arXiv preprint arXiv:2006.13979*.

Cristea, D., Pistol, I., Boghiu, e., Bibiri, A.-D., Gîfu, D., Scutelnicu, A., Plamada-Onofrei, M., Trandabat, D., and Bugeag, G. (2020). Cobiliro: A research platform for bimodal corpora. In *Proceedings of the 1st International Workshop on Language Technology Platforms*, pages 22–27.

Devlin, J., Chang, M.-W., Lee, K., and Toutanova, K. (2019). Bert: Pre-training of deep bidirectional transformers for language understanding. In *NAACL-HLT (1)*.

Gales, M. J., Knill, K. M., Ragni, A., and Rath, S. P. (2014). Speech recognition and keyword spotting for low-resource languages: Babel project research at cued. In *Fourth International workshop on spoken language technologies for under-resourced languages (SLTU-2014)*, pages 16–23. International Speech Communication Association (ISCA).

Garofolo, J. S., Lamel, L. F., Fisher, W. M., Fiscus, J. G., and Pallett, D. S. (1993). Darpa timit acoustic-phonetic continous speech corpus cd-rom. nist speech disc 1-1.1. *NASA STI/Recon technical report n*, 93:27403.

Georgescu, A. L., Caranica, A., Cucu, H., and Burileanu, C. (2018). Rodigits-a romanian connected digits speech corpus for automatic speech and speaker recognition. *University Politehnica of Bucharest Scientific Bulletin (submitted to)*.

Georgescu, A.-L., Cucu, H., and Burileanu, C. (2019). Kaldi-based dnn architectures for speech recognition in romanian. In *2019 International Conference on Speech Technology and Human-Computer Dialogue (SpeD)*, pages 1–6. IEEE.

Georgescu, A.-L., Cucu, H., Buzo, A., and Burileanu, C. (2020). Rsc: A romanian read speech corpus for automatic speech recognition. In *Proceedings of The 12th Language Resources and Evaluation Conference*, pages 6606–6612.

Graves, A., Fernández, S., Gomez, F., and Schmidhuber, J. (2006). Connectionist temporal classification: labelling unsegmented sequence data with recurrent neural networks. In *Proceedings of the 23rd international conference on Machine learning*, pages 369–376.

Hannun, A. (2017). Sequence modeling with ctc. *Distill*. https://distill.pub/2017/ctc.

Heafield, K. (2011). Kenlm: Faster and smaller language model queries. In *Proceedings of the sixth workshop on statistical machine translation*, pages 187–197.

Huang, J., Li, Y., Tao, J., Lian, Z., et al. (2018). Speech emotion recognition from variable-length inputs with triplet loss function. In *Interspeech*, pages 3673–3677.

Jang, E., Gu, S., and Poole, B. (2016). Categorical reparameterization with gumbel-softmax. *arXiv preprint arXiv:1611.01144*.

Kahn, J., Rivière, M., Zheng, W., Kharitonov, E., Xu, Q., Mazaré, P.-E., Karadayi, J., Liptchinsky, V., Collobert, R., Fuegen, C., et al. (2020). Libri-light: A benchmark for asr with limited or no supervision. In *ICASSP 2020-2020 IEEE International Conference on Acoustics, Speech and Signal Processing (ICASSP)*, pages 7669–7673. IEEE.

LeCun, Y., Bengio, Y., and Hinton, G. (2015). Deep learning. *nature*, 521(7553):436–444.

LeCun, Y., Bottou, L., Bengio, Y., and Haffner, P. (1998). Gradient-based learning applied to document recognition. *Proceedings of the IEEE*, 86(11):2278–2324.

Liu, Y., Ott, M., Goyal, N., Du, J., Joshi, M., Chen, D., Levy, O., Lewis, M., Zettlemoyer, L., and Stoyanov, V. (2019). Roberta: A robustly optimized bert pretraining approach. *arXiv preprint arXiv:1907.11692*.

Mititelu, V. B., Tufiş, D., and Irimia, E. (2018). The reference corpus of the contemporary romanian language (corola). In *Proceedings of the Eleventh International Conference on Language Resources and Evaluation (LREC 2018)*.

Oh Song, H., Xiang, Y., Jegelka, S., and Savarese, S. (2016). Deep metric learning via lifted structured feature embedding. In *Proceedings of the IEEE conference on computer vision and pattern recognition*, pages 4004–4012.

Panayotov, V., Chen, G., Povey, D., and Khudanpur, S. (2015). Librispeech: an asr corpus based on public domain audio books. In *2015 IEEE international conference on acoustics, speech and signal processing (ICASSP)*, pages 5206–5210. IEEE.

Park, D. S., Chan, W., Zhang, Y., Chiu, C.-C., Zoph, B., Cubuk, E. D., and Le, Q. V. (2019). Specaugment: A simple data augmentation method for automatic speech recognition. *arXiv preprint arXiv:1904.08779*.

Pascanu, R., Mikolov, T., and Bengio, Y. (2013). On the difficulty of training recurrent neural networks. In Dasgupta, S. and McAllester, D., editors, *Proceedings of the 30th International Conference on Machine Learning*, volume 28 of *Proceedings of Machine Learning Research*, pages 1310–1318, Atlanta, Georgia, USA. PMLR.

Paul, D. B. and Baker, J. (1992). The design for the wall street journal-based csr corpus. In *Speech and Natural Language: Proceedings of a Workshop Held at Harriman, New York, February 23-26, 1992*.

Pratap, V., Xu, Q., Sriram, A., Synnaeve, G., and Collobert, R. (2020). Mls: A large-scale multilingual dataset for speech research. In *INTERSPEECH*.

Păiș, V., Ion, R., Avram, A.-M., Irimia, E., Barbu Mititelu, V., and Mitrofan, M. (2021). Human-machine interaction speech corpus from the ROBIN project. In *2021 International Conference on Speech Technology and Human-Computer Dialogue (SpeD)*, pages 91–96.

Păiș, V., Ion, R., and Tufiș, D. (2020). A processing platform relating data and tools for Romanian language. In *Proceedings of the 1st International Workshop on Language Technology Platforms*, pages 81–88, Marseille, France. European Language Resources Association.

Păiș, V. and Tufiș, D. (2021). Capitalization and punctuation restoration: a survey. *Artificial Intelligence Review*.

Radford, A., Kim, J. W., Hallacy, C., Ramesh, A., Goh, G., Agarwal, S., Sastry, G., Askell, A., Mishkin, P., Clark, J., et al. (2021). Learning transferable visual models from natural language supervision. *arXiv preprint arXiv:2103.00020*.

Radford, A., Wu, J., Child, R., Luan, D., Amodei, D., Sutskever, I., et al. (2019). Language models are unsupervised multitask learners. *OpenAI blog*, 1(8):9.

Robinson, J. D., Chuang, C.-Y., Sra, S., and Jegelka, S. (2020). Contrastive learning with hard negative samples. In *International Conference on Learning Representations*.

Schneider, S., Baevski, A., Collobert, R., and Auli, M. (2019). wav2vec: Unsupervised pre-training for speech recognition. In *INTERSPEECH*.

Schroff, F., Kalenichenko, D., and Philbin, J. (2015). Facenet: A unified embedding for face recognition and clustering. In *Proceedings of the IEEE conference on computer vision and pattern recognition*, pages 815–823.

Stan, A., Dinescu, F., Țiple, C., Meza, Ș., Orza, B., Chirilă, M., and Giurgiu, M. (2017). The swara speech corpus: A large parallel romanian read speech dataset. In *2017 International Conference on Speech Technology and Human-Computer Dialogue (SpeD)*, pages 1–6. IEEE.

Stan, A., Yamagishi, J., King, S., and Aylett, M. (2011). The Romanian speech synthesis (RSS) corpus: Building a high quality HMM-based speech synthesis system using a high sampling rate. *Speech Communication*, 53(3):442–450.

Straka, M., Hajic, J., and Straková, J. (2016). Udpipe: trainable pipeline for processing conll-u files performing tokenization, morphological analysis, pos tagging and parsing. In *Proceedings of the Tenth International Conference on Language Resources and Evaluation (LREC'16)*, pages 4290–4297.

Tufiș, D., Barbu Mititelu, V., Irimia, E., Păiș, V., Ion, R., Diewald, N., Mitrofan, M., and Onofrei, M. (2019). Little strokes fell great oaks. creating CoRoLa, the reference corpus of contemporary Romanian. *Revue Roumaine de Linguistique*.

Ungureanu, D., Badeanu, M., Marica, G.-C., Dascalu, M., and Tufiș, D. I. (2021). Establishing a baseline of Romanian speech-to-text models. In *2021 International Conference on Speech Technology and Human-Computer Dialogue (SpeD)*, pages 132–138. IEEE.

van den Oord, A., Kalchbrenner, N., Espeholt, L., Kavukcuoglu, K., Vinyals, O., and Graves, A. (2016). Conditional image generation with pixelcnn decoders. In *NIPS*, pages 4790–4798.

van den Oord, A., Vinyals, O., and Kavukcuoglu, K. (2017). Neural discrete representation learning. In *NIPS*, pages 6309–6318.

Vaswani, A., Shazeer, N., Parmar, N., Uszkoreit, J., Jones, L., Gomez, A. N., Kaiser, Ł., and Polosukhin, I. (2017). Attention is all you need. In *Advances in neural information processing systems*, pages 5998–6008.

Wang, C., Rivière, M., Lee, A., Wu, A., Talnikar, C., Haziza, D., Williamson, M., Pino, J., and Dupoux, E. (2021). Voxpopuli: A large-scale multilingual speech corpus for representation learning, semi-supervised learning and interpretation. *arXiv preprint arXiv:2101.00390*.

In: Speech Recognition Technology ... ISBN: 978-1-68507-929-1
Editor: Vasile-Florian Păiş 

**Chapter 3**

# The Impact of Speech Recognition Performance on Human-Computer Interaction

**Vasile-Florian Păiş*, Andrei-Marius Avram, Radu Ion and Dan Tufiş**
Research Institute for Artificial Intelligence
"Mihai Drăgănescu", Romanian Academy,
Bucharest, Romania

**Abstract**

Spoken Human-Computer Interaction (HCI) assumes either simple command recognition, processing and feedback or complex dialogue in which the machine (a regular computer or a robot) can understand the questions addressed to it and respond appropriately, given the current context of the dialogue. The automatic speech recognition (ASR) system plays a key role in transcribing spoken utterances into text that is going to be further analysed in a natural language processing pipeline. However, when using such a system, there is usually a trade-off between the accuracy of the recognized text and the computation time required, both impacting the human experience. Low accuracy means that the robot may be unable to process the request, thus leading to improper feedback. High processing time makes the robot appear slow to the human user, thus potentially decreasing the interest in continuing the interaction.

*Corresponding Author's Email: vasile@racai.ro.

Performance analysis of the ASR component by itself, as well as the impact it has on the overall spoken dialogue system, led us to seek ways to improve the accuracy of the recognized text, while still complying with the low-latency required by a fluent user experience. In this context, we present two approaches: language-model based correction of the recognized text and tuning the ASR system with an additional speech dataset recorded especially for this purpose. The dedicated open-source Romanian speech dataset resulted from the ROBIN project will also be described, along with the impact it had on the overall system.

**Keywords:** human-computer interaction, automatic speech recognition, performance evaluation

# 1. Introduction

Human-Computer Interaction (HCI) or Human-Machine Interaction (HMI) lies at the crossroads of several research areas including artificial intelligence, cognitive psychology, computer science, interface design and many others. It can be studied either in a uni-modal context (focusing on either text, speech or vision) or in a multi-modal context (focusing on a combination of different signals) (Jaimes and Sebe, 2007). For the purposes of this work, we are considering a speech-based HCI context, where speech is used by both humans and machines. This involves at least three components: an automatic speech recognition (ASR) engine, a dialogue manager and a text-to-speech (TTS) component.

Advances in audio feature extraction (Gupta et al., 2018) and application of deep neural networks for speech recognition (Amodei et al., 2016) allow for increased performance of ASR systems. However, inherent problems associated with audio data, such as low-quality audio signals or transcriptions, differences in annotation styles (e.g., having samples that both removed or added filler words) and different recording settings (Raju et al., 2020), lower the final performance of the automatically generated transcripts. Furthermore, in low-resource settings, characterized by a small number of high-quality speech resources available for training purposes, the performance of ASR output is further decreased.

Following the acquisition of the input speech data that leads to an automatic transcript, an HCI system needs to process the resulting textual output using natural language processing techniques (NLP) (e.g., part-of-speech (POS) tagging, dependency parsing (DP), named entity recognition (NER), term extraction, semantic textual similarity (STS) ). Existing language processing components are usually developed using corpora of texts reflecting proper language usage in written documents. However, primary ASR output does not usually contain character capitalization and punctuation marks. Therefore, prior to applying other algorithms, restoring punctuation marks and proper capitalizing is a required step. In addition, the predicted transcripts may contain out-of-vocabulary words that were approximated by the ASR system based on the pattern it has learned from data, leading to incorrect predictions from the NLP systems that work with these transcriptions.

A dialogue can be defined as multiple exchanges between two speakers. An exchange represents two consecutive turns between the speakers, while a turn is defined as one or more utterances from the same speaker. In an HCI scenario, the human turn represents the input to an ASR system, while the computer turn is synthesized by a TTS system. In between lies the main component of a dialogue system: the dialogue manager. Based on the input received from the human speaker, the dialogue manager defines the next utterance(s) to be generated by the computer system (Deriu et al., 2021). The final component of a speech-based HCI system is the TTS module. This transforms the utterances generated by the dialogue manager into an audio signal, that is understandable by the human user.

As (Dix et al., 2004) noted, it is important to design interactive computer systems to be effective, efficient, easy and enjoyable to use. In the context of speech-based human-computer interaction, we consider that this translates into fast and meaningful audio responses. To obtain low latency between input and output, all the components involved in the pipeline must ensure high-speed processing. The accuracy and usability of the computer's audio response relies heavily on the result of the dialogue manager, which in turn depends on the ASR transcript.

For the purposes of this work, we focus primarily on the ASR component of a speech-based dialogue system, studying its impact on the rest of the processing chain and finally on the human user. This chapter synthesizes our experience gathered from recent national and international projects with an emphasis on spoken human-computer interaction. In the

ROBIN[1] project we experimented with different communication scenarios between a human user and the Pepper[2] robot in specific micro-worlds, while in the ENRICH4ALL[3] project we are exploring the interaction with an E-Government chatbot. This work allowed us to construct a neural-based, high-speed ASR system for the Romanian language, that is suitable for usage in low-latency environments such as spoken interaction with robots.

The rest of this work is structured as follows: Section 2 presents the general architecture of a speech-based dialogue system; Section 3 gives implementation details from the ROBIN project; Section 4 describes ASR enhancements leading to an increased performance of the dialogue system; Section 5 evaluates the impact of the proposed enhancements; and finally in Section 5.2 conclusions are formulated.

## 2. Architecture of a Speech-Based Dialogue System

A speech-based dialogue system, regardless of its implementation (as a desktop computer program, a robot application, an online chatbot) must allow queries to be performed using human voice and send back synthesized speech responses to the same user. As depicted in Figure 1, this process involves the following components: a human user, a recording device, the ASR system, the dialogue manager, a database, the TTS system and a sound rendering device.

The human users who interact with the machine use their own voice to formulate queries to the system. During the development and initial testing phases, the users are usually the developers of the system, meaning that they should be highly familiar with its characteristics, and that their voices may have been used to actually train the ASR model. These factors might make the team to overestimate the performance of the overall system and might lead to a release in production of a brittle version. However, during advanced testing and real-world usage, it is expected to have new users who are not familiar with the technical aspects of the application and whose feedback is essential in remedying the previously mentioned problems. It is highly important that system performance is tested against pre-

[1] http://aimas.cs.pub.ro/robin/
[2] https://robots.ieee.org/robots/pepper/
[3] https://www.racai.ro/p/enrich4all/

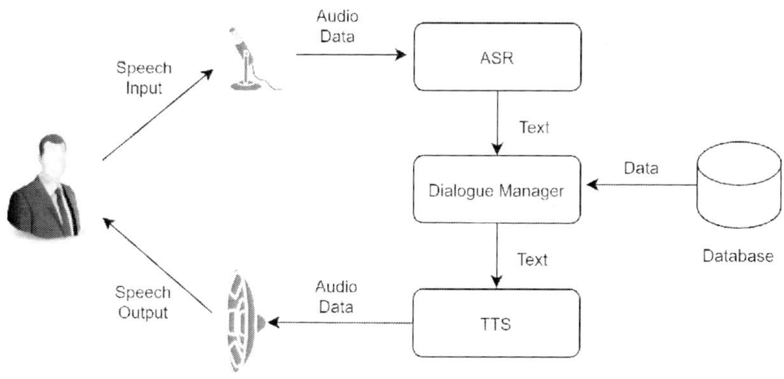


Figure 1. General architecture of a speech-based dialogue system.

viously unseen data (that was not used during model training). For speech recognition applications, performance should be evaluated not just on new sentences but also on new speakers.

Depending on the hardware platform being used, the recording device may represent a computer microphone, headphones with microphone, bluetooth headset, an embedded microphone within a robot or some other physical device. The recording device together with the recording software library will take the user's speech and produce a digital representation, in the form of audio data. Obviously, high-quality recording devices will lead to high-quality recordings that usually allow for improved ASR performance. Nevertheless, the recording device and associated software libraries must allow for recording a signal with characteristics similar to those used for training the ASR model. Operations such as downsampling (lowering the sample rate) or noise filtering may be required prior to sending the recorded signal to the ASR system. If these operations are not supported by the device itself or associated libraries, then additional software functions must be employed, while taking into consideration possible perturbations introduced by these new library routines.

The ASR component receives the recorded audio data and transforms it into a text representation, suitable for further processing. During development and testing, the real-time recording can be replaced by pre-recorded sound files of similar characteristics as those produced by the recording device. In this way, the entire system can be tested automatically without requiring a human tester. Usually the transcription is lower-cased, without punctuation and without sentence delimiters. Depending on the algorithms implemented further in the pipeline, obtaining "rich transcripts" (with correct casing and punctuation) may be a required processing step. At the speech recognition step we are interested in obtaining accurate transcriptions. These are characterized by a low character error rate (CER) and a low word error rate (WER). If using rich transcripts, we are also interested in obtaining high precision and recall in placing corresponding punctuation after each transcribed word.

The dialogue manager receives the transcript from the ASR system (either a regular transcript or a rich transcript). Then it tries to make sense of the user's query. If this is not possible, a standard message is usually returned, asking the user to repeat or rephrase the query. The dialogue manager usually makes use of a database with world or micro-world knowledge. This is useful either for directly retrieving relevant information or for populating slots in template messages. Finally, the answer is communicated as text sentences to the next component.

The TTS system is the last software component in the processing chain. It takes the text produced by the dialogue manager and transforms it into an audio signal. The audio signal is then rendered by a hardware component and presented to the human user. This completes a dialogue exchange between the human and the machine. The speech produced in the user's turn is travelling from the microphone to the ASR system and to the dialogue manager. The dialogue manager then generates the answer associated with the machine's turn which then travels via the TTS system to the hardware speaker. At this stage we are interested in producing an intelligible voice signal, as close as possible to the way a human would pronounce the message.

If we consider the hardware latency introduced by the hardware microphone and speakers to be negligible, then the overall system delay, as perceived by the human user, is given by the sum of the processing times $T$ associated with the software components: $T_{ASR}$, $T_{DM}$ and $T_{TTS}$, as described in Equation 1. To improve the user experience we need to minimize this perceived delay. Part of this equation is the time required for ASR processing, therefore this value also needs to be minimized.

$$T = T_{ASR} + T_{DM} + T_{TTS} \tag{1}$$

Apart from the delay, human users also look at the answers given by the system. If the system is always asking for clarifications, not being able to understand the user's query, or is providing unrelated results, the overall user experience is compromised. In this context, the dialogue manager plays the most important role. Nevertheless, it relies on the input provided by the ASR system. Therefore, once again it seems that speech recognition has a high impact on the overall performance of a speech-based HCI system.

For the purposes of the general diagram shown in Figure 1, we consider the ASR system to be the component that transforms audio data into text suitable for processing by the dialogue manager. However, this system usually has an internal structure comprising multiple pre-processing and post-processing modules. This is presented in Figure 2.

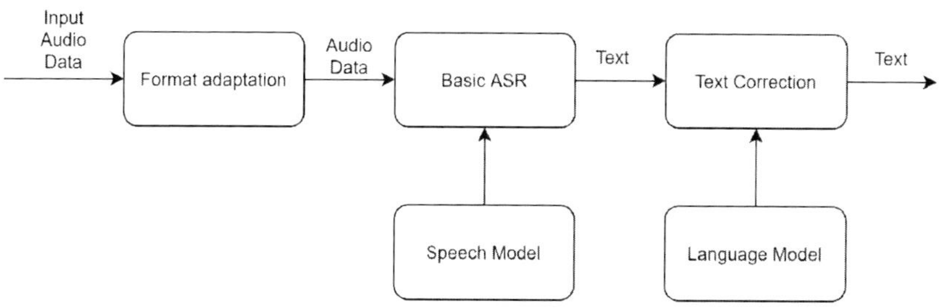


Figure 2. Detailed architecture of a generic ASR system.

Depending on the speech datasets used for training the speech model, pre-processing of the incoming audio data may be required. This includes format adaptation and filters. Format adaptation will convert the input signal into a format similar to the one seen during training (same sample rate, audio channels). Furthermore, audio filters may be used to keep only frequencies associated with human voice and discard others (usually associated with background noise).

The basic ASR component from Figure 2 needs an acoustic model, generated during the training phase. It will receive an audio stream in a compatible format and will produce an associated transcript. The transcript generated by the basic ASR component usually contains errors that can be further corrected using a language model. Additionally, the transcript can be enriched with automatically generated capitalization and punctuation in this post-processing step. This is implemented as a final post-processing operation before sending the text to the dialogue manager. More information about punctuation restoration is available in Chapter 5 of this book and in the survey of Păiş and Tufiş (2021). All these operations are generically called "text correction" in Figure 2 and represent the last block in this ASR processing chain.

# 3. Implementation Details

After covering the general architecture of speech-based HCI systems, we provide some implementation details from the ROBIN project. The resulting system follows the described general architecture, while having project-specific adaptations. Each component will be described in a corresponding subsection.

## 3.1. Automatic Speech Recognition

To solve the speech recognition task, we employed an end-to-end neural architecture that closely follows the original DeepSpeech2 model (Amodei et al., 2016), the only differences being the number of layers and neurons employed in each layer, that were reduced in order to better reflect the quantity of data we had at our disposal (Avram et al., 2020). The input of the model was generated by splitting the raw audio into 20 ms windows with a 10 ms stride and extracting the Mel-frequency cepstral coefficients (MFCCs) (Logan, 2000) from each frame. Then, each window was fed to a two-layered convolutional neural network (LeCun et al., 1998) whose role was to extract features from the spectrogram. The first layer uses a (41, 11) kernel and a (2, 2) stride, while the second layer has a kernel size of (21, 11) and a stride of (2, 1). Both layers employ a channel size of 32.

Each feature extracted by the convolutional layers is flattened and then the whole sequence is processed by four layers of bidirectional long-short term memory cells (LSTM) (Hochreiter and Schmidhuber, 1997) with 768 neurons. The role of these layers is to produce a contextualized representation based on the previous, present and future spectrogram features. Each contextualized representation is mapped into a vector of size 33 using a fully connected layer, with each entrance constituting the logit for one of the letters in Romanian, space, hyphen or a special token (i.e., the blank token) necessary to compute the CTC (Graves et al., 2006) loss. In addition, the DeepSpeech2 model comes with a batch normalization (Ioffe and Szegedy, 2015) after each layer except the last one that aids in the training more stable and faster.

The model was trained on a labeled speech corpus that contained approximately 230 hours of Romanian audio. The main part of the corpus comes from the oral component of CoRoLa (Mititelu et al., 2014) which contains mostly professional recordings from various sources (e.g., radio stations or recording studios). In the context of the RETEROM project[4], additional labeled audios were included in CoRoLa and thus in the overall training corpus of the DeepSpeech2 model. Other resources employed are represented by Romanian Digits (RoDigits) (Georgescu et al., 2018), Romanian part of Common Voice (RCV) (Ardila et al., 2020), Romanian Speech Synthesis (RSS) (Stan et al., 2011) and Romanian Read Speech Corpus (RSC) (Georgescu et al., 2020). In addition, three augmentation techniques were used on the audio data in order to improve the generalization capabilities of the model and reduce overfitting: (1) volume perturbation, (2) speed perturbation and (3) spectral augmentation (Park et al., 2019).

An N-gram based language model was further developed using the KenLM toolkit (Heafield, 2011) in order to improve the probabilities of the letters so that they produce transcripts that better align with Romanian text. The language model used 5-grams and was trained on a corpus composed of OSCAR - a corpus obtained by filtering Common Crawl[5] and the written part of CoRoLa, which totaled 10.2 GB of text after a cleaning procedure was applied. To further improve the performance of the language model, a grid search on the validation set was used to find its optimal hyperparameters $\alpha$ and $\beta$. $\alpha$ specifies the importance to place on the N-gram language model, while $\beta$ is a penalty term to consider the sequence length in the scores.

The Romanian DeepSpeech2 model was evaluated on a test set that contained 5,000 samples extracted randomly from the speech corpus. The results are outlined in Table 1. The raw model that did not employ the language model obtained a WER of 15.57% and a CER of 4.52%. Using the default hyperparameters of the KenLM $\alpha = 0.6$ and $\beta = 0.7$, the

[4]https://www.racai.ro/p/reterom/

[5]https://commoncrawl.org/

WER was improved by over 5.6% and the CER was improved by over 0.9%. After the grid search found the optimal hyperparameters $\alpha = 0.32$ and $\beta = 1.65$, the model obtained a final WER of 9.91% and CER of 2.81%. The results of the model with the language model trained on either CoRoLa or OSCAR, with and without the optimal hyperparameters, are also depicted in the table. It can be observed that the language model trained on the joint corpus obtained superior results in comparison with those trained on either of the individual corpora. The response time of the model was also tested using a CPU and a GPU, obtaining average response times of 600 ms and 70 ms, respectively, allowing the ASR module to respond in near real-time.

**Table 1. DeepSpeech2 evaluation results with various language model configurations: without a language model, non-/optimized language model trained on CoRoLa, non-/optimized language model trained on OSCAR, and non-/optimized language model trained on both CoRoLa and OSCAR**

| Model | N-Opt. WER | N-Opt. CER | Opt. WER | Opt. CER |
|---|---|---|---|---|
| DS2 | 15.57 | 4.52 | - | - |
| DS2+LMCoRoLa | 10.47 | 3.69 | 10.45 | 2.96 |
| DS2+LMOSCAR | 10.75 | 3.80 | 10.67 | 2.90 |
| DS2+LMCoRoLa+OSCAR | **9.92** | **3.61** | **9.91** | **2.81** |

The trained weights of the model, the code utilized for training and evaluating the model, and a script that creates an API for transcribing audio files were open-sourced for public usage[6]. Furthermore, the ASR component was integrated in the RELATE (Păiş et al., 2020; Păiş, 2020) platform and is available for online testing[7].

## 3.2. Dialogue Manager

The ROBIN Dialogue Manager (RDM, Ion et al. (2020)) was designed to work in a *micro-world*, that is, with a set of assumptions on the conversation limits, objects and facts from the targeted universe of discourse

[6]https://github.com/racai-ai/RobinASR

[7]https://relate.racai.ro/index.php?path=robin/asrdev

(e.g., a user asking for information in a computer store or a student asking for directions in a building), and with a *domain-aware ASR system* that is able to recognize quasi-English pronunciations of the domain-specific terms in Romanian. For instance, for the domain of selling computer-related hardware, the specialized ASR system has to recognize terms such as "uindăus" for "Windows" or "gi fors" for "GeForce". Without domain-specific tuning for ASR, these terms cannot be recognized properly. We will evaluate how the domain-specific ASR behaves in RDM as compared to the baseline ASR, in Subsection 5.1.

RDM is a Java application that is hosted on GitHub [8]. Each micro-world can be defined in a `.mw` file where objects from the universe of discourse and associated facts can be recorded. The objects from the universe of discourse are typed (e.g., they can be PERSONs, TIMEs, AMOUNTs or generic nouns such as "computer", "harddisk", etc.) and references of these objects can be enumerated with the REFERENCE keyword as in "Apple MacBook Air 13" is a reference of type "computer". TRUE predicates record which facts are true about the references in the `.mw` file, such as the store has some "Apple MacBook Air 13" laptops in stock. More information about the syntax and usage of `.mw` files can be found in the RDM paper and in the example files on GitHub[9].

The main dialogue loop of RDM works in the following way:

1. Microphone waits for input, automatically detecting speech and recording it until the user has stopped speaking.

2. The (configurable) ASR system takes the recorded wave file and produces the text for the associated speech act.

3. The text of the spoken utterance is automatically corrected using DICTionary statements from the `.mw` file statically mapping incorrectly transcribed strings to their correct form, as well as web services that deal with known errors produced by the configured ASR system.

4. The correct version of the textual user utterance is automatically POS

[8]https://github.com/racai-ai/ROBINDialog

[9]See the example files from the https://github.com/racai-ai/ROBINDialog/tree/master/src/main/resources folder.

tagged and dependency parsed, using the TEPROLIN Romanian text processing platform[10] (Ion, 2018).

5. All predicates are identified, with their compulsory arguments (i.e., subjects and direct objects), and matched with the predicates that are listed in the associated `.mw` file. The best match is used to utter the response back to the user.

6. The dialogue state is preserved for the active dialogue (RDM cannot handle multiple speakers at one time), and if the user is asking for more information about an event, the previously best matched predicate is used to supply this information. For instance, if the user is asking e.g., "Do you have a Windows 10 laptop?" and afterwards, "Does it have at least 8 GB of memory?", the second question refers to the set of laptops with Windows 10. More details about state preservation are found in Ion et al. (2020).

The RDM is quite fast[11] in the text processing and inference sections, with response times below one second for most of the received questions. Working with very specific micro-world scenarios, the questions are usually short (10 to 20 words) and so are the answers. To this processing time, the ASR and TTS computing times are added. Overall, we did not observe response times larger than three seconds for the whole cycle: ASR, text processing and TTS.

RDM was evaluated during the ROBIN project and *the performance largely depends on the accuracy of the ASR system*: if the text is correctly transcribed, the expected predicate is matched and thus, the correct answer is sent back to the user. The accuracy of the transcription depends on the quality of the recorded sound: we have experimented with sensitive microphones that were very close to the user's mouth as well as with environmental microphones that were further away from the speaker (at least two meters, also recording background noise). Thus, the ASR system was very good at recognizing good quality speech (empirically measured at approximately 9/10 words correct) and only average at recognizing noisy speech (6/10 words correct). Consequently, a dual-microphone speech enhancement algorithm (such as the one described by Yousefian and Loizou

[10] https://relate.racai.ro/index.php?path=teprolin/complete

[11] A video demonstration of RDM can be found at https://youtu.be/ZCWkoPPHReg

(2012)) would certainly help with improving the word recognition accuracy rate.

### 3.3. Text-to-Speech

RDM uses the SSLA text-to-speech library (Boroş et al., 2018) which is a statistical parametric speech synthesis algorithm that offers constant quality and a small memory footprint. It models frame-by-frame speech parameters such as spectral envelope, phone-state duration and voice pitch using decision trees. The input models are fully compatible with the HTS Toolkit (Tokuda et al., 2000) and only multinomial training is supported.

The feature set that SSLA uses is defined based on the phonetic context, syllable information, global context information (e.g., declarative, interrogative or exclamatory sentences) and local morpho-syntactic information. Please refer to Boroş et al. (2018) for an in-depth presentation of this feature set.

Evaluating RDM, we noted that SSLA produced very clear Romanian speech, easily intelligible, with approximately a second of processing. Numbers, dates and times, amounts of different kinds (e.g., mass, money, etc.) are automatically transcribed by RDM into text that can be readily synthesized into speech (e.g., "123" is transcribed into "o sută douăzeci şi trei" / "one hundred twenty three" and "08:00" is transcribed into "ora opt fix" / "eight o'clock sharp").

## 4. ASR Enhancements Leading to Increased Performance of the Overall System

As discussed in Section 1 and Section 2, the ASR component (with its subcomponents) has a huge impact on the entire system. This can be described in terms of total processing time required between the end of the human user's turn and the beginning of the computer's turn (see Equation 1) and in terms of the user's satisfaction when presented with an answer. In this section, we present techniques covering both the response time and the user's satisfaction, that were applied in our projects.

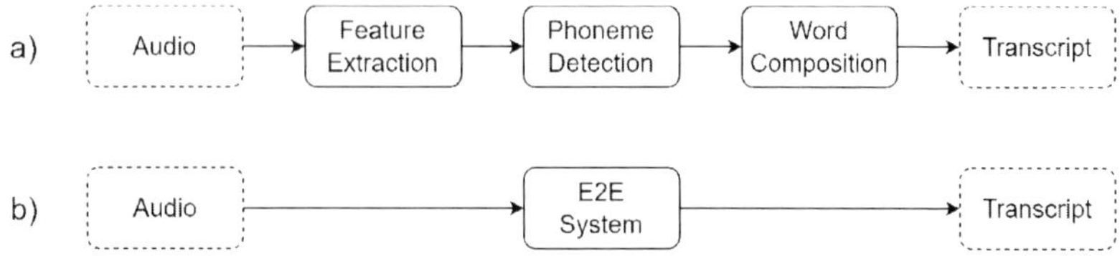


Figure 3. Architecture of (a) a pipeline ASR system and (b) an end-to-end ASR system.

## 4.1. End-to-End Neural ASR System

End-to-end (E2E) learning is one of the hottest topics in the deep learning and it refers to the possibility of training a single model for a complex problem (i.e., a deep neural network), bypassing the intermediate components that are usually present in traditional pipeline machine learning designs. E2E systems take advantage of deep neural network architecture which uses several layers to model complex problems and, similar to the human brain, each layer can specialize to perform intermediate tasks necessary to solve such problems.

The traditional design that was used to create ASR systems is a pipeline structure composed of three components: (1) *feature extraction* to extract the spectral information from the raw audio input, (2) *phoneme detection* to generate phonetical labels for each windows in the spectrogram and (3) *word composition* that uses the phonemes to generate the final transcription (see Figure 3). One limitation of this design is that the components are usually optimized in isolation, agnostic of the others, making each component brittle to the errors produced back in the pipeline. For instance, several wrongly predicted phonemes might confuse the word composition model, which has been trained mostly on correctly labeled data, causing the final transcript to contain words that were not uttered in the audio file. In addition, even if a suitable configuration is found, when one of the components needs to be updated, all the other ones have to be adjusted as well, in order to create an optimized system.

An E2E architecture solves these issues by replacing the three components in the pipeline architecture with a single component[12], usually a

[12]Some E2E systems keep the feature extraction component and use the spectrogram instead as input. However, this limits the generalization capabilities of the model and most

deep neural network, making the overall system more tightly connected and robust to potential errors (see Figure 3b). Another benefit of the E2E architecture is that it does not require deep knowledge of the subject (e.g., how to process phonemes) and only the input/output needs to be specified, the model being able to figure the best combination of patterns by itself. However, E2E models have their caveats including the high amount of data required for training or the difficulty in validating them due to their black-box nature (Goodfellow et al., 2016).

## 4.2. Fine-Tuning the ASR System with Domain-Specific Data

Adaptation of ASR systems to specific requirements has already been proposed and used in a variety of contexts. For example, ASR adaptation to speakers, as discussed in (Sari et al., 2020) and (Turan et al., 2020), is useful when the speaker is known in advance. Furthermore, when insufficient domain-specific data are available, domain adaptation techniques such as machine translation (MT) (Cucu et al., 2012; Mani et al., 2020) can be used. Since in our projects we are dealing with micro-worlds and the system is interacting with unknown speakers, we decided to increase the domain-specific data available and fine-tune the ASR system based on this new data.

We recorded a new dataset named "ROBIN Technical Acquisition Speech Corpus" (Păiş et al., 2021). For this purpose, a number of 711 sentences were created based on the specific micro-world scenario, related to the acquisition of computer hardware in an electronics shop. In the case of English words, in order to control the pronunciation, they were spelled as they would be read, instead of the English form. Considering this example sentence "Care e cel mai scump leptop huauei, cu placă grafică dedicată gi fors o mie şaizeci ti ai şi şase gigabaiţi RAM?" ("What is the most expensive Huawei laptop, with dedicated graphics unit GeForce 1060 Ti and 6 Gb of RAM?"), the words "laptop", "Huawei" and "GeForce 1060 Ti" are written as they should be pronounced ("leptop", "huauei", "gi fors o mie şaizeci ti ai" respectively). This ensures a good alignment between sound and text, ensuring its usability for ASR training.

The 711 sentences were divided in 4 groups, and 6 speakers (3 men and

---

of recent state-of-the-arts extract learnable features with convolutional networks directly from the audio.

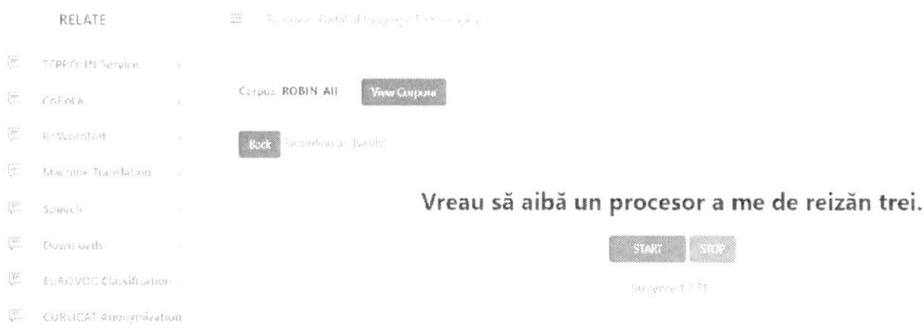


Figure 4. Recording interface within the RELATE platform.

3 women of different ages, using both off-the-shelf and dedicated recording equipment), selected from the ROBIN project's team, recorded a minimum of two groups of sentences. This resulted in a total of 3,786 audio files. Recording was performed using a dedicated component within the RELATE platform (Păiş et al., 2020). In this component, the user is presented with a single sentence to be spoken. The sentence is clearly made visible, by using a larger font and a different color, compared to the other interface elements. The user is given time to read and understand the sentence before pronouncing it. Thus, the user must press a "Record" button in order to start the recording. After recording one or multiple sentences, the user can access a list of the recordings and can decide to listen or download specific audio files. If the speaker realizes that a certain file is compromised (there was background noise or he made a mistake), then that file can be deleted and the corresponding sentence will be presented again for recording. Figure 4 presents an example sentence within the recording component.

The text component of the corpus was tokenized and annotated for lemma, part-of-speech and dependencies using UDPipe (Straka et al., 2016). The actual corpus processing was handled in the RELATE platform, by using the integration of multiple pipelines (Păiş, 2020), including UDPipe. The end product for the text component of the corpus was a collection of files named *Sn.txt*, for raw text files, and *Sn.conllu*, for annotated files. In this case, *Sn* stands for sentence number *n*. The *conllu* extension of the annotated documents indicates their format, which is the CoNLL-U format[13], fully described as part of the Universal Dependencies project. It is a column-based, tab-separated, format specifying 10 columns: word index, word form, lemma, universal part-of-speech tag[14], language-specific part-of-speech tag, morphological features, head of the current word, universal dependency relation, enhanced dependency graph and any other annotation. In our case, columns 9 (enhanced dependency graph) and 10 (other annotation) are always empty, while the rest of the columns are filled with corresponding information. Statistics regarding the text component of the corpus are given in Table 2. More information is available in (Păiș et al., 2021).

**Table 2. Text statistics**

| **Statistic** | **Value** |
|---|---|
| Number of text files | 711 |
| Total text size | 57Kb |
| Maximum file size | 122b |
| Minimum file size | 3b |
| Maximum number of characters | 115 |
| Maximum number of tokens | 26 |
| Minimum number of tokens | 2 |
| Average file size | 81.8b |
| Number of tokens | 11,927 |
| Unique tokens | 222 |
| Unique lemmas | 191 |
| Hapax legomena | 58 |

The audio component of the corpus is represented by WAV files. They follow the naming convention *Sn_s.wav*, where *n* represents the sentence number, similar to the text component file naming, and *s* represents the speaker number. By using this file naming scheme it is very easy to identify recordings corresponding to a certain sentence (by using the sentence number *n*) or recordings realized by the same speaker (by using the speaker

[13]https://universaldependencies.org/format.html
[14]https://universaldependencies.org/u/pos/index.html

number *s*). The files were recorded using recording devices available to the speakers (laptop microphone, headset, dedicated microphone) and converted to the same audio format using 44.1 KHz sample rate, 1 channel, and Signed Int16 PCM encoding. The total duration of the audio corpus is 6 hours and 25 minutes. More statistics about the audio component are provided in Table 3.

**Table 3. Audio statistics**

| Statistic | Value |
|---|---|
| Number of WAV files | 3,786 |
| Total duration | 6h25m03s |
| Minimum duration | 1.02s |
| Maximum duration | 12.91s |
| Average duration | 6.10s |
| Total size | 1.89Gb |
| Sample rate | 44.1KHz |
| Channels | 1 |
| Encoding | Signed Int16 PCM |

In addition to the text and audio data, we generated metadata associated with the corpus. This contains information about each speaker (gender, age interval, hardware recording device, number of recorded sentences), as well as overall corpus information. This enables further use of the corpus, by selecting only certain speakers (based on gender for example). For anonymization purposes, the age associated with speakers is given only as intervals (using a 10-year period) and not an actual number. Metadata is provided in a JSON file present in the dataset archive.

The ROBIN Technical Acquisition Speech Corpus dataset was used to train a new ASR model with domain-specific information in order to improve the performance in transcribing audio samples in the micro-world scenario of the ROBIN project. We used the above introduced DeepSpeech2 architecture, training the model from scratch, using randomly initialized weights, or fine-tuning the already existing version on the dataset. The KenLM language model that was employed to add a Romanian language bias when predicting transcriptions was upgraded in the fine-tuned version to better mimic the textual distribution found in the micro-worlds, by retraining it on a corpus that also contains the textual part of RTASC. A thorough analysis of their performance, together with the impact of the fine-tuning process is presented in the next section.

# 5. Impact of ASR Enhancements

In this section we present the effects of the ASR enhancements on both the dialogue manager and the overall system. We considered both the responses from the DM and the time delay before the user receives the response. Both are important aspects leading to an improved user experience.

## 5.1. Evaluation of RDM with a Fine-Tuned ASR System

We have evaluated RDM on the micro-world pertaining to the computer and computer hardware selling. In this domain, the ASR system is expected to cope with different (and sometimes incorrect) Romanian pronunciations of computer terminology and trademarks. For instance, say that the correct Romanian transcription of the English "Windows 10" phrase is "uindăus ten". There are pronunciations such as "uindos ten" or even "uindos zece" where the numeral "ten" is translated into Romanian. The ASR system was expected to recognize all of these possible pronunciations and this was one of the principles of constructing the ROBIN Technical Acquisition Speech Corpus.

The DeepSpeech2 model, fine-tuned using the new ROBIN Technical Acquisition Speech Corpus, was tested on a set of 50 test questions, from the same domain as the technical corpus, that were not included in the corpus. The same test was performed with the baseline ASR system that formed the basis of the fine-tuned system. Two male speakers (first one recorded sentences for the ROBIN Technical Acquisition Speech Corpus and the second one was new) read the test questions, using the recording equipment that each had available[15], and we measured the Word Error Rate (WER – the percent of wrongly recognized words out of the total words) with the baseline ASR model and with the fine-tuned.

[15]The new speaker used a webcam-grade microphone and the technical corpus contributor used a sensitive microphone in a quiet room.

**Table 4. WER on the ROBIN Technical Acquisition Speech Corpus test set**

| Speaker | Baseline WER | Fine-tuned WER |
|---|---|---|
| Male speaker 1 | 39.65% | 29.54% |
| Male speaker 2 | 59.92% | 45.79% |

**Test sentence**: Aveţi [redacted] cu 32[redacted] de RAM?
**Reference**: aveţi leptop asus cu treizeci şi doi de gigabaiţi de ram
**Baseline ASR**: aveţi [redacted] cu treizeci şi doi de [redacted] de ram
**Fine-tuned ASR**: aveţi [redacted] cu treizeci şi doi de [redacted] de ram

Figure 5. WER improving due to fine-tuning.

Table 4 shows that fine-tuning ASR systems works especially for the recognition of the domain-specific terminology. Speaker one used a sensitive microphone which explains his lower WERs, but in both cases, the reduction due to fine-tuning is significant. Inspecting the output of the fine-tuned ASR system, we discover that, in the vast majority of cases, the main difference is in the recognition of computer terminology and trademarks. Figure 5 gives an example of the differences in terminology recognition.

The fine-tuned ASR system may recognize a term properly or it may misspell it slightly, but in the latter case, it does much better than the baseline ASR system which fails completely. Figure 6 exemplifies this: "Apple" is wrongly transcribed as "pol" or "păr" by the baseline system and "M1" is misspelled as "emunu" instead of the expected "em unu" by the fine-tuned system. This type of errors directly influences the performance of the RDM, which fuzzy matches predicate arguments: if an argument is only misspelled, it will still be matched while if the argument is completely wrongly recognized, it will not match at all.

**Test sentence**: Vreau un [redacted] cu procesor [redacted].
**Reference**: vreau un [redacted] cu procesor [redacted]
**Baseline ASR**: vreau un [redacted] cu procesor [redacted]
**Fine-tuned ASR**: vreau un [redacted] cu procesor [redacted]

Figure 6. Fine-tuning misspellings vs. baseline errors.

The two ASR systems behave similarly when there are no specific terms. This is an indication that the baseline (general-domain) ASR system has not been degraded by the fine-tuning procedure. Figure 7 shows a general language sentence that is almost correctly recognized by both ASR systems (the only difference is the word "jocul" vs. the correct "jocurile").

**Test sentence**: Care este cel mai ieftin sistem pe care mă pot juca jocuri grafice?
**Reference**: care este cel mai ieftin sistem pe care mă pot juca jocuri grafice
**Baseline ASR**: care este cel mai ieftin sistem pe care mă pot juca [redacted] grafice
**Fine-tuned ASR**: care este cel mai ieftin sistem pe care mă pot juca jocuri grafice

Figure 7. General language is recognized properly by both ASR systems.

Using transcriptions of Male speaker 1 (the one who had the lowest WER, see Table 4), RDM was checked to see if it could find the relevant predicate (together with its arguments) when working with the baseline ASR system versus the fine-tuned ASR system. We found that with the baseline system, RDM picked up the relevant predicate in 23 transcriptions out of the total 50. The correct predicate identification rate grew to

40/50 when using the fine-tuned system. A total of 6/50 transcriptions were generated incorrectly by both systems, and thus, the identification of the relevant predicate was impossible.

## 5.2. Overall System Response Time

In Section 2, equation 1, we considered the overall response time as the sum of the response times associated with individual system components. We ignored things such as network time or time passing the message between components, since these are very small compared to the processing time required by each component. Thus in order to reduce the overall processing time, we need to focus on reducing each individual component's latency. Due to architectural constraints, the DM time is $T_{DM} \approx 500ms$, while the TTS time is in the interval $[500ms, 1200ms]$, depending on the length of the generated response, with an average value of $T_{TTSAVG} \approx 850ms$. Considering these processing times fixed, we were able to investigate the effects of the proposed ASR architecture on the overall system time. Nevertheless, it should be noted that TTS synthesis time can also be reduced using specific techniques. For improved TTS systems see Chapter 7 of this book and the work of Dumitrache and Rebedea (2020).

Given the end-to-end neural architecture for the ASR system, it is possible to execute it on CPU or GPU. Due to the massive parallelization of the processing flow, GPU computations are less time consuming. The ASR system was tested on an Intel i7-7700K CPU and achieved an average $T_{ASR-CPU} = 600ms$ (considering micro-world specific dialogues). Then, it was tested on an NVIDIA 1080 Ti GPU and it achieved an average $T_{ASR-GPU} = 70ms$. More experiments are described in (Avram et al., 2020).

By adding the invidual times, and considering the average TTS time, we achieve an overall response time $T_{CPU} = 1950ms$ and $T_{GPU} = 1420ms$. We consider both to be good response times, allowing the user to have an enjoyable experience interacting with the robot. Furthermore, the neural architecture used for the ASR system allowed us to decrease the response time, which in turn led to an improved overall time, especially when executing the ASR component on a GPU.

## Conclusion

Our work within the ROBIN project has shown that the performance of the ASR component has a direct impact on the overall system performance in the context of a speech-based HCI. Different ASR specific enhancements, used within the ROBIN project, were presented with their respective influence reflected on the entire speech-based dialogue system. Part of this work, a new Romanian speech dataset was constructed. It was presented in Section 4.2 and is available for download from the Zenodo platform[16], under a Creative Commons Attribution Non Commercial No Derivatives 4.0 International license[17].

The resulting ASR models were also exposed in the RELATE platform[18]. This allows for any online user to test the models and also run further text analysis on the automatic transcriptions. The models can be tested either by directly recording speech or by uploading a pre-recorded WAV file. Nevertheless, for improved performance, the user should limit the queries to micro-world specific topics.

Furthermore, the ASR system was used to construct a Romanian to English speech-to-speech translation mechanism (Avram et al., 2021) that is available within the RELATE platform[19]. The Speech-to-Speech translation system is composed of four families of components that were integrated into a cascaded manner: (1) automatic speech recognition, (2) transcription correction, (3) machine translation and (4) text-to-speech. Each component contains one or several models from which the user can choose, allowing high flexibility in how the overall system is configured. The first module contains both the general ASR trained on the 230 hours of Romanian audio data and the fine-tuned ROBIN Technical Acquisition Speech Corpus presented in this work. The second component contains a single model which capitalizes the words from a list of known named entities and replaces the predicted words with words from a known vocabulary. The machine translation component was developed in the "CEF Automated Translation toolkit for the Rotating Presidency of the Council

[16]https://doi.org/10.5281/zenodo.4626539

[17]https://creativecommons.org/licenses/by-nc-nd/4.0/legalcode

[18]https://relate.racai.ro/index.php?path=robin/asr

[19]https://relate.racai.ro/index.php?path=translate/speech_ro_en

of the EU" project under the coordination of TILDE[20]. For the fourth component, the English speech synthesizer, we used the pretrained Tacotron2 with Dynamic Convolution Attention (Battenberg et al., 2020) offered by MozillaTTS[21].

## References

Amodei, D., Ananthanarayanan, S., Anubhai, R., Bai, J., Battenberg, E., Case, C., Casper, J., Catanzaro, B., Cheng, Q., Chen, G., et al. (2016). Deep speech 2: End-to-end speech recognition in English and Mandarin. In *International conference on machine learning*, pages 173–182. PMLR.

Ardila, R., Branson, M., Davis, K., Kohler, M., Meyer, J., Henretty, M., Morais, R., Saunders, L., Tyers, F., and Weber, G. (2020). Common voice: A massively-multilingual speech corpus. In *Proceedings of the 12th Language Resources and Evaluation Conference*, pages 4218–4222.

Avram, A.-M., Păiş, V., and Tufiş, D. (2020). Towards a Romanian end-to-end automatic speech recognition based on DeepSpeech2. In *Proc. Rom. Acad. Ser. A*, volume 21, pages 395–402.

Avram, A.-M., Păiş, V., and Tufiş, D. (2021). A modular approach for Romanian-English speech translation. In Mtais, E., Meziane, F., Horacek, H., and Kapetanios, E., editors, *Natural Language Processing and Information Systems*, pages 57–63, Cham. Springer International Publishing.

Battenberg, E., Skerry-Ryan, R., Mariooryad, S., Stanton, D., Kao, D., Shannon, M., and Bagby, T. (2020). Location-relative attention mechanisms for robust long-form speech synthesis. In *ICASSP 2020-2020 IEEE International Conference on Acoustics, Speech and Signal Processing (ICASSP)*, pages 6194–6198. IEEE.

Boroş, T., Ştefan Daniel Dumitrescu, and Păiş, V. (2018). Tools and resources for Romanian text-to-speech and speech-to-text applications.

[20] https://ro.presidencymt.eu/#/text

[21] https://github.com/mozilla/TTS

Cucu, H., Besacier, L., Burileanu, C., and Buzo, A. (2012). Asr domain adaptation methods for low-resourced languages: Application to Romanian language. In *2012 Proceedings of the 20th European Signal Processing Conference (EUSIPCO)*, pages 1648–1652.

Deriu, J., Rodrigo, A., Otegi, A., Echegoyen, G., Rosset, S., Agirre, E., and Cieliebak, M. (2021). Survey on evaluation methods for dialogue systems. *Artificial Intelligence Review*, 54(1):755–810.

Dix, A., Finlay, J., Abowd, G., and Beale, R. (2004). *Human-computer interaction*. Pearson/Prentice-Hall, Harlow, England ; New York, 3rd ed edition.

Dumitrache, M. and Rebedea, T. (2020). Exploring end-to-end neural text-to-speech synthesis for Romanian. In Barbu Mititelu, V., Irimia, E., Tufiș, D., and Dan, C., editors, *Proceedings of the 15th International Conference Linguistic Resources and Tools for Natural Language Processing*, pages 93–102, Bucharest, Iași and online.

Georgescu, A. L., Caranica, A., Cucu, H., and Burileanu, C. (2018). RODIGITS-a Romanian connected-digits speech corpus for automatic speech and speaker recognition. *University Politehnica of Bucharest Scientific Bulletin (submitted to)*.

Georgescu, A.-L., Cucu, H., Buzo, A., and Burileanu, C. (2020). RSC: A Romanian read speech corpus for automatic speech recognition. In *Proceedings of The 12th Language Resources and Evaluation Conference*, pages 6606–6612.

Goodfellow, I., Bengio, Y., and Courville, A. (2016). *Deep learning*. MIT press.

Graves, A., Fernández, S., Gomez, F., and Schmidhuber, J. (2006). Connectionist temporal classification: labelling unsegmented sequence data with recurrent neural networks. In *Proceedings of the 23rd international conference on Machine learning*, pages 369–376.

Gupta, D., Bansal, P., and Choudhary, K. (2018). The state of the art of feature extraction techniques in speech recognition. In Agrawal, S. S., Devi,

A., Wason, R., and Bansal, P., editors, *Speech and Language Processing for Human-Machine Communications*, pages 195–207, Singapore. Springer Singapore.

Heafield, K. (2011). KenLM: Faster and smaller language model queries. In *Proceedings of the sixth workshop on statistical machine translation*, pages 187–197.

Hochreiter, S. and Schmidhuber, J. (1997). Long short-term memory. *Neural computation*, 9(8):1735–1780.

Ioffe, S. and Szegedy, C. (2015). Batch normalization: Accelerating deep network training by reducing internal covariate shift. In *International conference on machine learning*, pages 448–456. PMLR.

Ion, R. (2018). TEPROLIN: An extensible, online text preprocessing platform for Romanian. In *Proceedings of the International Conference on Linguistic Resources and Tools for Processing Romanian Language (ConsILR 2018)*, Iaşi, Romnia.

Ion, R., Badea, V. G., Cioroiu, G., Barbu Mititelu, V., Irimia, E., Mitrofan, M., and Tufiş, D. (2020). A dialog manager for micro-worlds. *Studies in Informatics and Control*, 29(4):411–420.

Jaimes, A. and Sebe, N. (2007). Multimodal human-computer interaction: A survey. *Computer Vision and Image Understanding*, 108(1):116–134. Special Issue on Vision for Human-Computer Interaction.

LeCun, Y., Bottou, L., Bengio, Y., and Haffner, P. (1998). Gradient-based learning applied to document recognition. *Proceedings of the IEEE*, 86(11):2278–2324.

Logan, B. (2000). Mel frequency cepstral coefficients for music modeling. In *In International Symposium on Music Information Retrieval*. Citeseer.

Mani, A., Palaskar, S., Meripo, N. V., Konam, S., and Metze, F. (2020). Asr error correction and domain adaptation using machine translation. In *ICASSP 2020 - 2020 IEEE International Conference on Acoustics, Speech and Signal Processing (ICASSP)*, pages 6344–6348.

Mititelu, V. B., Irimia, E., and Tufiş, D. (2014). CoRoLathe reference corpus of contemporary Romanian language. In *Proceedings of the Ninth International Conference on Language Resources and Evaluation (LREC'14)*, pages 1235–1239.

Park, D. S., Chan, W., Zhang, Y., Chiu, C.-C., Zoph, B., Cubuk, E. D., and Le, Q. V. (2019). Specaugment: A simple data augmentation method for automatic speech recognition. *arXiv preprint arXiv:1904.08779.*

Păiş, V., Ion, R., Barbu Mititelu, V., Irimia, E., Mitrofan, M., and Avram, A. (2021). ROBIN technical acquisition speech corpus.

Păiș, V. (2020). Multiple annotation pipelines inside the RELATE platform. In *The 15th International Conference on Linguistic Resources and Tools for Natural Language Processing*, pages 65–75.

Păiș, V., Ion, R., Avram, A.-M., Irimia, E., Mititelu, V. B., and Mitrofan, M. (2021). Human-machine interaction speech corpus from the robin project. In *2021 International Conference on Speech Technology and Human-Computer Dialogue (SpeD)*, pages 91–96.

Păiș, V., Ion, R., and Tufiş, D. (2020). A processing platform relating data and tools for Romanian language. In *Proceedings of the 1st International Workshop on Language Technology Platforms*, pages 81–88, Marseille, France. European Language Resources Association.

Păiş, V. and Tufiş, D. (2021). Capitalization and punctuation restoration: a survey. *Artificial Intelligence Review.*

Raju, S., Jagtap, V., Kulkarni, P., Ravikanth, M., and Rafeeq, M. (2020). Speech recognition to build context: A survey. In *2020 International Conference on Computer Science, Engineering and Applications (ICCSEA)*, pages 1–7.

Sari, L., Moritz, N., Hori, T., and Roux, J. L. (2020). Unsupervised speaker adaptation using attention-based speaker memory for end-to-end asr. In *ICASSP 2020 - 2020 IEEE International Conference on Acoustics, Speech and Signal Processing (ICASSP)*, pages 7384–7388.

Stan, A., Yamagishi, J., King, S., and Aylett, M. (2011). The Romanian speech synthesis (RSS) corpus: Building a high quality HMM-based speech synthesis system using a high sampling rate. *Speech Communication*, 53(3):442–450.

Straka, M., Hajič, J., and Straková, J. (2016). UDPipe: Trainable pipeline for processing CoNLL-U files performing tokenization, morphological analysis, POS tagging and parsing. In *Proceedings of the Tenth International Conference on Language Resources and Evaluation (LREC'16)*, pages 4290–4297, Portorož, Slovenia. European Language Resources Association (ELRA).

Tokuda, K., Yoshimura, T., Masuko, T., Kobayashi, T., and Kitamura, T. (2000). Speech parameter generation algorithms for HMM-based speech synthesis. In *Proc. of ICASSP*, pages 1315–1318.

Turan, M. T., Vincent, E., and Jouvet, D. (2020). Achieving Multi-Accent ASR via Unsupervised Acoustic Model Adaptation. In *Interspeech 2020*, pages 1286–1290. ISCA.

Yousefian, N. and Loizou, P. C. (2012). A dual-microphone speech enhancement algorithm based on the coherence function. *IEEE Transactions on audio, speech, and language processing*, 20(2):599–609.

In: Speech Recognition Technology ... ISBN: 978-1-68507-929-1
Editor: Vasile-Florian Păiş 

Chapter 4

# The Role of Automatic Speech Recognition Systems in Developing Medical Applications

**Maria Mitrofan***
Research Institute for Artificial Intelligence
"Mihai Drăgănescu", Romanian Academy,
Bucharest, Romania

**Abstract**

Technological progress in recent years has impacted the medical system, leading to the emergence of new technologies specific to the medical field. Important resources have been directed to transform the medical system. The most recent include digital scribes, voice biomarkers and medical IoT. In some segments, the performance of the systems was improved by the use of technologies such as automatic speech recognition and natural language processing. While medical notes were shorthanded in the 20th century, today the healthcare system has begun to adopt ASR-based technologies to transcribe conversations between doctors and patients. An ASR technology that can accelerate transcription of the clinical conversation has an immediate positive impact on the medical act.

ASR-centered technologies are now part of the offering of big software development companies, such as Google, Amazon, IBM, etc. These companies and others, including many startups, have

*Corresponding Author's Email: maria@racai.ro.

entered the race to offer different types of Machine Learning technologies that support medical services to facilitate the work of clinical workers: electronic health records and automated digital scribes use ASR and NLP to automatically transcribe patient-clinician conversations and medical notes. Voice biomarkers are being used to develop automated solutions that can identify and monitor health conditions such as Parkinson's Disease or screen potential COVID-19 infections. The IoT computing paradigm is being used within a medical context in what is known as the Internet of Medical Things to deliver low latency Edge computing that enables a new generation of medical apps.

**Keywords:** ASR, NLP, medical, EHR, vocal biomarkers, IoMT

## 1. Introduction

In the last few years, digital health technology has seen a radical transformation, largely due to the interest in modernizing the medical system worldwide and in improving medical acts. This has been made possible by using recent developments in Artificial Intelligence and Machine Learning research and in the rise of Big Data platforms and Cloud computing that enable the automation of essential parts of the medical process.

Recently, AI systems such as medical scribes have employed the advances in automatic speech recognition (ASR) and natural language processing (NLP) to develop intelligent clinical environments. Both ASR and NLP are key areas that can contribute to the development of medical technologies. Although ASR began to be used in the medical field in the 1980s, it is only in the 21st century that the quality of ASR has increased so that it can be considered useful in transcribing medical conversations. Even though the development of ASR systems for the medical domain currently presents a number of challenges, the latest studies report a performance of ASR closer to that of human scribes.

State-of-the-art ASR and NLP systems have enabled research and development in a wide range of clinical processes, such as electronic health records that automatically transcribe doctor-patient conversations, technologies that use ASR to identify vocal biomarkers that can detect medical conditions, and the Internet of Medical Things (IoMT) that uses computing and sensors to deliver smart health applications.

This paper will further present recent ASR-based technologies that contribute to smart healthcare systems

## 2. General Overview of ASR

Automatic speech recognition (ASR) enables users to transform speech audio signals (word sequences) into corresponding texts. However, when compared with other types of signals (e.g., images) speech recognition is difficult, because speech displays a large range of variability in speech signals. This variability is caused by the complex interaction of various factors such as speaker characteristics, environmental noise, channel distortion (e.g., microphone issues), speech style and rate, and dialect differences. A successful ASR system must deal with all of these (Yu and Deng, 2016).

Traditional ASR systems encompass multiple components that work together much like in a pipeline system. A typical architecture contains signal processing and feature extraction, ASR models, and hypothesis search that combines model scores for a given feature vector sequence and hypothesized word sequence that outputs the word sequence with the highest score. In the signal processing and feature extraction module, the audio signal is taken as input and is then enhanced by removing noise and distortions. Subsequently, the signal is converted from the time domain to the frequency domain. Finally, significant feature vectors are extracted that are suitable for the following acoustic models (Aldarmaki et al., 2021). Additionally, "rich transcripts" require proper capitalization and punctuation restoration (Păiş and Tufiş, 2021).

ASR models are composed of three main components: an acoustic model, a phonetic dictionary, and a language model (see Fig.1). The Acoustic Model (AM) estimates the probability that a given speech signal has been generated by a corresponding sequence of words by incorporating knowledge about acoustics and phonetics which can be modeled using Hidden Markov Models (HMMs) (Juang and Rabiner, 1991) and Gaussian Mixture Models (GMMs) (Zhang et al., 1994). The language model (LM) estimates the probability of a hypothesized word sequence, or LM score, by learning the correlation between words from a training corpus that is, usually, a text. Language models are used to improve the accuracy of acoustic models by integrating linguistic knowledge.

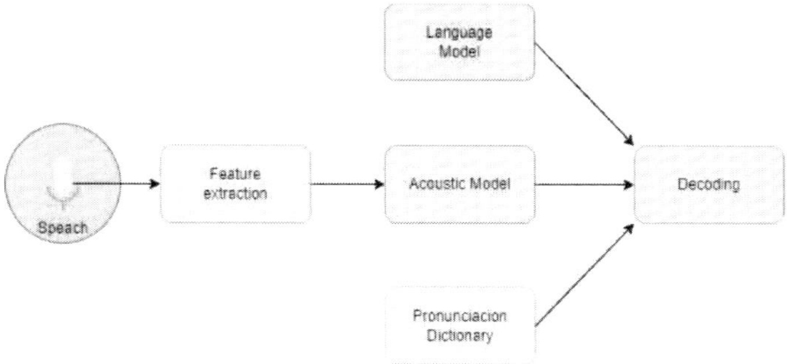


Figure 1. Typical Traditional Pipeline ASR Architecture.

The accuracy of ASR was significantly improved when traditional GMMs were replaced by deep neural networks (DNNs). This hybrid modeling replaced the acoustic likelihood evaluation, but still kept all the components such as the acoustic model and language model. Since the introduction of deep learning in ASR (Hinton et al., 2012), a variety of neural network architectures for acoustic modeling have been explored (Miao et al., 2015), (Zhang et al., 2015)), such as recurrent neural networks (RNNs) and long short-term memory (LSTM) neural networks (Hochreiter and Schmidhuber, 1997).

Recently, the speech community made a breakthrough by transitioning from hybrid modeling to end-to-end (E2E) modeling ((Bahdanau et al., 2016), (Prabhavalkar et al., 2017)), which directly translates an input speech sequence into an output token sequence using a single network. End-to-end systems refer to a unitary architecture, capable of receiving raw audio or speech features as input and outputting words. Unlike in a pipeline system, all the component, such as the feature extractor, the acoustic model, and even sometimes the language model are integrated into a single network (Li, 2021).

# 3. NLP Applications in Medical Domain

The rapid development of emerging AI technologies has led to the emergence of numerous smart applications in various healthcare fields. One of the main AI-based technologies is natural language processing (NLP), and due to its ability to analyse and process texts, NLP plays a key role in the development of smart healthcare technologies. For example, ASR systems that use NLP are among the most advanced due to NLP capability to simulate real conversations.

In the following, we present three of the most relevant tasks of NLP that together with ASR contribute to the development of intelligent medical applications: named entity recognition (NER), classification and summarization.

## 3.1. Named Entity Recognition

Extracting relevant information from clinician-patient transcripts and translating it into a structured form can help reduce physicians' burnout caused by bureaucratic problems. Although it is well known that the task of information extraction (IE) from medical transcripts is not a trivial one, it is of interest to both academia and industry. Named entity recognition (NER) is a key component of the pipeline for extracting information from medical texts because it can help identify medical named entities such as diseases, drugs, surgery reports, anatomical parts, treatment, etc. Therefore, we will present current state-of-the-art results obtained following the latest studies in this field.

One of the first relevant works in extracting entities from transcripts based on clinical conversations is presented in (Finley et al., 2018). They used hierarchical recurrent neural networks (RNNs) to tag sentences and turns with their predicted class. In the next stage, the sentences classified as such were preprocessed using a series of heuristics such as: regular expressions used to identify predictable entities (medication dosages, temporal expressions), and complete or partial string matches with ontologies. Although the models presented in this paper have contributed to the development of applications in this field, they also have some drawbacks, such as the fact that removing sentences from context can lead to misinterpretations.

(Du et al., 2019), developed an application designed to extract symptoms mentioned in clinical conversations. The authors proposed two deep learning approaches to identify symptom names: a hierarchical Span-Attribute Tagging (SAT) model and a sequence-to-sequence model able to infer the symptoms and their status from speaker turns using a sliding window over the conversation. The system was trained on a corpus consisting of 3,000 conversations, manually annotated by medical scribes. This approach achieved an F-score between 0.5 and 0.8, depending on the complexity of the symptom.

(Patel et al., 2020), work also focused on extracting Medication Regimen information from doctor-patient transcripts. They extracted three types of attributes corresponding to medications: frequency, route and change. The corpus used in this paper consists of 63,000 medical transcripts, all of them being annotated by human annotators with MR tags. The framework developed was based on weak supervision and used noisy classification labels. This approach achieved an F1-score of 0.66 for frequency identification, 0.58 for route of the medicine and 0.33 for identification of the change in treatment.

(Shafran et al., 2020), trained a state-of-the-art tagging model in order to extract medications mentions, symptoms and medical conditions. For this work, a corpus of 6,000 doctor-patient conversations was annotated by medical scribes. The Span-Attribute Tagging model was used to identify clinically relevant spans and to tag the spans with the specific labels. This approach obtained an F1-score of 0.9 for medications, 0.72 for symptoms and 0.57 for conditions.

(Selvaraj and Konam, 2021), implemented Question Answering (QA) models based on a sequence-to-sequence attention model, and pointer-generator networks (PGNets) (See et al., 2017) augmented with Co-Attentions in order to extract Medical Regimen (MR) from transcribed medical conversations. Medication Regimen extraction is defined by the identification of dosages and frequencies from the medication mentioned in the conversations. Due to the complexity of the transcripts, the system is designed to extract information from a segment of the transcript and not the entire transcript. The study used 6,693 real clinician-patient conversations. This approach obtained an F1-score of 0.89 for dosage and 0.46 for medication frequency.

(Krishna et al., 2021), developed a system capable of identifying relevant diagnoses mentioned in the conversation and organ system abnormalities reported by the patient. They used neural approaches (e.g., BERT models (Devlin et al., 2018)) combined with traditional learning approaches in order to tackle the multi-label classification challenges. The main problems of this task are the large size of the conversations, each conversation containing approximately 1,500 words, and the irrelevant information they contain. For this work, a corpus of 6,862 physician-patient conversation transcripts with corresponding annotated notes was used. It includes transcripts from cardiology (2,732), family medicine (2,731), interventional cardiology (989), and internal medicine (410). They reported an F1-score of 0.86.

One of the biomedical entity types of relevance for medicine or biosciences are chemical compounds and drugs. The correct detection these entities is critical for other text mining applications building on them, such as adverse drug-reaction detection, medication-related fake news or drug-target extraction (Gonzalez-Agirre et al., 2019). In this context, (Ion et al., 2019) proposed an ensemble system combining a gazetteer-based baseline and a RNN-based NER system, leading to an F1 score of 0.85 when applied on Spanish language. (Păi and Mitrofan, 2021), while focusing on named entity recognition of professions and occupations in health-related social media, proposed combining multiple word embedding representations. Experiments show that domain-specific embeddings produce better results than general-domain embeddings. However, a combination of these achieves the highest F1 score.

Considering the Romanian language, (Mitrofan, 2019) considered the field of biomedical named entity recognition. This lead to the creation of the SiMoNERo Romanian medical treebank (Mititelu and Mitrofan, 2020), containing named entity annotations. (Petrea et al., 2009) introduce a spontaneous speech database for the Romanian language with medical applicability. The authors also acknowledge the challenge of creating a spontaneous speech recognition tool for Romanian language with medical applicability for the benefit of persons with difficulties in mobility, communication and even common people. Even though not focusing on the medical domain, (Avram et al., 2020) propose constructing an end-to-end neural ASR for Romanian language based on the DeepSpeech2 architecture, while (Ungureanu et al., 2021) propose establishing a baseline for Romanian speech-to-text models. In this context, the integration of different ASR and biomedical NER systems in the RELATE platform for processing Romanian language ((Păi et al., 2020), (Pi, 2020)) is expected to foster further research in this area.

**Table 1. F1 scores for different entity extraction models**

| Study | Type of network | Type of entities | F1-score |
|---|---|---|---|
| (Finley et al., 2018) | RNN | medication dosage, temporal expression, symptom | - |
| (Du et al., 2019) | SAT and seq2seq | symptom, status | 0.5-0.8 |
| (Patel et al., 2020) | NN | frequency, route, change | 66.90, 58.09 , 33.54 |
| (Shafran et al., 2020) | SAT | condition, symptom, medication | 57, 72, 90 |
| (Selvaraj and Konam, 2021) | seq2seq | dosage, frequency | 89.57, 45,94 |
| (Krishna et al., 2021) | NN | diagnosis | 86.12 |

## 3.2. Classification

As a classic task of NLP, text classification plays an essential role in more complex NLP tasks such as text retrieval or data mining. However, medical text categorization can be considered a specific area of text classification, because most of the time it has to deal with problems such as high dimensionality or data sparsity. Usually, medical transcripts contain detailed information, a patient's medical history and the effect of the prescriptions, hence complex medical vocabularies that classification models have to deal with. In the following, current state-of-the-art results for the classification of medical transcripts are presented.

(Jeblee et al., 2019), developed a system that extracts relevant information from a set of 800 transcripts of conversations between a patient and a physician. This study can be seen as a starting point for a system that automatically generates clinical notes from dialogues. To extract and classify relevant information from the transcripts, the authors used models such as neural networks (NNs), latent Dirichlet allocation (LDA) (Blei et al., 2003) and support vector machines (SVMs). The system developed consists of an automated pipeline that contains the following modules: text preprocessing, medical entity extraction and classification of utterance type, attribute, relevant sections of a clinical note and primary diagnosis. To understand the context of each conversation, each utterance is classified in one of the six classes: statement, question, answear, backchannel, positive answer, negative answer or excluded (unclear utterance). For this type of classification, a two-layer bidirectional gated recurrent unit (GRU) (Cho et al., 2014) neural network was used, and an F1-score of 0.71 was obtained. After the relevant entities were identified they were classified according to two attribute types: pertinence (relevance) and modality (whether the mentioned events took place or not). The attribute classifier is based on SVM and achieved an F1-score of 0.62 for pertinence and 0.77 for modality.

The extracted entities were also classified according to relevant sections of a usual clinical note: subjective (S), objective (O), assessment (A), plan (P) and none if the entity is relevant or not to a note. For the SOAP classification the authors used neural models that achieved an F1-score of 0.60. Another task in the pipeline was primary diagnosis classification with the help of which the main diagnosis of a note was identified. The models used for this type of classification are based on SVM, logistic regression and random forest models and achieved an average F1-score of 0.78.

Using recent advances in both ASR and NLP (Schloss and Konam, 2020), have taken a step forward in automatically generating medical notes. Their study presents a system designed to classify both utterances from medical dialogues according to SOAP sections and the speaker role (doctor, patient, caregiver and other). A hierarchical encoder-decoder architecture was trained on 8,130 medical conversations and obtained an F1-score of 0.48 for SOAP sections and 0.59 for speaker classification.

Additionally, a recent work on the classification of medical transcripts is presented in (Ferracane and Konam, 2020). In order to classify the utterance according to SOAP classes (subjective, objective, assessment, plan and none), the authors trained a model based on biLSTMs and LSTMs neural networks and obtained an F1-score of 0.38. The lack of heterogeneity of the results was justified by the diversity of the training data (63,000 annotated transcripts). They split all the files into 18 advantages and disadvantages groups based on gender, ethnicity, age, socioeconomic status, mental health, obesity and location, so they could observe a statistically relevant difference that occurs in the case of the advantaged group.

## 3.3. Summarization

Automatic conversation summarization between physicians and patients can reduce the amount of information that physicians need to process in order to systematize medical records. A summary is defined as a reductive transformation of source text to summary text through content reduction selection and/or generalization on what is important in the source (Jones, 2007). As the main purpose of the summarization is to extract the essential information and reduce the redundancies, it can be a useful tool that can help clinicians structure medical information. Therefore, there is a growing interest in developing this NLP task in the medical domain. If, for medical staff understanding and extracting information from a physician-patient conversation is a trivial task, for automated NLP systems, it can be a challenge due to the specific elements of medical language and the variability of conversations.

(Liu et al., 2019), describe a proposed an architecture able to extract key information and to identify the topic spanned across turns from multiple utterances. Utilizing the hierarchical structure of the conversations they integrated attention mechanisms at the topic level in an adapted pointer-generator neural network. This approach proves to attain robust performance, outperforms the baseline and maintains its behavior even in the case of a small set of training data.

One of the recent attempts to systematize relevant aspects of a medical encounter that can be used for later medical decisions is done by (Joshi et al., 2020). They used an extension of a pointer generator network (PGNet) where they introduced a penalty to the generator distribution and added medical concepts and explicit models for identifying negations. The authors of the study showed that this approach can capture relevant information in 80% of the conversations, therefore, this system can be considered a viable alternative to manually summarizing the information in medical notes.

(Enarvi et al., 2020), describe an end-to-end neural summarization architecture that generates medical reports from physician-patient conversation transcripts. The reported results were obtained using a corpus of 800,000 ambulatory orthopedic surgery encounters from 280 physicians. The input of the system is represented by a sequence of tokens generated in the ASR phase. Each medical report is divided into four main sections and each section is generated by a seq2seq neural model. The authors stated that seq2seq models, in particular Transformer, are superior to models based on RNN because they have the capability to extract key information from clinical conversation transcripts and to summarize the relevant information extracted.

# 4. ASR Applications in Medical Domain

## 4.1. Digital Scribes for Medical Domain

In recent years, an acknowledged problem in healthcare has been represented by clinicians burnout (Friedberg et al., 2014). Usually, the clinician needs to dedicate a large amount of its working time to clinical documentation, this situation leading to information loss (Shachak et al., 2009) and distractions (Campbell et al., 2006).

Even though the majority of clinicians have hired medical scribes which seems to be the perfect solution, the direct medical costs have increased substantially. Therefore, with the hope that both the effort and time invested by clinicians in the documentation process will be reduced, interest in digital scribe systems has increased. Using these types of systems, the clinician-patient relationship improves, developing better patient-centered care.

A digital scribe (or a speech recognition-assisted documentation system) is an automated system that uses as input clinician-patient conversations and automatically extracts information useful for the clinical encounter note. In theory, a digital scribe is able to perform the same function as human medical scribes (Finley et al., 2018). From a technical point of view, a digital scribe is a pipeline that employs technologies from both ASR and NLP in order to provide clinicians with tools able to produce medical notes based on clinician-patient conversations.

The typical infrastructure of a digital scribe contains a microphone used to record the conversation between the patient and the clinician, an ASR system used to convert the audio to text, a set of NLP models used to extract information from the transcript, summarize the relevant information and generate the final medical note (see Fig. 2).

### 4.1.1. Challenges of Developing Digital Scribes for the Medical Domain

There are imminent challenges and risks for each step from a digital scribe pipeline, some of which are described below.

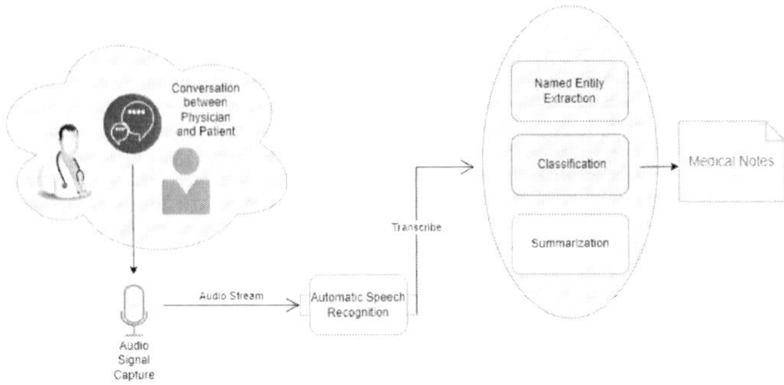


Figure 2. Medical Scribe Architecture.

The first task that any digital scribe system must be able to do is audio recording of a clinician-patient conversation. Even if it appears to be an easy step to take, in practice, there are many variables that can influence the quality of the recording. The diversity of the acoustic environments, the position of the recording device, background noise, and long-form content have a strong impact on the quality of the recording. Several works showed that the word error rate based on commercial ASR engines for medical conversations was at least 35%. Moreover, a typical clinician-patient conversation takes place between more than two participants, thus adding a supplementary level of complexity and potential error to the ASR system. To tackle the problem of diarization, (Shafey et al., 2019) proposed a system based on a recurrent neural network that improved the word-level diarization error rate from 15.8% to 2.2%. As (Quiroz et al., 2019) stated, medical speech differs from conversational speech in several ways.

In medical conversations, different linguistic phenomena are present, such as disfluencies, nonlexical pauses, repeated words, restarted sentences, lack of clear juncture for phrases, and perhaps the feature that has the most semnificative impact on the performance of a medical ASR is complex medical terminology, which includes numerous new terms. (Chang et al., 2002) have shown that in every 5-10 medical abstracts there is one new abbreviation. This feature of medical vocabulary is the main reason why most ASR systems have been trained and tested in a single medical field.

After the ASR system has rendered the transcript corresponding to the doctor-patient conversation, the next step in the pipeline of a digital scribe

```
Dr: Did your mother or your father have diabetes
or cadio-vascular diseases?
P:  Yes, my mother had diabetes.
Dr: Type 2 diabetes?
P:  Yes, and my father died from a stroke.
Dr: Currently what treatment do you have at home?
P:  Aspenter 75 mg 1 cp/day, Noliprel 5 mg 1cp/day,
Rosucard 40 mg 1cp/day.
Dr: Ok. How have you been diagnosed with type 2 diabetes?
P:  I did my annual check-up because I was very
thirsty and I was drinking around 3-4 liters of water per day.
Dr: Did you also have some other symptoms such as
blurry vision, weight loss or asthenia?
P:  Yes, blurry vision and weight loss.
I lost around 4 kilos in 1 month.
```

Figure 3. Example of clinician-patient conversation.

is the one in which the text is structured in a useful form for the next processing steps. Although this stage of processing should not pose any problem, in the case of medical conversations, the texts produced often do not have a linear chain of topics discussed. Namely, the topic of the conversation may be changed from one speaker turn to another.

Figure 3 shows that during a conversation between doctor and patient, a series of transitions are made from one subject to another, often without a connection between them. Therefore, for a digital scribe to generate coherent medical notes, the system needs to identify clear boundaries of each topic, connect disparate information throughout the conversation, and concatenate it into a coherent and relevant form.

Currently, numerous semantic taxonomies and tools are used for extracting relevant information from medical unstructured texts. Two such tools, that allow the user to map text with Unified Medical Language System (UMLS)[1] concepts, are MetaMap[2] and cTAKES[3]. MetaMap was developed by the National Library of Medicine (NLM) in order to map biomedical text to concepts in UMLS. It combines computational linguistic techniques with NLP approaches. The Clinical Text Analysis and Knowledge Extraction System (cTAKES) uses machine learning and rule-based techniques to standardize medical concepts and to extract information from medical texts. Even though these tools are widely used and known in the

[1]https://www.nlm.nih.gov/research/umls/index.html

[2]https://lhncbc.nlm.nih.gov/ii/tools/MetaMap.html

[3]https://ctakes.apache.org/

biomedical field, both were designed and developed for written texts, and not for spoken medical conversations. This is the main cause of inaccuracies and word mismatching when tools designed for medical written language are used for spoken language. For example, using MetaMAP to map concepts from a spoken conversation may result in the extraction of irrelevant information.

The process of developing ASR systems for the medical domain is also hampered by the lack of structured medical data. Firstly, obtaining and sharing medical data can be difficult or sometimes impossible because of privacy issues. Secondly, data obtained from real-life conversations between clinicians and patients prove to be very noisy data that requires significant pre-processing work. Consequently, clean and structured medical data can be considered valuable assets for both academia and industry, and obtaining a real data set from hospitals or medical clinics to apply deep learning methods can be extremely tedious. A solution to annotate large amounts of data may be crowdsourcing, but unlike other areas, there is a need for domain knowledge.

Although the list of challenges can be long, the need for virtual writers with performances close to human ones, makes increasing efforts to be focused on the development of these technologies.

## 4.2. Software and Platforms with ASR-Based Capabilities in the Medical Domain

Medical ASR, due to its immediate applicability, is a topic of research also for specialized companies. In this chapter information related to several commercially available products is also included. The advent of performant ASR and NLP happening in the last years allowed the emergence of a new paradigm of medical software services generating a new ecosystem of applications centered around automation and AI. This includes, for instance, smart assistants, speech recognition platforms used for dictation, Electronic Health Record systems (EHRs) and more. All of these have enabled clinicians to interact with patients while the software does most of the patient encounter workflow: it listens to the conversation between the physician and the patient while performing a transcription, it can automatically write clinical documentation, automatically retrieve relevant information and so on. In addition to the rise of ML technologies, the success of these applications has also been made possible by the use of cloud and big data infrastructures to support the technical demands of such applications.

Examples of such software and platforms offering ASR based capabilities are as follows:

- Modal Fluency Direct[4] from 3M is a cloud based front-end EMR using speech recognition technologies to deliver real time automated and interactive intelligence to clinicians.

- Dragon Medical One[5] from Nuance recently introduced what it refers to as ambient clinical intelligence (ACI) into its services by automatically writing clinical documentation that includes data concerning the history of illnesses, physical exams, assessments, and treatment plans. All the information is then inputted into the EHR. The company claims that when the patient and clinician speak naturally, it can translate nonclinical terms into clinical terminology while summarizing natural language into coherent sentences.

- Kiroku[6] is one of the platforms targeting the specific niche of dentistry and claims that users can reduce the time they spend creating clinical notes by 50%.

- Suki[7] is providing both a speech platform and a voice-driven digital assistant designed for clinicians allowing them to speak their notes into an EHR, claiming to reduce documentation time by 76% on average. It can copy notes from previous patient encounters, and show the physician details on a specific patients medications while retrieving their vital signs and problem lists. The platform was tested by The American Academy of Family Physicians in its Innovation Laboratory during a pilot project [8]. Ten clinicians in three medical domains concluded that the results were compelling with a 62%

[4]https://www.3m.com/3M/en/_US/health-information-systems-us/create-time-to-care/clinician-solutions/speech-recognition/fluency-direct/

[5]https://www.nuance.com/healthcare/provider-solutions/speech-recognition/dragon-medical-one.html

[6]https://trykiroku.com/

[7]https://www.suki.ai/s3

[8]https://www.aafp.org/dam/AAFP/documents/media_center/charts-graphs/digitalassistant-innovationlab–phase-1-whitepaper.pdf

decrease in documentation time per patient, a 51% decrease in documentation time during clinic hours, and a 70% decrease in after-hours charting.

- DeepScribe[9] claims that its proprietary ambient scribe technology automatically listens to natural patient conversations without any prompting. Then the AI-based solution extracts medically-relevant information, summarizes the interaction into cohesive sentences, and directly integrates notes into the appropriate fields in an EHR system.

- Abridge[10] provides audio based solutions that record and summarize medical conversations. For clinicians, the platform uses algorithms that quickly produce a SOAP outline type of documentation. What sets Abridge apart from other companies is that they also offer an application available on iOS and Android that can be used by patients to record their conversation, generate interactive transcripts and obtain key points such as medication instructions.

The examples above are systems targeting end users on both sides of the spectrum, namely patients and clinicians.

Another class of platforms are those offered by Microsoft, IBM, Google and Amazon, where they provide access to development frameworks and APIs that can be used by other companies and developers to incorporate ASR and NLP capabilities in their own apps.

One concern, however, is the actual performance of ASR and NLP within specific medical contexts. For instance, this study from 2018 (Kodish-Wachs et al., 2018) targeting conversational medical speech found a wide range of word errors across the most known general purpose ASR engines, with values ranging from 65% to 34% (ASR engines that were tested included Microsoft, IBM, Amazon, Nuance, Google and others).

(Chiu et al., 2017) presented state-of-the-art papers for speech recognition for medical conversations and reported that Connectionist Temporal Classification (CTC) phoneme-based models were able to achieve a word error rate of 20.1%, and Listen Attend and Spell (LAS) grapheme-based models were able to achieve a word error rate of 18.3%. For comparison,

[9] https://www.deepscribe.ai/
[10] https://www.abridge.com/

a study made on several ASR implementations, reported a word error rate of 2.98% obtained with Nvidia Quartznet models (Georgescu et al., 2021).

Another work (Miner et al., 2020), dealing with the accuracy of ASR in psychotherapy using Google Cloud Speech-to-Text with a sample of patient-therapist audio recordings collected as part of a US-based clinical trial, had a transcription word error rate of 25%. For clinician-identified harm-related sentences, the word error rate was 34%. The conclusion of the study was that, as of the time of the study, ASR in the psychotherapy context may support understanding of language patterns but may not be ready for individual-level safety surveillance.

Recently, in a paper published by Google (Soltau et al., 2021), pertaining to extracting clinically relevant information from speech data using a Recurrent Neural Network Transducer (RNN-T) network (Graves, 2012) achieved a WER of 20% on the ASR task. This is comparable to other models in recent work but the novelty is that using an RNN-T model with a fixed-alignment loss achieved is relatively simpler. The authors also mention that it will be available as Google APIs.

In conclusion, although these commercial products represent possible viable solutions for different areas of the medical field, most of them need validation in terms of clinical utility. Although each product presented promises to help the medical field, the performances are not transparent and therefore a technical validation is not yet possible. In order to prove their clinical utility, all these products must provide technical validity, clinical validity, usability, and utility. Without a transparent presentation of these research phases, it is difficult to determine whether they are really useful or not.

### 4.2.1. Case Study: Amazon Medical

- **Amazon Transcribe Medical**

  The following is a short description of Amazon's offering that specifically targets the medical domain. Amazon Transcribe Medical[11] is Amazon's medical ASR service that allows transcription of medical related speech. It is available to use through two modes: real-time streaming transcription (using a microphone) and batch transcription (through an uploaded file). When an audio stream is sent to Amazon

[11] Amazon Transcribe Medical

Transcribe Medical, it returns a stream of JSON objects containing the audio transcription. Batch mode also supports channel identification to separate and transcribe channels and identify speakers in single-channel audio files. For better results, the medical specialty of the clinician in the transcription job or stream needs to be provided.

Currently, the following medical specialties are supported in streaming transcription only: Cardiology, Neurology, Oncology and Urology. Family medicine, Internal medicine, Obstetrics and Gynecology (OB-GYN) and Pediatrics are supported in both streaming and batch modes. Medical custom vocabularies can also be used to improve transcription accuracy. Amazon Transcribe uses APIs to interact with the system. For instance, to start a medical transcription job, one can use the StartMedicalTranscriptionJob[12] API, and to retrieve information on a medical transcription job, one can use the GetMedicalTranscriptionJob[13] API.

- **Amazon Comprehend Medical**

  Amazon Comprehend Medical[14] is the natural language processing (NLP) service offered by Amazon that uses a pretrained model to detect meaningful information in unstructured clinical text (e.g., physicians notes, discharge summaries, test results, case notes). These are known in NLP as named entities and are textual references to medical information such as medical conditions, medications, and protected health information. In some cases, these entities are linked to standardized ontologies (including RxNorm[15], ICD-10-CM[16], and SNOMED CT[17] knowledge bases).

  All results include a confidence score, which indicates the confidence that the NLP engine has in the accuracy of the detected entities. Entities can be detected in several categories: Anatomy (e.g., parts of the body), Medical Condition (e.g., symptoms, diagnosis), Medication, Protected Health Information (patient's personal infor-

[12]https://docs.aws.amazon.com/transcribe/latest/dg/transcribe-medical.html
[13]https://docs.aws.amazon.com/transcribe/latest/dg/transcribe-medical.html
[14]https://aws.amazon.com/comprehend/medical/
[15]https://www.nlm.nih.gov/research/umls/rxnorm/index.html
[16]https://www.cdc.gov/nchs/icd/icd10cm.htm
[17]https://www.snomed.org/

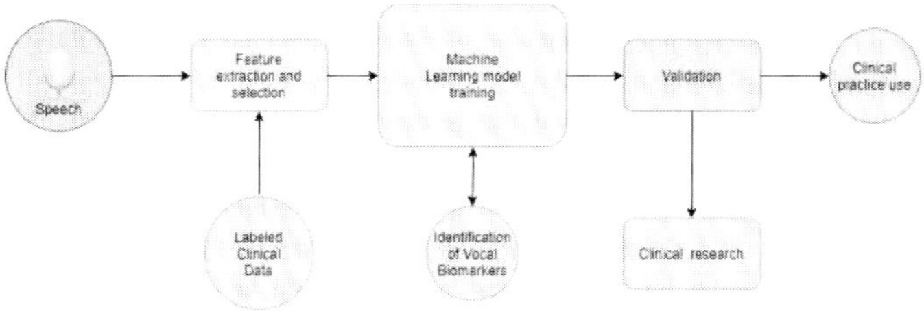


Figure 4. Classic Architecture of a Voice Biomarker.

mation), Test Treatment Procedure (procedures that are used to determine a medical condition) and Time Expression (entities related to time). At the time of writing of this chapter Amazon Comprehend Medical[18] can analyse text only in English (US-EN).

## 4.3. ASR and Vocal Biomarkers

Diseases can affect various organs that can subsequently affect the human voice. Speech is therefore a novel biomarker that can be used in screening patients, diagnosing conditions, or in grading the severity of the stages of an illness. Recent examples include research on vocal biomarkers related to Parkinson's Disease, Alzheimer's Disease and Mild Cognitive Impairment, Multiple Sclerosis and Rheumatoid Arthritis, Mental Health, Cardiometabolic and Cardiovascular Diseases, COVID-19 and Other Conditions with Respiratory Symptoms (Fagherazzi et al., 2021). One advantage of speech as a biomarker is that it is noninvasive (Quatieri et al., 2020) (see Fig. 4).

For instance, for Alzheimer's disease (AD), using the state-of-the-art end-to-end (E2E) ASR pretrained model wav2vec2.0 achieved accuracy of 83.2% and 78.0% in the Chinese language in the long-audio and short-audio competition tracks of the 2021 NCMMSC Alzheimer's Disease Recognition Challenge (Quiroz et al., 2019), respectively.

Another study on the automatic detection of AD (Sadeghian et al., 2021) described a fully automatic speech recognition system using a combination of Hidden Markov Model (HMM) and Deep Neural Network

[18] https://docs.aws.amazon.com/comprehend-medical/latest/dev/comprehendmedical-welcome.html

(DNN) methods and reported an accuracy of 94.5%, albeit using a small sample size.

Reporting on the 2021 ADReSSo Challenge shared task (Luz et al., 2021) a study (Luz et al., 2021) using Google Cloud-based Speech Recognizer for automatically transcribing the audio and a combination of acoustic and linguistic features extracted directly from audio recording, without human intervention, achieved a baseline accuracy of 78.87% for the AD classification task and 68.75% accuracy for the cognitive decline prediction task.

For Parkinson's Disease (PD), a study (Tracy et al., 2020) focusing on the clinical utility investigated using classic machine learning models - L2-regularized logistic regression, random forest, and gradient boosted decision trees - reported an AUC score of 85%.

Within the COVID-19 global pandemic context, a study (Han et al., 2020) reports an average accuracy of 69% in estimating the severity of illness, based on the number of days in hospitalization. Another study (Maor et al., 2021) performed on 80 subjects reported an area under the curve (AUC) of 72% in associating the vocal biomarker with SARS-CoV-2. When added to a self-reported symptom classifier, the AUC was 85%.

State-of-the-art ASR systems combined with the use of vocal biomarkers are enabling the development of health-related frameworks and software directly targeting the automation of clinical processes.

Surfboard[19] is an open-source Python library for extracting audio features with applications to the medical domain. Developed by the Novoic company[20] it was built on top of packages such as LibROSA[21] and pysptk[22], and it can be used both programmatically in python or by a command-line interface. Surfboard's architecture includes extracting components as single values or time series - in which case statistics can be extracted from the time series to create time-independent features. These features can be fed, for instance, into a multilayer perceptron (MLP), a common use case for audio classification tasks. In (Lenain et al., 2020) is preented a use case on classifying Parkinson's disease sufferers versus healthy controls on the mPower dataset (the outcome of the mobile Parkin-

[19] https://pypi.org/project/surfboard/

[20] https://novoic.com/

[21] https://librosa.org/doc/latest/index.html#

[22] https://pysptk.readthedocs.io/en/latest/

son Disease study (Bot et al., 2016) done with surveys and tasks that activate phone sensors to collect and track health and symptoms of Parkinson Disease (PD) progression including audio recordings). The results reported included an AUC score of 85% when the training and testing sets were randomly sampled and 69% for the situation where the training and testing sets were disjointed by participants.

Vocalis Health[23] is an AI company specializing in health tech that has developed a voice-enabled AI platform that creates proprietary vocal biomarkers for healthcare screening and continuous remote monitoring of health. Vocalis Health is identifying disease-specific vocal biomarkers to go through various validations. Voice samples are collected from users that are then analysed, verified, and labeled with an associated medical record. The Vocalis Health technology transforms the audio recordings into visual images. A unique signature is generated per disease/condition and for each patient. A validation procedure is then conducted on the training data of a specific vocal biomarker.

VocalisCheck[24] is a software solution that assesses the voice of a person whose COVID-19 status is unknown, without additional information or prior knowledge about the individual user. The system provides an API that can be used to provide a quick voice check which can be integrated into workflows and it is available as a software-only product with a cloud-based algorithm database. A single voice sample is recorded using a mobile app or web-based tool, and a cloud-based AI analytics engine provides feedback within a minute or two.

VocalisTrack[25] is another solution that enables chronic patients to be tracked at home using voice. It is a stand-alone, AI-based software tool that analyses voice recordings of patients who record their voice via the app on their smartphone. Analysing the data from this app, VocalisTrack offers the clinical care team ongoing insights about the patients current shortness of breath. It uses the patients smartphone without additional hardware or physical examination and it detects changes in patients' shortness of breath. This in turn allows the care team to potentially take clinical actions. The company claims that the software has a sensitivity of 95% and a specificity of 93%, for identifying changes in shortness of breath.

[23] https://vocalishealth.com/

[24] https://vocalishealth.com/vocalis-health-products/vocalischeck

[25] https://vocalishealth.com/vocalis-health-products/vocalistrack

Sonde[26] is another company that provides different solutions for preventative healthcare. Its product, Mental Health, is a voice-powered mental fitness tracking and journaling product that can help users monitor their mental fitness. Objective changes in mental fitness can be measured through changes in vocal features. Their respiratory health product detects and monitors for symptoms of COVID-19, asthma, COPD, and several other pulmonary conditions. The company claims that respiratory fitness health checks and tracking can be estimated from just 6 seconds of voice on a smartphone. It provides information on various symptoms like coughing, shortness of breath, difficult breathing, chest tightness. It is available through an API or directly through the app. The Sonde Platform Service API allows partners to access Sonde Vocal Biomarkers based Health Check with their apps. The API is recieves vocal samples and returns a risk score from 0 to 100.

Cortis AI technology[27], Audia, is used in the company's solution in triage for call centers that can analyse patient consultations in text, video, or audio formats, and detect whether there is a high risk of COVID-19. The company claims that Audia has already learned from more than 100,000 medical interviews about COVID-19.

Winterlight[28] has developed a tablet-based technology that assesses cognitive health (including memory, thinking, and reasoning) by analysing hundreds of language markers from short snippets of speech. By analysing speech alone, the app can detect cognitive impairment associated with dementia and mental illness by using 550 features of speech and language. The company has provided an API that can be used to receive analyses for speech data already collected or to integrate with other apps or devices that continuously collect speech to receive results.

Kintsugi[29] is a company developing speech recognition based software targeting mental health use cases. The company uses voice biomarkers to measure and predict well-being. The technology is available on smartphones and home devices as an app. It provides access to various well-being exercises and quizzes that are clinically validated that the company claims challenge cognitive distortions. The software allows the tracking of

[26] https://www.sondehealth.com/

[27] https://www.corti.ai/

[28] https://winterlightlabs.com/

[29] https://kintsugihello.com/

the progress over time with journal entries and emotional wellness markers.

Audeering[30] is a company that cooperates with the University of Augsburg to carry out research studies on a voice-based COVID-19 test. They collect data samples, audio recordings, and related health data. The company claims that its AI system can achieve an accuracy of up to 82%. It can detect emotions, scenes, and many other features from audio. The SoundLab[31] software can monitor health developments, provide analysis for diagnosis, and collect data for the development of voice biomarkers. Human experts can use health data enriched by AI technology for diagnoses.

## 4.4. Medical IOT and ASR

The Internet of Things (IoT) is a paradigm of integration between IT technologies, devices, and sensors that has enabled the emergence of a new generation of applications (see fig. 5). While it is usually thought of in connection to smart home appliances, it has also been part of a wide range of smart automation in all kinds of fields, such as agriculture, transportation, and energy management. Taking advantage of classic cloud technologies and newer architecture approaches such as Edge and Fog computing, the IoT has allowed the development of real-time healthcare solutions labeled as medical IoT (or IoMT) that are intelligent.

This has become of increased relevance even more so within the global pandemic context where physical access to healthcare can be an issue due to various factors, such as social restrictions, huge numbers of screenings that need to be done in a short amount of time, and all sorts of health risk concerns. IoT technologies take advantage of a complex number and types of signals, and one of the important applications is the combination of these signals with speech to deliver enhanced clinical solutions ((Greco et al., 2020), (Amin and Hossain, 2020)).

One example of the convergence of AI and IoT in healthcare is described by (Muhammad and Alhussein, 2021). In this study, a smart healthcare framework for Voice Pathology Detection (VPD) is proposed that captures electroglottograph (EGG) and voice signals that are further transformed into spectrograms on the Edge Layer of the IoT System. These are

[30] https://www.audeering.com/

[31] https://soundlab.cs.princeton.edu/software/

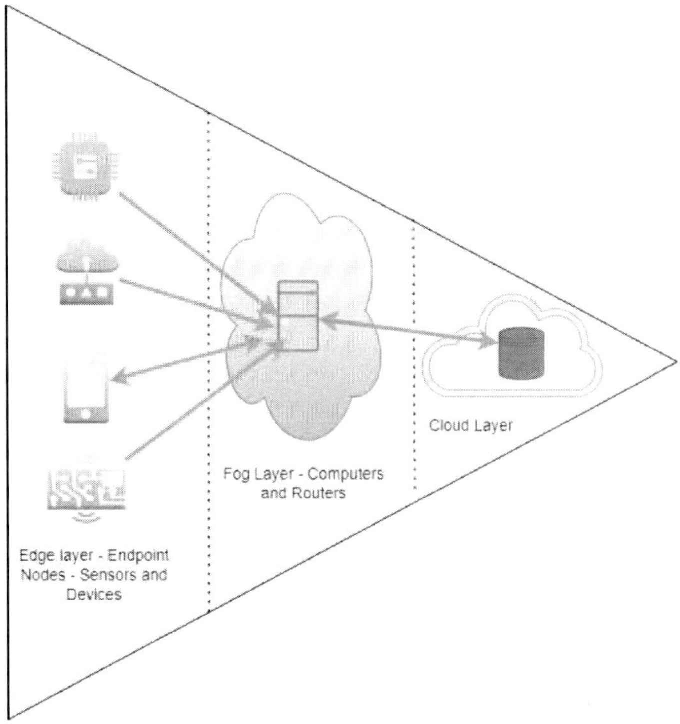


Figure 5. IoT architecture.

sent to the Cloud Layer of the system where features are extracted from the spectrograms using a CNN and are merged and processed using a bidirectional long short-term memory network (LSTM). The results are then sent back to the app users. The paper reports an accuracy of 95.65% evaluated on the fused signals of voice and EGG.

In (Baucas and Spachos, 2020) a Remote Patient Monitoring (RPM) solution architecture is described and investigated. To address issues related to patient privacy, real-time data flow, and patient-service interaction, the system uses an IoT-framework consisting of Raspberry-Pi for monitoring, recording, filtering, and preprocessing of voice signals and an NVIDIA Jetson TX1 kit for video monitoring and complex processing of the framework - the Fog layer of the IoT system. Based on the input from the users, if assistance is requested and detected by the ASR module, then the system will stream data into the Cloud layer, where it can be further assessed by a medical center, or a remote interactive session is initiated when needed. Using the Google Speech Command dataset, an accuracy of 96.8% was achieved. For these types of real-world use cases, another important evaluation criterion is the system response time, and its latency. For this purpose, the study compared the system configured with Edge processing as already described with a Cloud-only configuration where the Raspberry-Pi end nodes send the data directly in the Cloud where it is processed. In a scenario where three equipped rooms are sending data, the average latency time of the Edge setup was 0.16 ms as opposed to 20.02 ms obtained in the Cloud-only setup.

From the above two mentioned use cases, one can see that an advantage of the IoT is that it can push the processing of machine learning (ML) algorithms at any of the layers, thus creating scenarios where extremely large amounts of data can be manipulated.

Another example of benefits from merging ML technology - specifically regarding ASR - with IoT frameworks in healthcare is given by (Ramallo-González et al., 2021). In this paper, an open IoT platform has been explored that attempts to bridge data acquisition, aggregation, and machine learning technologies to combat the COVID-19 pandemic. The platform uses sensors to perform voice data collection, using ASR to infer breathing rhythms, coughing, sneezing, together with oxygen saturation monitoring and temperature monitoring (done at in-house fixed points and using a Markov Chain to derive a classification of health/disease patterns). The collected information is sent through the fusion and storage layer using the NGSI protocol[32]. The Analytics Support Layer and the Service Layer are used to enable the gathering of insights into COVID-19 patterns and the ability to provide feedback and act using, for instance, conversational bots.

## Conclusion

The performance of ASR and NLP systems has increased rapidly over the years allowing these technologies to be used in healthcare-related contexts where accuracy and latency are critical in building real-world use case scenarios. Both ASR and NLP are an essential part of the interface between

[32] https://knowage.readthedocs.io/en/6.1.1/user/NGSI/README/index.html

health workers and patients and the automation of clinical processes.

In the case of NLP, techniques such as Named Entity Recognition, Classification and Summarization enable software such as Digital Medical Scribes to deliver the needed functionality. ASR seems to be the gateway for many of the medical use cases that have been taken up by research institutes or by medical companies. This is the case for EHR platforms that are becoming an industry norm for medical services.

One of the domains where ASR has a lot of impact is in clinical research and the development of Vocal Biomarker technology. For instance, Parkinsons Disease and Alzheimers Disease research has used ASR technologies to develop methods for automatic screening and monitoring of patients. Usage of vocal biomarkers-enabled technology is being used to research improvements in real-time triage and monitoring of patients in epidemic crises such as COVID-19.

ASR is also part of the emergence of the Medical IoT domain that brings together IoT frameworks with medical use cases that leverage the power of edge computing for fast feedback and merging of signals from various medical sensors to enhance ML algorithms featurization. There are, however, some concerns related to the availability of medical voice corpora that would allow the ML algorithms to be trained on a much wider range of data. However, it is also true that the medical domain is benefiting from the use of ASR and NLP, and this is expected to be even more so in the future.

## References

Aldarmaki, H., Ullah, A., and Zaki, N. (2021). Unsupervised automatic speech recognition: A review. *arXiv preprint arXiv:2106.04897*.

Amin, S. U. and Hossain, M. S. (2020). Edge intelligence and internet of things in healthcare: A survey. *IEEE Access*, 9:45–59.

Avram, A.-M., Vasile, P., and Tufis, D. (2020). Towards a Romanian end-to-end automatic speech recognition based on DeepSpeech2. In *Proc. Rom. Acad. Ser. A*, volume 21, pages 395–402.

Bahdanau, D., Chorowski, J., Serdyuk, D., Brakel, P., and Bengio, Y. (2016). End-to-end attention-based large vocabulary speech recognition. In *2016 IEEE international conference on acoustics, speech and signal processing (ICASSP)*, pages 4945–4949. IEEE.

Baucas, M. J. and Spachos, P. (2020). Fog and iot-based remote patient monitoring architecture using speech recognition. In *2020 IEEE Symposium on Computers and Communications (ISCC)*, pages 1–6. IEEE.

Blei, D. M., Ng, A. Y., and Jordan, M. I. (2003). Latent dirichlet allocation. *the Journal of machine Learning research*, 3:993–1022.

Bot, B. M., Suver, C., Neto, E. C., Kellen, M., Klein, A., Bare, C., Doerr, M., Pratap, A., Wilbanks, J., Dorsey, E. R., et al. (2016). The mpower study, parkinson disease mobile data collected using researchkit. *Scientific data*, 3(1):1–9.

Campbell, E. M., Sittig, D. F., Ash, J. S., Guappone, K. P., and Dykstra, R. H. (2006). Types of unintended consequences related to computerized provider order entry. *Journal of the American Medical Informatics Association*, 13(5):547–556.

Chang, J., Schutze, H., and Altman, R. (2002). Creating an online dictionary of abbreviations from medline. *Journal of the American Medical Informatics Association*, page 612620.

Chiu, C.-C., Tripathi, A., Chou, K., Co, C., Jaitly, N., Jaunzeikare, D., Kannan, A., Nguyen, P., Sak, H., Sankar, A., et al. (2017). Speech recognition for medical conversations. *arXiv preprint arXiv:1711.07274*.

Cho, K., Van Merriënboer, B., Gulcehre, C., Bahdanau, D., Bougares, F., Schwenk, H., and Bengio, Y. (2014). Learning phrase representations using rnn encoder-decoder for statistical machine translation. *arXiv preprint arXiv:1406.1078*.

Devlin, J., Chang, M.-W., Lee, K., and Toutanova, K. (2018). Bert: Pre-training of deep bidirectional transformers for language understanding. *arXiv preprint arXiv:1810.04805*.

Du, N., Chen, K., Kannan, A., Tran, L., Chen, Y., and Shafran, I. (2019). Extracting symptoms and their status from clinical conversations. *arXiv preprint arXiv:1906.02239*.

Enarvi, S., Amoia, M., Teba, M. D.-A., Delaney, B., Diehl, F., Hahn, S., Harris, K., McGrath, L., Pan, Y., Pinto, J., et al. (2020). Generating medical reports from patient-doctor conversations using sequence-to-sequence models. In *Proceedings of the first workshop on natural language processing for medical conversations*, pages 22–30.

Fagherazzi, G., Fischer, A., Ismael, M., and Despotovic, V. (2021). Voice for health: The use of vocal biomarkers from research to clinical practice. *Digital biomarkers*, 5(1):78–88.

Ferracane, E. and Konam, S. (2020). Towards fairness in classifying medical conversations into soap sections. *arXiv preprint arXiv:2012.07749*.

Finley, G., Edwards, E., Robinson, A., Brenndoerfer, M., Sadoughi, N., Fone, J., Axtmann, N., Miller, M., and Suendermann-Oeft, D. (2018). An automated medical scribe for documenting clinical encounters. In *Proceedings of the 2018 Conference of the North American Chapter of the Association for Computational Linguistics: Demonstrations*, pages 11–15.

Friedberg, M. W., Chen, P. G., Van Busum, K. R., Aunon, F., Pham, C., Caloyeras, J., Mattke, S., Pitchforth, E., Quigley, D. D., Brook, R. H., et al. (2014). Factors affecting physician professional satisfaction and their implications for patient care, health systems, and health policy. *Rand health quarterly*, 3(4).

Georgescu, A.-L., Pappalardo, A., Cucu, H., and Blott, M. (2021). Performance vs. hardware requirements in state-of-the-art automatic speech recognition. *EURASIP Journal on Audio, Speech, and Music Processing*, 2021(1):1–30.

Gonzalez-Agirre, A., Marimon, M., Intxaurrondo, A., Rabal, O., Villegas, M., and Krallinger, M. (2019). Pharmaconer: Pharmacological substances, compounds and proteins named entity recognition track. In *Proceedings of The 5th Workshop on BioNLP Open Shared Tasks*, pages 1–10.

Graves, A. (2012). Sequence transduction with recurrent neural networks. *arXiv preprint arXiv:1211.3711*.

Greco, L., Percannella, G., Ritrovato, P., Tortorella, F., and Vento, M. (2020). Trends in iot based solutions for health care: Moving ai to the edge. *Pattern recognition letters*, 135:346–353.

Han, J., Qian, K., Song, M., Yang, Z., Ren, Z., Liu, S., Liu, J., Zheng, H., Ji, W., Koike, T., et al. (2020). An early study on intelligent analysis of speech under covid-19: Severity, sleep quality, fatigue, and anxiety. *arXiv preprint arXiv:2005.00096*.

Hinton, G., Deng, L., Yu, D., Dahl, G. E., Mohamed, A.-r., Jaitly, N., Senior, A., Vanhoucke, V., Nguyen, P., Sainath, T. N., et al. (2012). Deep neural networks for acoustic modeling in speech recognition: The shared views of four research groups. *IEEE Signal processing magazine*, 29(6):82–97.

Hochreiter, S. and Schmidhuber, J. (1997). Long short-term memory. *Neural computation*, 9(8):1735–1780.

Ion, R., Păi, V. F., and Mitrofan, M. (2019). Racais system at pharmaconer 2019. In *Proceedings of The 5th Workshop on BioNLP Open Shared Tasks*, pages 90–99.

Jeblee, S., Khan Khattak, F., Crampton, N., Mamdani, M., and Rudzicz, F. (2019). Extracting relevant information from physician-patient dialogues for automated clinical note taking. In *Proceedings of the Tenth International Workshop on Health Text Mining and Information Analysis (LOUHI 2019)*, pages 65–74, Hong Kong. Association for Computational Linguistics.

Jones, K. S. (2007). Automatic summarising: The state of the art. *Information Processing & Management*, 43(6):1449–1481.

Joshi, A., Katariya, N., Amatriain, X., and Kannan, A. (2020). Dr. summarize: Global summarization of medical dialogue by exploiting local structures. *arXiv preprint arXiv:2009.08666*.

Juang, B. H. and Rabiner, L. R. (1991). Hidden markov models for speech recognition. *Technometrics*, 33(3):251–272.

Kodish-Wachs, J., Agassi, E., Kenny III, P., and Overhage, J. M. (2018). A systematic comparison of contemporary automatic speech recognition engines for conversational clinical speech. In *AMIA Annual Symposium Proceedings*, volume 2018, page 683. American Medical Informatics Association.

Krishna, K., Pavel, A., Schloss, B., Bigham, J. P., and Lipton, Z. C. (2021). Extracting structured data from physician-patient conversations by predicting noteworthy utterances. In *Explainable AI in Healthcare and Medicine*, pages 155–169. Springer.

Lenain, R., Weston, J., Shivkumar, A., and Fristed, E. (2020). Surfboard: Audio feature extraction for modern machine learning. *arXiv preprint arXiv:2005.08848*.

Li, J. (2021). Recent advances in end-to-end automatic speech recognition. *arXiv preprint arXiv:2111.01690*.

Liu, Z., Ng, A., Lee, S., Aw, A. T., and Chen, N. F. (2019). Topic-aware pointer-generator networks for summarizing spoken conversations. In *2019 IEEE Automatic Speech Recognition and Understanding Workshop (ASRU)*, pages 814–821. IEEE.

Luz, S., Haider, F., de la Fuente, S., Fromm, D., and MacWhinney, B. (2021). Detecting cognitive decline using speech only: The adresso challenge. *arXiv preprint arXiv:2104.09356*.

Maor, E., Tsur, N., Barkai, G., Meister, I., Makmel, S., Friedman, E., Aronovich, D., Mevorach, D., Lerman, A., Zimlichman, E., et al. (2021). Noninvasive vocal biomarker is associated with severe acute respiratory syndrome coronavirus 2 infection. *Mayo Clinic Proceedings: Innovations, Quality & Outcomes*.

Miao, Y., Gowayyed, M., and Metze, F. (2015). Eesen: End-to-end speech recognition using deep rnn models and wfst-based decoding. In *2015 IEEE Workshop on Automatic Speech Recognition and Understanding (ASRU)*, pages 167–174. IEEE.

Miner, A. S., Haque, A., Fries, J. A., Fleming, S. L., Wilfley, D. E., Wilson, G. T., Milstein, A., Jurafsky, D., Arnow, B. A., Agras, W. S., et al. (2020). Assessing the accuracy of automatic speech recognition for psychotherapy. *NPJ digital medicine*, 3(1):1–8.

Mititelu, V. B. and Mitrofan, M. (2020). The Romanian medical treebank-SiMoNERo. *ISSN 1843-911X*, page 7.

Mitrofan, M. (2019). *Extragere de cunostinte din texte în limba româna si date structurate cu aplicatii în domeniul medical*. PhD thesis, Romanian Academy.

Muhammad, G. and Alhussein, M. (2021). Convergence of artificial intelligence and internet of things in smart healthcare: A case study of voice pathology detection. *IEEE Access*.

Păiş, V., Ion, R., and Tufiş, D. (2020). A processing platform relating data and tools for Romanian language. In *Proceedings of the 1st International Workshop on Language Technology Platforms*, pages 81–88.

Păiş, V. and Mitrofan, M. (2021). Assessing multiple word embeddings for named entity recognition of professions and occupations in health-related social media. In *Proceedings of the Sixth Social Media Mining for Health (# SMM4H) Workshop and Shared Task*, pages 128–130.

Păiş, V. and Tufiş, D. (2021). Capitalization and punctuation restoration: a survey. *Artificial Intelligence Review*, pages 1–42.

Patel, D., Konam, S., and Selvaraj, S. P. (2020). Weakly supervised medication regimen extraction from medical conversations. *arXiv preprint arXiv:2010.05317*.

Petrea, C., Ghelmez-Hanes, D., Popescu, V., Buzo, A., and Burileanu, C. (2009). Spontaneous speech database for the Romanian language with medical applicability. *BIOSTEC, Porto*.

Pi, V. (2020). Multiple annotation pipelines inside the relate platform. In *The 15th International Conference on Linguistic Resources and Tools for Natural Language Processing*, pages 65–75.

Prabhavalkar, R., Rao, K., Sainath, T. N., Li, B., Johnson, L., and Jaitly, N. (2017). A comparison of sequence-to-sequence models for speech recognition. In *Interspeech*, pages 939–943.

Quatieri, T. F., Williamson, J. R., Lammert, A. C., Heaton, K. J., and Palmer, J. S. (2020). Noninvasive biomarkers of neurobehavioral performance. *LINCOLN LABORATORY JOURNAL*, 24(1).

Quiroz, J. C., Laranjo, L., Kocaballi, A. B., Berkovsky, S., Rezazadegan, D., and Coiera, E. (2019). Challenges of developing a digital scribe to reduce clinical documentation burden. *NPJ digital medicine*, 2(1):1–6.

Ramallo-González, A. P., González-Vidal, A., and Skarmeta, A. F. (2021). Ciotvid: Towards an open iot-platform for infective pandemic diseases such as covid-19. *Sensors*, 21(2):484.

Sadeghian, R., Schaffer, J. D., and Zahorian, S. A. (2021). Towards an automatic speech-based diagnostic test for alzheimers disease. *Frontiers in Computer Science*, 3:13.

Schloss, B. and Konam, S. (2020). Towards an automated soap note: classifying utterances from medical conversations. In *Machine Learning for Healthcare Conference*, pages 610–631. PMLR.

See, A., Liu, P. J., and Manning, C. D. (2017). Get to the point: Summarization with pointer-generator networks. *arXiv preprint arXiv:1704.04368*.

Selvaraj, S. P. and Konam, S. (2021). Medication regimen extraction from medical conversations. In *Explainable AI in Healthcare and Medicine*, pages 195–209. Springer.

Shachak, A., Hadas-Dayagi, M., Ziv, A., and Reis, S. (2009). Primary care physicians use of an electronic medical record system: a cognitive task analysis. *Journal of general internal medicine*, 24(3):341–348.

Shafey, L. E., Soltau, H., and Shafran, I. (2019). Joint speech recognition and speaker diarization via sequence transduction. *arXiv preprint arXiv:1907.05337*.

Shafran, I., Du, N., Tran, L., Perry, A., Keyes, L., Knichel, M., Domin, A., Huang, L., Chen, Y., Li, G., et al. (2020). The medical scribe: corpus development and model performance analyses. *arXiv preprint arXiv:2003.11531*.

Soltau, H., Wang, M., Shafran, I., and Shafey, L. E. (2021). Understanding medical conversations: Rich transcription, confidence scores & information extraction. *arXiv preprint arXiv:2104.02219*.

Tracy, J. M., Özkanca, Y., Atkins, D. C., and Ghomi, R. H. (2020). Investigating voice as a biomarker: Deep phenotyping methods for early detection of parkinson's disease. *Journal of biomedical informatics*, 104:103362.

Ungureanu, D., Badeanu, M., Marica, G.-C., Dascalu, M., and Tufis, D. I. (2021). Establishing a baseline of Romanian speech-to-text models. In *2021 International Conference on Speech Technology and Human-Computer Dialogue (SpeD)*, pages 132–138.

Yu, D. and Deng, L. (2016). *Automatic Speech Recognition*. Springer.

Zhang, S., Jiang, H., Wei, S., and Dai, L. (2015). Feedforward sequential memory neural networks without recurrent feedback. *arXiv preprint arXiv:1510.02693*.

Zhang, Y., Alder, M., and Togneri, R. (1994). Using gaussian mixture modeling in speech recognition. In *Proceedings of ICASSP'94. IEEE International Conference on Acoustics, Speech and Signal Processing*, volume 1, pages I–613. IEEE.

In: Speech Recognition Technology ... ISBN: 978-1-68507-929-1
Editor: Vasile-Florian Păiş 

**Chapter 5**

# Punctuation Recovery for Romanian Transcribed Documents

**Vasile-Florian Păiş***
Research Institute for Artificial Intelligence
"Mihai Drăgănescu", Romanian Academy
Bucharest, Romania

**Abstract**

An automatic speech recognition system (ASR) turns sounds into transcribed text. The resulting documents usually lack punctuation marks, which makes them difficult to read. In addition, more advanced text analysis algorithms, such as named entity recognition and information extraction, have problems with unpunctuated documents. This chapter gives an introduction to punctuation restoration in general and presents specific experiments regarding punctuation recovery for the Romanian language. In this context, a tool is introduced for converting a tokenized corpus into a format usable for training punctuation restoration models. The tool is used to convert several existing corpora, which are then used to train and evaluate models. The resulting system and model are integrated in the RELATE platform for processing the Romanian language and are available for online usage and download. The system employs current state-of-the-art technologies such as contextualized word embedding representations and transformer-based neural networks. It

*Corresponding Author's Email: vasile@racai.ro.

must be noted that even though ASR produces lots of unpunctuated data, this is not the only source of unpunctuated documents. Social media posts, short text messages, micro-blogging and optical character recognition (OCR) are examples of other domains where punctuation restoration plays a key role in pre-processing the raw text.

**Keywords:** punctuation restoration, Romanian language

# 1. Introduction

Proper use of capital letters and punctuation marks influences the way human readers understand text documents. By removing periods indicating the end of sentences and commas the text becomes difficult to read and sometimes ambiguous. The reader may be unable to properly understand the information conveyed by a certain document. In this context, Jones et al. (2003) studied the impact of capitalization and punctuation on the readability of speech-to-text transcripts. This is particularly important since the vast majority of automatic speech recognition (ASR) systems produce transcripts in lower case form and without any punctuation marks. Furthermore, works such as Tündik et al. (2018) and more recently Datta et al. (2020) show that deaf or hard-of-hearing subjects perceive a larger improvement when punctuation is added compared to regular readers, without hearing difficulties. Even more, in the case of specialised domains such as the medical domain, punctuation marks make an important contribution to text understanding. Barbu Mititelu and Mitrofan (2020) showed that for Romanian language, medical texts have a higher frequency of punctuation signs, than general purpose texts.

In the case of artificial intelligence (AI) algorithms, punctuation provides important clues for segmentation and more advanced text analysis, including part-of-speech tagging, named entity recognition, dependency parsing and machine translation. Already in 1994, Jones (1994) showed that "for longer sentences of real language a grammar which makes use of punctuation massively outperforms an otherwise similar grammar that ignores it". Furthermore, Makhoul et al. (2005) showed that correct comma positioning has a large impact on both entity and relation extraction. Thus, current state-of-the-art language models, including BERT (Devlin et al., 2019), ELMo (Peters et al., 2018a) and OpenAIs GPT-2 (Radford et al.,

2019), make use of punctuation and it becomes part of their respective vocabularies.

Considering a text without any punctuation, the task of punctuation restoration aims at inserting appropriate punctuation marks. Given that commas and periods usually occur in larger numbers than other marks, many studies focus on the restoration of these two punctuation marks. Nevertheless, other marks such as exclamation marks, question marks, colons, semicolons and quotation marks have been considered in the literature. In the case of ASR transcriptions, the text documents resulting after punctuation restoration are sometimes referred to as "rich transcriptions". In this context, one of the first initiatives concerning automatic rich transcriptions of spoken language started in 2002 in the context of the DARPA Effective, Affordable Reusable Speech-to-text (EARS)[1] programme which supported the goal of significantly advancing the state-of-the-art in the hardest speech recognition challenges, including rich transcriptions of language (Liu et al., 2005).

Considering a sequence of words $\{w_1, w_2, w_3, ..., w_n\}$, the task of punctuation restoration aims at obtaining a new sequence $\{p_1, p_2, p_3, ..., p_n\}$, with $p_i \in P$, where $p_i$ is the punctuation mark following the word $w_i$ and $P$ is the set of available punctuation marks. Thus, punctuation restoration can be expressed as a sequence-to-sequence operation, mapping the sequence of words to a sequence of marks. Furthermore, since not all words are followed by a punctuation mark, $P$ includes a symbol specifying the lack of a mark, usually noted as $O$. For example, if we are interested in predicting only commas and periods, $P = \{COMMA, PERIOD, O\}$. If we take the transcribed sentence *"preedintele a vizitat romnia suedia i danemarca"* (*"the president travelled to romania sweden and denmark"*), this becomes a sequence of 7 words {*"preedintele", "a", "vizitat", "romnia", "suedia", "i", "danemarca"*}. Therefore we expect a corresponding sequence of 7 punctuation marks to be predicted by a punctuation restoration system. In this case, a correct sequence would be: $\{O, O, O, COMMA, O, O, PERIOD\}$. This corresponds to the sentence *"preedintele a vizitat romnia, suedia i danemarca."*

[1] http://mi.eng.cam.ac.uk/research/projects/EARS/ears_summary.html

In addition to punctuation restoration, capitalization or truecasing is the process of turning a lower-cased text document into a form having appropriate letter casing. Although different from punctuation restoration, these two tasks are sometimes intertwined. Proper punctuation sometimes provides strong clues towards letter casing. One such example is the first letter uppercase following an end-of-sentence period. Both tasks are useful post-processing steps after obtaining the raw output of an ASR system.

In a recent survey, Păiş and Tufiş (2021) provide details on the evolution of both punctuation restoration and capitalization algorithms as well as information regarding current state-of-the-art approaches for the two tasks. The approaches used for recovering punctuation marks follow the general evolution of artificial intelligence algorithms. Early attempts make use of rule-based systems, while recent models employ deep neural network architectures, including transformer-based (Vaswani et al., 2018) models.

Apart from ASR output, other sources of text can benefit from punctuation restoration algorithms. These include optical character recognition (OCR) (Miller et al., 2000), short text messages (SMS), chats, tweets or any micro-blogging activities in general (Baldwin et al., 2013; Nebhi et al., 2015). However, in the case of ASR systems, punctuation restoration algorithms can also employ cues extracted from speech. Acoustic information involves prosody which comprises features such as pause duration between words, pitch-intensity and per-word timing. Furthermore, as shown in (Vaissiere, 1983), prosodic cues seem to be relevant to discourse structure across languages. In this context, authors have tried creating either prosodic-only models or combined models considering both prosody and text. Batista et al. (2009) investigated prosodic information for both words and syllables, showing that word-based features are the most reliable features for both English and Portuguese. Furthermore, Che et al. (2016) proposed using two parallel neural network models (one dedicated to text features and one dedicated to prosody features), and only combined them in the final stage of the overall neural network.

Data augmentation is a known technique for improving the quality of neural network-based models by increasing the availability of training data with automatically generated new data samples. In this context, Soboleva et al. (2020) experimented with a multi-speaker, prosody aware, text-to-speech (TTS) system for generating additional audio segments to increase the available training data for a punctuation restoration system. Experiments show promising results for certain punctuation marks, but indicate that the best results for comma prediction can be achieved using only human recorded audio without any synthesized segments.

Since punctuation restoration models can be trained by using only text data, augmentation techniques specific to text-only files can also be used. General natural language augmentation frameworks have been proposed, such as the NL-Augmenter[2] (Dhole et al., 2021). However, not all possible transformations are relevant to punctuation restoration, usable in the context of ASR transcripts. In this context, we aim to both vary the number of punctuation marks and introduce perturbations similar to the errors caused by speech recognition algorithms. Inspired by the work of Wei and Zou (2019), Alam et al. (2020) propose emulating ASR errors by means of simple text operations, such as insertion, substitution and deletion. These operations can be applied randomly at the word level. Furthermore, since ASR errors may result in out-of-vocabulary words (erroneously recognized words), the authors propose randomly inserting the "unknown" token.

Recent works on punctuation restoration for the English language usually rely on datasets from the International Workshop on Spoken Language Translation (IWSLT). These are machine translation datasets that are focused on the automatic transcription and translation of TED and TEDx talks (public speeches covering many different topics)[3]. One dataset that was used for evaluating a number of recent works is from the IWSLT 2011 evaluation campaign (Federico et al., 2011). It is comprised of monolingual and parallel corpora of TED talks that are copyright of the TED Conference LLC and distributed under the Creative Commons Attribution-NonCommercial-NoDerivs 3.0 license[4]. The first paper to use this dataset for punctuation prediction evaluation was Peitz et al. (2011). However, as also happens with later papers, only a fraction of the corpus was used for the punctuation restoration task. In this case, only text documents belonging to the English-to-French translation track.

Chen et al. (2021) propose a discriminative self-training approach for punctuation prediction, incorporating large sets of unlabeled spoken language data. The authors make use of pre-trained language models and human-labeled speech transcripts to first train a teacher model. Then the

---

[2]https://github.com/GEM-benchmark/NL-Augmenter

[3]http://www.ted.com

[4]http://creativecommons.org/licenses/by-nc-nd/3.0/

teacher model was used to insert punctuation into ASR transcripts. Finally, a student model is trained using pre-trained language models, human-labeled data and automatically labeled data (from the teacher model). A weighted loss is used to combine the loss on human-labeled data and automatically labeled data. This accounts for the inherent noise associated with the automatic labeling approach. Furthermore, the authors also explore label smoothing (Szegedy et al., 2016) to improve training with noisy labels. The proposed approach achieves state-of-the-art performance on the IWSLT 2011 English dataset as well as on a private Chinese dataset.

Shi et al. (2021) use an external part-of-speech (POS) tagger to provide additional information considered useful for restoring punctuation. Furthermore, the authors experiment with the Funnel Transformer (Dai et al., 2020) architecture to filter out sequential redundancy. To combine a language model with the POS predictions, the weights associated with the last layer of the POS tagger are used, similar to an embedding matrix. Thus, the last hidden states of the language model are combined with the last weights of the POS tagger and fed into a fusion layer. Unlike other approaches, such as Tilk and Alumäe (2015) and Yi and Tao (2019), which combines multiple embeddings by concatenation alone, Shi et al. (2021) employ a self-attention encoder (Vaswani et al., 2017) as the fusion layer, thus enabling both features to better interact with each other through the multi-head self-attention mechanism.

With regard to the Romanian language, Caranica et al. (2015) implement an n-gram model for joint capitalization and punctuation restoration (considering comma and period). Based on the work of Rosenfeld (2000), the model is created with $n = 3$ since this value represents a common choice for large training corpora. Furthermore, taking into account the observation that increasing n-gram order does not help as much as increasing the training data set (Gravano et al., 2009), the authors keep the $n$ value fixed. The proposed algorithm constructs all sequences of words considering all combinations of capitalization and following punctuation (comma, period, no punctuation). When all the words in the input line are processed, the word sequence with the highest probability is selected. Experiments are performed using two large internal datasets collected by web crawling, composed of news and talk-shows texts, split into training and evaluation sub-corpora. Training is performed using each corpus individually and also using a single merged corpus, while evaluation is performed on each of the two corpora evaluation subsets. The merged language model performs similarly to the model trained on the specific corpus, with individual differences ranging from 0% to 2%. The best reported F1 measure is 59% for both comma and period prediction.

Guerreiro et al. (2021) proposed constructing a single multilingual model for punctuation restoration of speech transcripts in multiple languages. Experiments are conducted using transcripts of TED Talks from the IWSLT 2017 and IWSLT 2011 evaluation campaigns. The multilingual model is compared against monolingual models for German, Dutch, Portuguese and Romanian languages. The authors used two setups: one for predicting only commas and periods and another for predicting also question marks (in addition to commas and periods). The model architecture contains three main elements: a transformer-based encoder model, an attention mechanism over the encoder layers, and a multinomial logistic regression classifier. The encoder model is either RoBERTa or XLM-RoBERTa. The results indicate that commas are more difficult to predict than periods, using pre-trained contextual models. Furthermore, the authors indicate similar results being obtained by the multilingual model and corresponding monolingual models (with F1 differences usually less than 1%). Considering the Romanian language, the multilingual model achieves an F1 score of 83.7% for period prediction and 70.8% for comma prediction, compared to the monolingual model achieving 83.1% and 69.2% respectively.

This chapter is structured as follows: Section 2 describes the relevant punctuation for the Romanian language; Section 3 describes the corpora and resources used for experimenting with punctuation restoration models in the Romanian language; Section 4 presents the algorithms used; and Section 5 presents the obtained results. Finally, in Section 5 conclusions are formulated.

## 2. Punctuation in Romanian Language

The Romanian alphabet is based on the Latin script with five additional letters using diacritics Ă, Â, Î, Ş, Ţ (with their corresponding lowercase forms: ă, â, î, ş, ţ). For the letters Ş, and Ţ, (lowercase forms: ş, ţ), two variants have circulated: one with a comma under the letter and another one with a cedilla. However, only the former is currently recommended by the

Romanian National Standardization Body (ASRO), corresponding to unicode characters U+0x218 (Ş), U+0x21A (Ţ), U+0x219 (ş) and U+0x21B (ţ). Many electronic texts are not written with diacritics. In order to automatically introduce diacritics, programs have been created to recover them in such texts (Nuțu et al., 2019; Dumitrescu and Boroș, 2013; Tufiș and Ceaușu, 2008).

Punctuation marks specific to the Romanian language include: comma, full stop, colon, exclamation mark, question mark, semicolon, quotation marks, apostrophe, hyphen, dash and round brackets. The quotation marks use double low (left) and right marks ( „ and ”, respectively). However, especially in electronic texts, the ASCII quotation mark character (ASCII character 0x22) may be encountered (this is a different character from the right quotation mark, which is the unicode character U+0x201D). Dialogues are introduced using quotation dashes ("-"). The Oxford comma, used in certain English language documents, is considered incorrect in the Romanian language. In titles, only the first letter of the first word is capitalized, and the rest of the title makes use of regular sentence capitalization. Names of months and days, as well as adjectives derived from proper names are not capitalized. Examples of correctly written words in Romanian and their corresponding English translation: *februarie* ("February"), *vineri* ("Friday"), *italian* ("Italian").

From the point of view of automatic punctuation restoration, different approaches can be foreseen depending on the specific mark. For example, dialogue dashes assume the algorithm is aware of the turns taken by the speakers. This is referred to as speaker diarization. A recent survey (Park et al., 2022) covers different techniques regarding speaker diarization using deep learning. In many cases, the hyphen is used similar to the apostrophe in English to denote a contraction. In this case, an n-gram model trained on a sufficiently large corpus can prove an effective tool for restoring hyphens. Moreover, a contraction lexicon[5] can also be used effectively for inserting hyphens specific to contractions.

Unlike Spanish, where question marks and exclamation marks come in two variants (at the beginning of a sentence and at the end), in Romanian there is a single variant. The question and exclamation marks are used only at the end of the sentence. They correspond to the regular ASCII characters

[5]https://en.wiktionary.org/wiki/Appendix:Romanian_contractions

"?" - 0x3F and "!" - 0x21.

While primarily investigating the English language, early work considered punctuation only as cues from the reader perspective to the possible prosodic and pause characteristics of the text (Markwardt, 1942). However, Nunberg (1990) argues for a much greater role associated with punctuation. Furthermore, punctuation marks are classified as delimiting, separating and disambiguating. Some marks, such as the comma, may belong to multiple categories since they are able to perform multiple roles. Păiș and Tufiș (2021) note that even with modern deep learning algorithms, commas seem to be the most difficult punctuation mark to predict in English. Previous observations regarding comma usage are also true for the Romanian language; therefore we expect similar difficulties in predicting commas.

# 3. Corpora and Resources

A punctuation restoration algorithm aims at predicting a punctuation mark (or the lack of any mark) after each token. This implies the usage of a tokenized text. Furthermore, any Romanian language corpus, using proper grammatical rules and of enough size (with regard to the number of tokens and punctuation marks) can be used for training a punctuation restoration system. In this context, we designed a tool that allows processing corpora expressed as CoNLL-U Plus[6] formatted files and produces other CoNLL-U Plus files useful for punctuation restoration (with punctuation tokens removed and containing an indication of the punctuation following each remaining token).

The CoNLL-U Plus format is used within the Universal Dependencies (UD)[7] project. It is intended as an extension of the basic CoNLL-U[8] format. In both formats, annotations are encoded in plain text UTF-8 files, using only the line feed (LF) character as a line break. There are three types of lines: word lines containing the annotation of a word/token in 10 fields separated by a single tab character; blank lines marking sentence boundaries; and comment lines starting with a hash (#) character. Sentences consist of one or more word lines, and word lines contain the following fields:

---

[6]https://universaldependencies.org/ext-format.html

[7]https://universaldependencies.org/

[8]https://universaldependencies.org/format.html

- ID: Word index within the sentence
- FORM: Word form or punctuation symbol
- LEMMA: Lemma or stem of word form
- UPOS: Universal part-of-speech tag[9]
- XPOS: Language-specific part-of-speech tag
- HEAD: Head of the current word (considering a dependency tree)
- DEPREL: Universal dependency relation to the HEAD
- DEPS: Enhanced dependency graph in the form of a list of head-deprel pairs
- MISC: Any other annotation.

While a CoNLL-U file always has precisely ten columns separated by TAB characters, a CoNLL-U Plus file can have any non-zero number of columns. The first line is used in this case to identify the columns being used. It must be a sentence-level comment, beginning with "# global.columns" and specifying the names of the columns used in the file. There are ten predefined column names that identify the original columns of the core CoNLL-U files (as identified in the above listing). A CoNLL-U Plus file may contain any subset of them with the addition of any other new columns.

The open source tool[10] that was developed for creating punctuation restoration training corpora produces a CoNLL-U Plus file with an eleventh column called "RACAI:PUNCTUATION". It contains information in the form "*<Punctuation>After=yes*", where *<Punctuation>* is one of period, comma, semicolon, colon, hyphen, question, exclamation. There can be multiple values separated by comma. For example, considering the text fragment "... XX S.R.L., cu sediul ..." ("... XX S.R.L., with headquarters ...") the last column associated with the token "L" will contain "PeriodAfter=yes, CommaAfter=yes". In this way it becomes possible to account for multiple punctuation marks following a single text token. A complete example is shown in Figure 1.

[9] https://universaldependencies.org/u/pos/
[10] https://github.com/racai-ai/PunctuationRestoration

```
# global.columns = ID FORM LEMMA UPOS XPOS FEATS HEAD DEPREL DEPS MISC RACAI:PUNCTUATION
# sent id = ro-mj-2011-00000G0001I4Q5GI5D13TF7DVAJMMEEK-s12
# text = Cu participarea reprezentantului Ministerului Public, procuror Carmen-Cătălina Gliga.
1	Cu	cu	ADP	Spsa	AdpType=Prep|Case=Acc	2	case	_	_	_
2	participarea	participare	NOUN	Ncfsry	Case=Nom|Definite=Def|Gender=Fem|Number=Sing	0	root	_	_	_
3	reprezentantului	reprezentant	NOUN	Ncmsoy	Case=Gen|Definite=Def|Gender=Masc|Number=Sing	2	nmod	_	_	_
4	Ministerului	minister	NOUN	Ncmsoy	Case=Gen|Definite=Def|Gender=Masc|Number=Sing	3	nmod	_	_	_
5	Public	public	ADJ	Afpms-n	Definite=Ind|Degree=Pos|Gender=Masc|Number=Sing	4	amod	_	_	CommaAfter=yes
7	procuror	procuror	NOUN	Ncms-n	Definite=Ind|Gender=Masc|Number=Sing	3	appos	_	_	_
8	CarmenCătălina	Carmen-Cătălina	PROPN	Np	_	7	nmod	_	_	_
9	Gliga	Gliga	PROPN	Np	_	8	flat	_	_	PeriodAfter=yes
```

Figure 1. Example corpus file used for training punctuation restoration systems.

In addition to converting the input files to a suitable format for training punctuation restoration, the conversion tool also performs basic filtering of input sentences. It makes sure there are only Romanian characters present in the data and that the resulting sentences contain at least three tokens (these are word tokens, since the punctuation tokens were converted to annotations following a word token).

In the context of the international project "Multilingual Resources for CEF.AT in the legal domain" (MARCELL)[11] a large comparable corpus of legal documents for 7 European Union (EU) languages was created (Váradi et al., 2020). This includes a monolingual sub-corpus for the Romanian language (Tufis et al., 2020). The Romanian corpus (MARCELL-RO), as well as the other MARCELL corpora, was already split at sentence and token level, lemmatized, and annotated at the token level. Annotations comprise part-of-speech tags, dependency parsing, and named entities and finally, the corpus was enriched with IATE terms and EUROVOC descriptors. All these annotations were realized using automatic processes and the end result was made available in CoNLL-U Plus format at the European Language Resource Coordination ELRC-SHARE[12] repository. The MARCELL-RO corpus was already exploited for named entity recognition (NER) in the Romanian legal domain, by producing the manually annotated sub-corpus LegalNERo (Păiș et al., 2021c) and training different NER systems (Păiș et al., 2021b).

Following the success of the MARCELL project, we went on to create a new large resource relevant to the Connecting Europe Facility (CEF) Automated Translation (AT) eTranslation platform, covering domains rel-

[11] https://marcell-project.eu/

[12] https://www.elrc-share.eu/

evant to all Digital Service Infrastructures (DSIs). Thus, in the context of the project "Curated Multilingual Resources for CEF.AT" (CURLICAT)[13], consortium partners aim to deliver language resources, in particular monolingual corpora, in the EU/CEF languages: Bulgarian, Croatian, Hungarian, Polish, Romanian, Slovak and Slovenian. All the targeted seven EU's official languages are under-resourced languages and consequently, languages without sufficient technological support. The monolingual corpora will represent the following specific domains: finance, health, scientific research, cultural heritage, education, economics, and politics. Even though the data will be cleared from the point of view of Intellectual Property Rights (IPR), there remains the problem of protecting potentially sensitive personal data. In this context, the previously constructed NER system, based on the LegalNERo corpus, was used to anonymize the CURLICAT corpus.

Considering the availability of the MARCELL-RO corpus, as well as its usage in other projects, it became a good choice for training punctuation restoration models for the Romanian language. Furthermore, its CoNLL-U Plus format ensured automatic compatibility with the previously described tool for producing a corpus suitable for punctuation restoration. To make the text more similar to the output of an ASR system, the documents were lowercased and sentence boundaries were removed. With regard to the punctuation marks, we focused only on comma and periods. Statistics are given in Table 1.

**Table 1. MARCELL-RO corpus statistics**

| **Statistic** | **Value** |
|---|---:|
| Number of tokens | 31,352,408 |
| Distinct tokens | 146,067 |
| Hapax legomena | 44,281 |
| Number of period marks | 1,427,242 |
| Number of comma marks | 1,917,506 |

To facilitate training of neural network models as well as comparison

[13]https://curlicat-project.eu/

with future algorithms, we created a split of the original corpus into three parts: a larger part used for training, a section used for model validation during training and a final part used for testing the end model on unseen text. We used an approximately 70%-15%-15% split for the three parts. The split was performed at the file level in the MARCELL-RO corpus and the resulting parts were aggregated into single files. Statistics on the splits are given in Table 2.

**Table 2. MARCELL-RO corpus splits statistics**

| Statistic | Value |
|---|---|
| Training | |
| Number of tokens | 21,988,358 |
| Distinct tokens | 126,040 |
| Hapax legomena | 40,076 |
| Number of period marks | 998,987 |
| Number of comma marks | 1,347,213 |
| Validation | |
| Number of tokens | 4,466,262 |
| Distinct tokens | 69,878 |
| Hapax legomena | 25,064 |
| Number of period marks | 205,474 |
| Number of comma marks | 273,860 |
| Testing | |
| Number of tokens | 4,897,788 |
| Distinct tokens | 71,275 |
| Hapax legomena | 24,612 |
| Number of period marks | 222,781 |
| Number of comma marks | 296,433 |

Each indicator provided in Table 2 is computed on an individual split of the corpus. Therefore, distinct tokens and hapax legomena refer to tokens present in the split (and not on the entire corpus, since entire corpus statistics are given in Table 1). The distribution of punctuation marks between the validation and testing sub-corpora is similar, thus allowing for the splits to be used for evaluating neural models. The entire corpus, in CoNLL-U Plus format, is available for download from the RELATE platform[14]. Furthermore, the splits can be downloaded as well[15], the archive containing in this case three files corresponding to the three splits.

RoRefTrees (RRT)[16] (Barbu Mititelu, 2018) is a corpus commonly used for training basic language resource kits (BLARK) for the Romanian language. It is the reference treebank in Universal Dependencies format (CoNLL-U) for standard Romanian. Tools providing part-of-speech tagging, lemmatization and dependency parsing, such as NLPCube (Boroș et al., 2018), Stanza (Qi et al., 2020) and UDPipe (Straka et al., 2016) commonly use Universal Dependency data for multilingual evaluation. This includes the Romanian RRT data for evaluation in the Romanian language. It contains 9,523 sentences, manually validated at the syntactic level, that reflect the contemporary language, covering a variety of genres. It is based on RACAI-RoTb (Irimia and Barbu Mititelu, 2015) and on UAIC-RoTb (Perez, 2014). The distribution of text genres in RoRefTrees is not balanced: literature - 1,818 sentences, law - 1,606 sentences, medical - 1,210 sentences, FrameNet translations - 1,092 sentences, academic writing - 950 sentences, news - 933 sentences, science - 362 sentences, wikipedia - 251 sentences, miscellanea - 1,301 sentences. These genres can be told apart by the sentences id.

The RRT corpus offers a common split into training (75%), validation (12.5%) and testing (12.5%). We processed the corpus splits individually for usage in punctuation restoration evaluation. Statistics are given in Table 3. As shown in this table, the size of the RRT corpus is much smaller than that of the MARCELL-RO corpus. RRT contains only approximately 0.5% of the comma and periods present in the MARCELL-RO corpus. Therefore, we consider that the RRT corpus is not suitable for training punctuation restoration models. However, since it is being used in different other natural language processing tasks, it can be used for testing pre-trained models.

Modern deep neural architectures make use of distributional word rep-

---

[14] https://relate.racai.ro/resources/punctuation_restoration/marcell_punctuation_restoration.tar.bz2

[15] https://relate.racai.ro/resources/punctuation_restoration/punctuation_corpus_train_dev_test.tar.bz2

[16] https://github.com/UniversalDependencies/UD_Romanian-RRT

**Table 3. RRT corpus splits statistics**

| Statistic | Value |
|---|---|
| Training | |
| Number of tokens | 105,528 |
| Distinct tokens | 22,246 |
| Hapax legomena | 13,226 |
| Number of period marks | 5,529 |
| Number of comma marks | 7,093 |
| Validation | |
| Number of tokens | 9,735 |
| Distinct tokens | 4,277 |
| Hapax legomena | 3,345 |
| Number of period marks | 524 |
| Number of comma marks | 689 |
| Testing | |
| Number of tokens | 9,326 |
| Distinct tokens | 3,982 |
| Hapax legomena | 3,054 |
| Number of period marks | 514 |
| Number of comma marks | 626 |

resentation models, also known as word embeddings. We can distinguish between static models, where each word has an associated vector representation that remains constant throughout the training process, and contextual models, where the associated representation is generated based on the context in which a word appears. Contextual representations have proven to be more useful for different natural language processing tasks, compared to static ones. However, training of contextual models requires large volumes of text and considerable processing power, thus making them very challenging to train. For English, there are multiple contextual models such as BERT (Devlin et al., 2019), RoBERTa (Liu et al., 2019), ELMo (Peters et al., 2018b) and XLNet (Yang et al., 2019). Many contextual models come in at least two variants: base and large. In the "large" variant, there are more neural layers with more artificial neuron cells present in the model's architecture, which leads to more parameters needing to be stored, resulting in an increase in model size. In turn, this leads to an increase in the memory required to load the model and also an increase in the CPU time needed when using the model.

For the Romanian language, a number of high-quality static word representation models have been proposed. Păiș and Tufiș (2018a) made use of the Representative Corpus of Contemporary Romanian Language (CoRoLa) (Barbu Mititelu et al., 2019, 2018; Tufiș and Cristea, 2017; Cristea et al., 2019) to train word embeddings using FastText (Bojanowski et al., 2017). These were evaluated against WikiPedia and Common Crawl based embeddings and were shown to provide better results, due to the content of the CoRoLa corpus. Additional word embeddings (Păiș and Tufiș, 2018b) were explored within the ReTeRom[17] project by making use of the word's lemma and part of speech. While training a NER system in the legal domain, word representations were created based on the MARCELL-RO corpus (Păiș et al., 2021b). In the biomedical domain, word embeddings were explored by Mitrofan (2019). In the retail banking domain word representations were explored by Raicu et al. (2020).

In recent years, contextual word representations for the Romanian language have become available. Dumitrescu et al. (2020) introduces two Romanian BERT variants by considering cased and uncased forms associated with Romanian words. Both variants follow the BERT-base architecture. Masala et al. (2020) introduces another Romanian BERT model, called RoBERT, using three architecture sizes, including a large version. The authors compare RoBERT with other models and show improvement on different tasks. Masala et al. (2021) proposes a new BERT model for legal judgement predictions, trained on a legal-domain corpus. Furthermore, (Zaharia et al., 2021) explore knowledge distillation (Hinton et al., 2015) on the Romanian BERT model. In addition to Romanian-only models, there are multilingual contextual models that include Romanian representations. These include mBERT (Devlin et al., 2019) and XLM-RoBERTa (Conneau et al., 2020).

[17] https://www.racai.ro/p/reterom/index_en.html

# 4. Algorithms

In (Avram et al., 2020) was proposed an algorithm for hyphen restoration making use of bigram and unigram models trained on the CoRoLa corpus, considering both words with hyphens and words without hyphens. To reduce the models size, for models containing words without hyphens, there were considered only words allowing also a form with a hyphen. Then, for text correction the algorithm first determines from the bigram model the frequencies of the word in context with hyphen and without. If the frequencies of appearance are equal, the unigram model is used to identify the most frequent form. To reduce the computation time required, only windows starting with the current word (the one that may need correction) are considered. Furthermore, since in some cases there may be several hyphenation variants associated with a certain word (either because they are valid or because of errors in the corpus), all of these forms were considered when determining the frequencies. The final algorithm is presented in Algorithm 1. The actual implementation[18] further optimizes on this by computing the frequencies only when they are actually needed and makes use of hash tables to efficiently query the models.

For comma and period, Păiș and Tufiș (2021) showed that the best performing models are based on transformer models. These are usually associated with contextual word representation models, such as BERT (Devlin et al., 2019) and RoBERTa (Liu et al., 2019). As already presented in Section 3, BERT models have recently become available for the Romanian language. Even though RoBERTa based models have shown better performance on some tasks, such models are not yet available for Romanian. Furthermore, previous works (Dima et al., 2020; Păiș and Mitrofan, 2021) have shown that combinations of embeddings (either static or contextual) have the ability to improve the results on different tasks when compared to single models. Due to hardware and time constraints we were not able to explore all the available models or any combinations of them. Instead we focused our experiments on a single model, namely the monolingual Romanian BERT model introduced in Dumitrescu et al. (2020).

For implementation purposes, we followed the approach described in Alam et al. (2020). The text is first tokenized, and then contextual representations are obtained through the BERT model. The embedding vectors

[18]https://github.com/racai-ai/RobinASRHyphenationCorrection

**Algorithm 1** Hyphen restoration algorithm

**for all** $W_k$ in ASR output **do**
  **if** $w_k$ allows one or more forms with hyphen **then**
    **for all** form with hyphen $H_j$ associated with $w_k$ **do**
      $FH2_j \leftarrow Freq(H_j, W_{k+1})$
      $FH1_j \leftarrow Freq(H_j)$
    **end for**
    $FH2 \leftarrow max(FH2_j)$
    $FW2 \leftarrow Freq(W_k, W_{k+1})$
    $FH1 \leftarrow max(FH1_j)$
    $FW1 \leftarrow Freq(W_k)$
    **if** $FH2 > FW2$ **then**
      correct $W_k$ using form $H_j$, where $j = argmax(FH2_j)$
    **end if**
    **if** $FH2 == FW2andFH1 > FW1$ **then**
      correct $W_k$ using form $H_j$, where $j = argmax(FH1_j)$
    **end if**
  **end if**
**end for**

are then passed through a bidirectional LSTM (BiLSTM) layer and finally through a linear layer which gives predictions regarding the punctuation mark following each input token.

Tokenization is handled by using the WordPiece (Schuster and Nakajima, 2012) subword tokenization algorithm. This is the default algorithm used by the BERT, DistilBERT (Sanh et al., 2020) and ELECTRA (Clark et al., 2020) models. It starts by initializing the vocabulary to include every character present in the training data and progressively learns a given number of merge rules. In contrast to other tokenization algorithms, WordPiece does not choose the most frequent symbol pair but the one that maximizes the likelihood of the training data once added to the vocabulary. Being a subword tokenization algorithm means that a word (especially a rare word) can be decomposed into multiple tokens. Since contextual embeddings are associated with each token and then passed through the network, predictions are given at the token (subword) level. In this case, to obtain the prediction associated with a given word, only the predicted punctuation

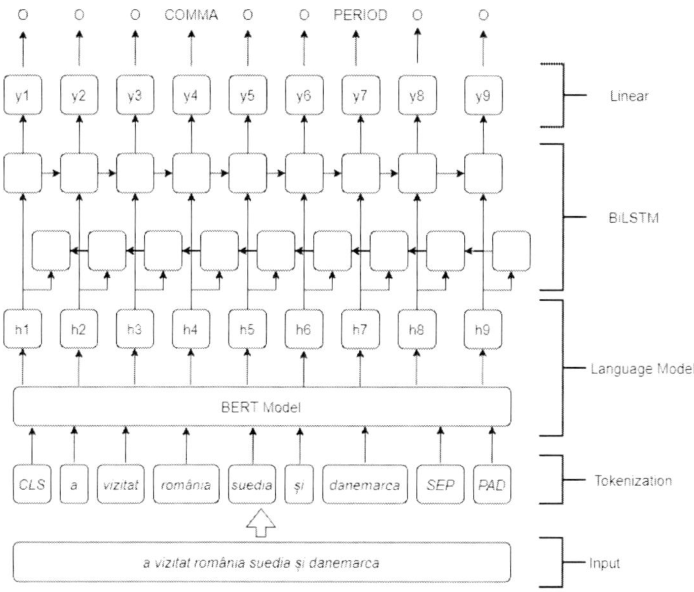


Figure 2. Model architecture.

mark associated with the last subword token is considered (for each word). The other predictions are ignored. The same approach is used when constructing the training data (only the last subword token is annotated with the following punctuation).

Figure 2 presents the general model architecture used for punctuation recovery. Apart from the regular tokens associated with words, BERT models make use of special tokens indicating start of sequence (CLS), end of sequence (SEP) and padding (PAD) when the sequence is smaller than the one accepted by the model. Contextual representations are obtained from the BERT model, in the form of floating point vectors of dimension 768 (corresponding to a BERT-base model). These are fed to the BiLSTM layer, thus allowing the network to make effective use of both past and future contexts for prediction. The outputs from the two LSTM layers (forward and backward) are concatenated at each time step and fed to a fully connected layer with three output neurons, which correspond to two punctuation marks (comma and period) and one "O" token (meaning there is no punctuation predicted). Predictions are obtained directly from the last linear layer by means of the $argmax$ function. Even though for some tasks it was shown that a final CRF layer may improve results, we did not employ such a layer.

Data augmentation is a known technique for improving results, especially in low resource scenarios. In our case the MARCELL-RO corpus is quite large, but it is a well written text. However, the ASR output does not always contain correctly transcribed text. Therefore, we used data augmentation to introduce noise in the documents, trying to make the training dataset look more like ASR output. Wei and Zou (2019) proposed four simple but powerful operations: synonym replacement, random insertion, random swap, and random deletion. The authors also studied the performance gains related to the size of augmented data. They discovered that too much augmentation can actually lead to decreased performance and proposed an augmentation parameter of 0.1 which works good in most scenarios. Building on their work, Alam et al. (2020) propose using only three augmentation operations: replacement, deletion and insertion. This is more similar to errors introduced during ASR transcription, where word swap is less likely to occur, compared to the other operations. Furthermore, with regard to replacement and insertion, Alam et al. (2020) propose using the “unknown” token. This would correspond to errors in recognizing certain words. The authors also suggest to use in addition to the overall augmentation parameter two other parameters specifically controlling the probabilities of substitutions and additions.

# 5. Results

The comma and period restoration algorithm described in Section 4 was trained on the training part of the dataset, using the validation split for evaluation during training. Finally it was tested using the test split. These splits were described in Section 3. We used the Romanian BERT model from Dumitrescu et al. (2020) with a learning rate of $5e-6$. With regard to data augmentation, we used an overall augmentation probability of $\alpha = 0.15$. Out of this, both the substitution and deletion rates were set to $\alpha_{sub} = \alpha_{del} = 0.4$. The insertion probability was then computed as $\alpha_{ins} = 1 - (\alpha_{sub} + \alpha_{del}) = 0.2$. Data augmentation was only used on the training split of the corpus. In the case of substitutions, the punctuation mark associated with the existing token was kept. In the case of insertions, it was assumed that no punctuation marks were necessary for the new tokens.

The model was trained on a machine with 2 GPUs for 10 epochs. The best validation accuracy was 0.98. This model was stored and then used for computing the precision, recall and F1 metrics on both the validation and testing datasets. The results on the validation set are given in Table 4 and for the testing dataset in Table 5.

**Table 4. Results on the MARCELL-RO validation dataset**

| Punctuation | Precision % | Recall % | F1 % |
|---|---|---|---|
| Comma | 88.03 | 86.61 | 87.31 |
| Period | 96.36 | 95.34 | 95.85 |
| MicroAvg | 91.61 | 90.35 | 90.98 |

**Table 5. Results on the MARCELL-RO testing dataset**

| Punctuation | Precision % | Recall % | F1 % |
|---|---|---|---|
| Comma | 87.87 | 86.48 | 87.17 |
| Period | 96.05 | 95.23 | 95.63 |
| MicroAvg | 91.39 | 90.23 | 90.81 |

The same model, obtained by training on the MARCELL-RO corpus, was tested on the RRT corpus splits. The results are given in Table 6 for all splits. As described in Section 3, the RRT corpus contains texts from multiple domains. We consider this to be the main reason behind the significant drop in performance compared to the MARCELL-RO-Test. The micro averaged F1 score has dropped from 90.81% (on MARCELL-RO-Test) to 74.70% (on RRT-Test), a 16.11% difference. This results from a decrease of 12.38% in period prediction performance and 19.84% in comma prediction. This confirms once again the difficulties associated with predicting commas. Period prediction seems to be more robust when considering different domains and styles associated with the text.

The hyphenation algorithm introduced in (Avram et al., 2020) and de-

**Table 6. Results on the RRT corpus splits**

| Punctuation | Precision % | Recall % | F1 % |
|---|---|---|---|
| Training | | | |
| Comma | 73.51 | 67.74 | 70.51 |
| Period | 82.57 | 83.96 | 83.26 |
| MicroAvg | 77.70 | 74.85 | 76.24 |
| Validation | | | |
| Comma | 73.34 | 64.30 | 68.52 |
| Period | 79.85 | 81.68 | 80.76 |
| MicroAvg | 76.40 | 71.81 | 74.03 |
| Testing | | | |
| Comma | 69.63 | 65.18 | 67.33 |
| Period | 81.92 | 84.63 | 83.25 |
| MicroAvg | 75.47 | 73.95 | 74.70 |

scribed in Section 4 was already integrated in the RELATE[19] (Păiș et al., 2020) platform. This platform contains multiple models, resources and tools for processing the Romanian language, resulting from different national and international research projects. It contains multiple BLARK pipelines (Păiș, 2020; Păiș et al., 2021a), allowing for lemmatization, morpho-syntactic annotations, dependency parsing (Ion, 2018) and text classification (Avram et al., 2021b). With regard to speech applications, it contains integrations of Automatic Speech Recognition (ASR) and Text-to-Speech (TTS) (Stan et al., 2011) modules, as well as more advanced speech processing, such as Speech-to-Speech translation (Avram et al., 2021a). In this context we decided to also integrate the punctuation restoration algorithm in the RELATE platform.

We considered that the best way to integrate the algorithm in the platform, as well as to allow its reuse in other applications, would be to expose the functionality as a REST web service. This means the implementation of an HTTP web server, exposing an endpoint that receives a text with accepted characteristics (lowercase, no punctuation, tokenized) and returns

[19]https://relate.racai.ro

the punctuation marks associated with each token. To allow processing of documents of any size, the server accepts both GET and POST HTTP requests. Furthermore, for error identification, the result is in JSON format, containing a *status* field, which can take the values *OK* and *ERROR*. In the case of normal operation, the returned JSON object also contains a *result* field with the predicted punctuation marks. An example API call is provided in Listing 1 and the resulting JSON response is given in Listing 2. In the call *\n* is used to indicate a new line character, in order to send the tokenized document. The example text contains 7 tokens, thus resulting in 7 punctuation marks being predicted in the resulting JSON. Each prediction corresponds to the punctuation mark following a token. The actual server implementation was realized in Python using the Flask[20] framework.

Listing 1. Example API call

```
http://127.0.0.1:5105/api/v1.0/punctuation?text=președintele
\na\nvizitat\nromânia\nsuedia\nși\ndanemarca
```

Listing 2. API call result

```
{
    result: "O O O COMMA O O PERIOD "
    status: "OK"
}
```

The RELATE platform is intended for processing both single documents and large collections of documents. In the first case, the user can access a simple web interface to enter the requested document. Then, the text is processed internally and the results are displayed in the same easy to use web interface. For this operation there is no account required. An example of the interface is presented in Figure 3 with the result in Figure 4.

In addition to the public web interface, the RELATE platform has an internal part, requiring an authenticated user. In this case, large corpora can be automatically processed by means of tasks. Each task is sent to an internal scheduler and executed in parallel by using multiple processes, potentially distributed on multiple servers. Punctuation restoration in this case starts by uploading an archive with text without punctuation, possibly

[20]https://flask.palletsprojects.com/en/2.0.x/

Figure 3. Web interface for punctuation restoration inside the RELATE platform.

Figure 4. Result given in the web interface for punctuation restoration inside the RELATE platform.

obtained from an ASR system. Then, the user needs to schedule a task in the platform. Finally, when the task finishes, the user can either access each file individually or download a new archive with the results.

## Conclusion

This chapter introduced the task of punctuation restoration. Experiments involving the Romanian language were described. For this purpose, a dedicated tool was first created to transform any CoNLL-U Plus formatted corpus into something suitable for training punctuation restoration algorithms.

Then, a large corpus, MARCELL-RO, was transformed and used for training a punctuation restoration algorithm. Finally, the resulting model was tested on the RRT corpus (which is commonly used for many Romanian language natural language processing tasks).

Experiments have shown that comma restoration is more challenging than period restoration in the Romanian language. This is similar to other languages, including English. Furthermore, when using a model in a different domain (the case of the MARCELL-RO based model used on the RRT corpus), period restoration works better (there is a smaller decrease in F1 score compared to comma prediction). Nevertheless, punctuation restoration is not yet a solved problem, since even a model trained on a large text corpus is not able to perform similarly on an out-of-domain text resource. Hence, there is no general model that can be used out-of-the-box on any general text or audio transcription.

When dealing with punctuation insertion into audio transcripts, the task is further complicated by the potential errors present in the text. Each ASR system is characterized by a certain amount of word errors. These can occur due to recording conditions, differences in the way sounds are pronounced by the speaker compared to the training set, words that sound similar, etc. Păiș and Tufiș (2021) indicated that current state-of-the-art models trained on text data suffer a performance decrease when applied to ASR transcriptions. However, even when training models using real transcriptions the overall system performance is still reduced when compared to the system restoring punctuation of correct text (with no word errors).

As mentioned in Section 1, punctuation restoration is useful in many cases where the text may not contain proper punctuation. For example in social media messages the user may omit punctuation or sometimes even use it in an incorrect way. However, when dealing with ASR transcriptions, having access to the sound data may provide additional cues that may help punctuation restoration (an example is pause duration or pitch variation which may provide hints for the end of sentences or commas). For the Romanian language experiments described in this chapter we used only text data for both training and evaluating the models. Therefore, a future research direction may involve extending the models with audio information in order to improve the creation of rich transcriptions.

## References

Alam, T., Khan, A., and Alam, F. (2020). Punctuation restoration using transformer models for high-and low-resource languages. In *Proceedings of the Sixth Workshop on Noisy User-generated Text (W-NUT 2020)*, pages 132–142, Online. Association for Computational Linguistics.

Avram, A.-M., Păiș, V., and Tufiș, D. (2020). Towards a Romanian end-to-end automatic speech recognition based on DeepSpeech2. *Proceedings of the Romanian Academy Series A*, 21:395–402.

Avram, A.-M., Păiș, V., and Tufiș, D. (2021a). A modular approach for Romanian-English speech translation. In Métais, E., Meziane, F., Horacek, H., and Kapetanios, E., editors, *Natural Language Processing and Information Systems*, pages 57–63, Cham. Springer International Publishing.

Avram, A.-M., Păiș, V., and Tufiș, D. (2021b). Pyeurovoc: A tool for multilingual legal document classification with eurovoc descriptors. In *Proceedings of Recent Advances in Natural Language Processing (RANLP2021)*, pages 92–101.

Baldwin, T., Cook, P., Lui, M., MacKinlay, A., and Wang, L. (2013). How noisy social media text, how diffrnt social media sources? In *Proceedings of the 6th International Joint Conference on Natural Language Processing*, pages 356–364.

Barbu Mititelu, V. (2018). *Modern Syntactic Analysis of Romanian*, pages 67–78. Editura Universității Alexandru Ioan Cuza, Iași.

Barbu Mititelu, V. and Mitrofan, M. (2020). The Romanian medical treebank - SiMoNERo. In Barbu Mititelu, V., Irimia, E., Tufiș, D., and Dan, C., editors, *Proceedings of the 15th International Conference Linguistic Resources and Tools for Natural Language Processing*, pages 7–16, online.

Barbu Mititelu, V., Tufiș, D., and Irimia, E. (2018). The reference corpus of the contemporary romanian language (corola). In *Proceedings of the Eleventh International Conference on Language Resources and Evaluation (LREC 2018)*, pages 1178–1185.

Barbu Mititelu, V., Tufiș, D., Irimia, E., Păiș, V., Ion, R., Diewald, N., Mitrofan, M., and Mihaela, O. (2019). Little strokes fell great oaks. Creating CoRoLa, the reference corpus of contemporary Romanian. In *Revue Roumaine de Linguistique, No./Issue 3*.

Batista, F., Trancoso, I., and Mamede, N. (2009). Automatic recovery of punctuation marks and capitalization information for iberian languages. In *Proceedings of the Joint SIG-IL/Microsoft Workshop on Speech and Language Technologies for Iberian Languages*, pages 99–102.

Bojanowski, P., Grave, E., Joulin, A., and Mikolov, T. (2017). Enriching word vectors with subword information. *Transactions of the Association for Computational Linguistics*, 5:135–146.

Boroș, T., Dumitrescu, S. D., and Burtica, R. (2018). NLP-cube: End-to-end raw text processing with neural networks. In *Proceedings of the CoNLL 2018 Shared Task: Multilingual Parsing from Raw Text to Universal Dependencies*, pages 171–179, Brussels, Belgium. Association for Computational Linguistics.

Caranica, A., Cucu, H., Buzo, A., and Burileanu, C. (2015). Capitalization and punctuation restoration for Romanian language. *UPB Scientific Bulletin, Series C*, 77:95–106.

Che, X., Luo, S., Yang, H., and Meinel, C. (2016). Sentence boundary detection based on parallel lexical and acoustic models. In *Proceedings of the Annual Conference of the International Speech Communication Association (INTERSPEECH)*, pages 2528–2532.

Chen, Q., Wang, W., Chen, M., and Zhang, Q. (2021). Discriminative Self-Training for Punctuation Prediction. In *Proc. Interspeech 2021*, pages 771–775.

Clark, K., Luong, M.-T., Le, Q. V., and Manning, C. D. (2020). ELECTRA: Pre-training text encoders as discriminators rather than generators. In *ICLR*.

Conneau, A., Khandelwal, K., Goyal, N., Chaudhary, V., Wenzek, G., Guzmán, F., Grave, E., Ott, M., Zettlemoyer, L., and Stoyanov, V. (2020). Unsupervised cross-lingual representation learning at scale. In

*Proceedings of the 58th Annual Meeting of the Association for Computational Linguistics*, pages 8440–8451, Online. Association for Computational Linguistics.

Cristea, D., Diewald, N., Haja, G., Mărănduc, C., Barbu Mititelu, V., and Onofrei, M. (2019). How to find a shining needle in the haystack. querying corola: solutions and perspectives. *RRL*, (3):279–292.

Dai, Z., Lai, G., Yang, Y., and Le, Q. (2020). Funnel-transformer: Filtering out sequential redundancy for efficient language processing. In Larochelle, H., Ranzato, M., Hadsell, R., Balcan, M. F., and Lin, H., editors, *Advances in Neural Information Processing Systems*, volume 33, pages 4271–4282. Curran Associates, Inc.

Datta, P., Jakubowicz, P., Vogler, C., and Kushalnagar, R. (2020). Readability of punctuation in automatic subtitles. In *Proceedings of the International Conference on Computers Helping People with Special Needs*, pages 195–201.

Devlin, J., Chang, M.-W., Lee, K., and Toutanova, K. (2019). Bert: Pre-training of deep bidirectional transformers for language understanding. In *Proceedings of the 2019 Conference of the North American Chapter of the Association for Computational Linguistics: Human Language Technologies, Volume 1 (Long and Short Papers)*, pages 4171–4186. Association for Computational Linguistics.

Dhole, K. D., Gangal, V., Gehrmann, S., Gupta, A., Li, Z., Mahamood, S., Mahendiran, A., Mille, S., Srivastava, A., Tan, S., Wu, T., Sohl-Dickstein, J., Choi, J. D., Hovy, E., Dusek, O., Ruder, S., Anand, S., Aneja, N., Banjade, R., Barthe, L., Behnke, H., Berlot-Attwell, I., Boyle, C., Brun, C., Cabezudo, M. A. S., Cahyawijaya, S., Chapuis, E., Che, W., Choudhary, M., Clauss, C., Colombo, P., Cornell, F., Dagan, G., Das, M., Dixit, T., Dopierre, T., Dray, P.-A., Dubey, S., Ekeinhor, T., Giovanni, M. D., Gupta, R., Gupta, R., Hamla, L., Han, S., Harel-Canada, F., Honore, A., Jindal, I., Joniak, P. K., Kleyko, D., Kovatchev, V., Krishna, K., Kumar, A., Langer, S., Lee, S. R., Levinson, C. J., Liang, H., Liang, K., Liu, Z., Lukyanenko, A., Marivate, V., de Melo, G., Meoni, S., Meyer, M., Mir, A., Moosavi, N. S., Muennighoff, N., Mun, T.

S. H., Murray, K., Namysl, M., Obedkova, M., Oli, P., Pasricha, N., Pfister, J., Plant, R., Prabhu, V., Păiș, V., Qin, L., Raji, S., Rajpoot, P. K., Raunak, V., Rinberg, R., Roberts, N., Rodriguez, J. D., Roux, C., S., V. P. H., Sai, A. B., Schmidt, R. M., Scialom, T., Sefara, T., Shamsi, S. N., Shen, X., Shi, H., Shi, Y., Shvets, A., Siegel, N., Sileo, D., Simon, J., Singh, C., Sitelew, R., Soni, P., Sorensen, T., Soto, W., Srivastava, A., Srivatsa, K. A., Sun, T., T, M. V., Tabassum, A., Tan, F. A., Teehan, R., Tiwari, M., Tolkiehn, M., Wang, A., Wang, Z., Wang, G., Wang, Z. J., Wei, F., Wilie, B., Winata, G. I., Wu, X., Wydmaski, W., Xie, T., Yaseen, U., Yee, M., Zhang, J., and Zhang, Y. (2021). NL-Augmenter: A Framework for Task-Sensitive Natural Language Augmentation.

Dima, G.-A., Avram, A.-M., and Cercel, D.-C. (2020). Approaching SMM4H 2020 with ensembles of BERT flavours. In *Proceedings of the Fifth Social Media Mining for Health Applications Workshop & Shared Task*, pages 153–157, Barcelona, Spain (Online). Association for Computational Linguistics.

Dumitrescu, S., Avram, A.-M., and Pyysalo, S. (2020). The birth of Romanian BERT. In *Proceedings of the 2020 Conference on Empirical Methods in Natural Language Processing: Findings*, pages 4324–4328.

Dumitrescu, S. D. and Boroș, T. (2013). A unified corpora-based approach to diacritic restoration and word casing. In *6th Language and Technology Conference (LTC 2013)*, Poznan, Poland.

Federico, M., Bentivogli, L., Paul, M., and Stueker, S. (2011). Overview of the IWSLT 2011 evaluation campaign. In *Proceedings of the International Workshop on Spoken Language Translation (IWSLT)*, pages 11–27.

Gravano, A., Jansche, M., and Bacchiani, M. (2009). Restoring punctuation and capitalization in transcribed speech. In *Proceedings of the IEEE International Conference on Acoustics, Speech, and Signal Processing (ICASSP)*, pages 4741–4744.

Guerreiro, N. M., Rei, R., and Batista, F. (2021). Towards better subtitles: A multilingual approach for punctuation restoration of speech transcripts. *Expert Systems with Applications*, 186:115740.

Hinton, G., Vinyals, O., and Dean, J. (2015). Distilling the knowledge in a neural network.

Ion, R. (2018). Teprolin: An extensible, online text preprocessing platform for romanian. In *The 13th International Conference on Linguistic Resources and Tools for Natural Language Processing*, pages 69–76.

Irimia, E. and Barbu Mititelu, V. (2015). RACAI-RoTb: nucleu de corpus de limbă română adnotat sintactic cu relații de dependență. *Revista Română de Interacțiune Om-Calculator*, 8(2):101–120.

Jones, B. E. M. (1994). Exploring the role of punctuation in parsing natural text. In *Proceedings of the 15th conference on Computational linguistics - Volume 1 (COLING 94)*, pages 421–425. Association for Computational Linguistics.

Jones, D. A., Wolf, F., Gibson, E., Williams, E., Fedorenko, E., Reynolds, D. A., and Zissman, M. (2003). Measuring the readability of automatic speech-to-text transcripts. In *Proceedings of the 8th European Conference on Speech Communication and Technology (EUROSPEECH)*, pages 1585–1588.

Liu, Y., Ott, M., Goyal, N., Du, J., Joshi, M., Chen, D., Levy, O., Lewis, M., Zettlemoyer, L., and Stoyanov, V. (2019). RoBERTa: A robustly optimized BERT pretraining approach.

Liu, Y., Shriberg, E., Stolcke, A., Peskin, B., Ang, J., Hillard, D., Ostendorf, M., Tomalin, M., Woodland, P., and Harper, M. (2005). Structural metadata research in the EARS program. In *Proceedings of IEEE International Conference on Acoustics, Speech, and Signal Processing (ICASSP 2005)*, pages 957–960.

Makhoul, J., Baron, A., Bulyko, I., Nguyen, L., Ramshaw, L. A., Stallard, D., Schwartz, R. M., and Xiang, B. (2005). The effects of speech recognition and punctuation on information extraction performance. In *INTERSPEECH 2005 - Eurospeech, 9th European Conference on Speech Communication and Technology, Lisbon, Portugal, September 4-8, 2005*, pages 57–60. ISCA.

Markwardt, A. H. (1942). *Introduction to the English Language*. Oxford University Press, New York.

Masala, M., Iacob, R. C. A., Uban, A. S., Cidota, M., Velicu, H., Rebedea, T., and Popescu, M. (2021). jurBERT: A Romanian BERT model for legal judgement prediction. In *Proceedings of the Natural Legal Language Processing Workshop 2021*, pages 86–94, Punta Cana, Dominican Republic. Association for Computational Linguistics.

Masala, M., Ruseti, S., and Dascalu, M. (2020). RoBERT – a Romanian BERT model. In *Proceedings of the 28th International Conference on Computational Linguistics*, pages 6626–6637, Barcelona, Spain (Online). International Committee on Computational Linguistics.

Miller, D., Boisen, S., Schwartz, R., Stone, R., and Weischedel, R. (2000). Named entity extraction from noisy input: Speech and ocr. In *Proceedings of the Sixth Conference on Applied Natural Language Processing*, pages 316–324.

Mitrofan, M. (2019). *Extragere de cunostinte din texte în limba româna si date structurate cu aplicatii în domeniul medical*. PhD thesis, Romanian Academy.

Nebhi, K., Bontcheva, K., and Gorrell, G. (2015). Restoring capitalization in #tweets. In *Proceedings of WWW Companion*, pages 1111–1115.

Nuțu, M., Lőrincz, B., and Stan, A. (2019). Deep learning for automatic diacritics restoration in Romanian. In *2019 IEEE 15th International Conference on Intelligent Computer Communication and Processing (ICCP)*, pages 235–240.

Nunberg, G. (1990). The linguistics of punctuation. In *CSLI Lecture Notes 18*.

Park, T. J., Kanda, N., Dimitriadis, D., Han, K. J., Watanabe, S., and Narayanan, S. (2022). A review of speaker diarization: Recent advances with deep learning. *Computer Speech & Language*, 72:101317.

Peitz, S., Freitag, M., Mauser, A., and Ney, H. (2011). Modeling punctuation prediction as machine translation. In *Proceedings of the International Workshop on Spoken Language Translation (IWSLT)*, pages 238–245.

Perez, C. A. (2014). *Linguistic Resources for Natural Language Processing*. PhD thesis, Faculty of Computer Science, Al. I. Cuza University, Iași.

Peters, M. E., Neumann, M., Iyyer, M., Gardner, M., Clark, C., Lee, K., and Zettlemoyer, L. (2018a). Deep contextualized word representations,. In *Proceedings of NAACL 2018*.

Peters, M. E., Neumann, M., Iyyer, M., Gardner, M., Clark, C., Lee, K., and Zettlemoyer, L. (2018b). Deep contextualized word representations. In *Proc. of NAACL*.

Păiș, V. (2020). Multiple annotation pipelines inside the relate platform. In *The 15th International Conference on Linguistic Resources and Tools for Natural Language Processing*, pages 65–75.

Păiș, V., Ion, R., Avram, A.-M., Mitrofan, M., and Tufiș, D. (2021a). In-depth evaluation of Romanian natural language processing pipelines. *Romanian Journal of Information Science and Technology (ROMJIST)*, 24(4):384–401.

Păiș, V. and Mitrofan, M. (2021). Assessing multiple word embeddings for named entity recognition of professions and occupations in health-related social media. In *Proceedings of the Sixth Social Media Mining for Health (#SMM4H) Workshop and Shared Task*, pages 128–130, Mexico City, Mexico. Association for Computational Linguistics.

Păiș, V., Mitrofan, M., Gasan, C. L., Coneschi, V., and Ianov, A. (2021b). Named entity recognition in the Romanian legal domain. In *Proceedings of the Natural Legal Language Processing Workshop 2021*, pages 9–18, Punta Cana, Dominican Republic. Association for Computational Linguistics.

Păiș, V., Mitrofan, M., Gasan, C. L., Ianov, A., Ghiță, C., Coneschi, V. S., and Onuț, A. (2021c). Romanian Named Entity Recognition in the Legal domain (LegalNERo).

Păiș, V. and Tufiș, D. (2018a). Computing distributed representations of words using the CoRoLa corpus. *Proceedings of the Romanian Academy Series A - Mathematics Physics Technical Sciences Information Science*, 19(2):185–191.

Păiș, V. and Tufiș, D. (2018b). More Romanian word embeddings from the RETEROM project. *Proceedings of the International Conference on Linguistic Resources and Tools for Processing Romanian Language - CONSILR*, pages 91–100.

Păiș, V. and Tufiș, D. (2021). Capitalization and punctuation restoration: a survey. *Artificial Intelligence Review*.

Păiș, V., Tufiș, D., and Ion, R. (2020). A processing platform relating data and tools for Romanian language. In *Proceedings of The 12th Language Resources and Evaluation Conference*, pages 81–88, Marseille, France. European Language Resources Association.

Qi, P., Zhang, Y., Zhang, Y., Bolton, J., and Manning, C. D. (2020). Stanza: A Python natural language processing toolkit for many human languages. In *Proceedings of the 58th Annual Meeting of the Association for Computational Linguistics: System Demonstrations*.

Radford, A., Wu, J., Child, R., Luan, D., Amodei, D., and Sutskever, I. (2019). Language models are unsupervised multitask learners. OpenAI blog.

Raicu, I., Boitout, N., Bologa, R., and Sturza, M. G. (2020). Word embeddings in Romanian for the retail banking domain. In *Proceedings of the IE 2020 International Conference*.

Rosenfeld, R. (2000). Two decades of statistical language modeling: where do we go from here? *Proceedings of the IEEE*, 88:1270–1278.

Sanh, V., Debut, L., Chaumond, J., and Wolf, T. (2020). Distilbert, a distilled version of bert: smaller, faster, cheaper and lighter.

Schuster, M. and Nakajima, K. (2012). Japanese and korean voice search. In *2012 IEEE International Conference on Acoustics, Speech and Signal Processing (ICASSP)*, pages 5149–5152.

Shi, N., Wang, W., Wang, B., Li, J., Liu, X., and Lin, Z. (2021). Incorporating External POS Tagger for Punctuation Restoration. In *Proc. Interspeech 2021*, pages 1987–1991.

Soboleva, D., Skopek, O., Šajgalík, M., Cărbune, V., Weissenberger, F., Proskurnia, J., Prisacari, B., Valcarce, D., Lu, J., Prabhavalkar, R., and Miklos, B. (2020). Replacing human audio with synthetic audio for on-device unspoken punctuation prediction.

Stan, A., Yamagishi, J., King, S., and Aylett, M. (2011). The Romanian speech synthesis (RSS) corpus: Building a high quality HMM-based speech synthesis system using a high sampling rate. *Speech Communication*, 53(3):442–450.

Straka, M., Hajič, J., and Straková, J. (2016). Udpipe: Trainable pipeline for processing conll-u files performing tokenization, morphological analysis, pos tagging and parsing. In *Proceedings of the Tenth International Conference on Language Resources and Evaluation (LREC 2016)*.

Szegedy, C., Vanhoucke, V., Ioffe, S., Shlens, J., and Wojna, Z. (2016). Rethinking the inception architecture for computer vision. In *2016 IEEE Conference on Computer Vision and Pattern Recognition (CVPR)*, pages 2818–2826, Los Alamitos, CA, USA. IEEE Computer Society.

Tilk, O. and Alumäe, T. (2015). LSTM for punctuation restoration in speech transcripts. In *Proceedings of the Sixteenth annual conference of the international speech communication association (INTERSPEECH)*, pages 683–687.

Tufiș, D. and Ceaușu, A. (2008). Diac+: A professional diacritics recovering system. In *Proceedings of the 6th Language Resources and Evaluation Conference - LREC 2008*, Marrakech, Morocco.

Tufiș, D. and Cristea, D. (2017). An outlook over CoRoLa: The reference corpus of contemporary written and spoken corpus. In *Proceedings of SpeD conference, (invited talk)*, Bucharest, Romania.

Tufis, D., Mitrofan, M., Păis, V., Ion, R., and Coman, A. (2020). Collection and annotation of the Romanian legal corpus. In *Proceedings of the 12th Language Resources and Evaluation Conference*, pages 2773–2777, Marseille, France. European Language Resources Association.

Tündik, M., Szaszák, G., Gosztolya, G., and Beke, A. (2018). User-centric evaluation of automatic punctuation in ASR closed captioning. In *Proceedings Interspeech 2018*, pages 2628–2632.

Vaissiere, J. (1983). *Language-independent prosodic features*, pages 53–66. Springer Verlag.

Váradi, T., Koeva, S., Yamalov, M., Tadić, M., Sass, B., Nitoń, B., Ogrodniczuk, M., Pęzik, P., Barbu Mititelu, V., Ion, R., Irimia, E., Mitrofan, M., Păis, V., Tufis, D., Garabík, R., Krek, S., Repar, A., Rihtar, M., and Brank, J. (2020). The MARCELL legislative corpus. In *Proceedings of the 12th Language Resources and Evaluation Conference*, pages 3761–3768, Marseille, France. European Language Resources Association.

Vaswani, A., Bengio, S., Brevdo, E., Chollet, F., Gomez, A. N., Gouws, S., Jones, L., Kaiser, Ł., Kalchbrenner, N., Parmar, N., Sepassi, R., Shazeer, N., and Uszkoreit, J. (2018). Tensor2tensor for neural machine translation.

Vaswani, A., Shazeer, N., Parmar, N., Uszkoreit, J., Jones, L., Gomez, A. N., ukasz Kaiser, and Polosukhin, I. (2017). Attention is all you need. In *Proceedings of the 31st International Conference on Neural Information Processing Systems (NIPS)*, pages 5998–6008.

Wei, J. and Zou, K. (2019). EDA: Easy data augmentation techniques for boosting performance on text classification tasks. In *Proceedings of the 2019 Conference on Empirical Methods in Natural Language Processing and the 9th International Joint Conference on Natural Language Processing (EMNLP-IJCNLP)*, pages 6382–6388, Hong Kong, China. Association for Computational Linguistics.

Yang, Z., Dai, Z., Yang, Y., Carbonell, J., Salakhutdinov, R. R., and Le, Q. V. (2019). Xlnet: Generalized autoregressive pretraining for language understanding. In Wallach, H., Larochelle, H., Beygelzimer, A., d'Alché-Buc, F., Fox, E., and Garnett, R., editors, *Advances in Neural Information Processing Systems*, volume 32. Curran Associates, Inc.

Yi, J. and Tao, J. (2019). Self-attention based model for punctuation prediction using word and speech embeddings. In *Proceedings of the IEEE*

*International Conference on Acoustics, Speech and Signal Processing (ICASSP)*, pages 7270–7274.

Zaharia, G.-E., Avram, A.-M., Cercel, D.-C., and Rebedea, T. (2021). Dialect identification through adversarial learning and knowledge distillation on Romanian BERT. In *Proceedings of the Eighth Workshop on NLP for Similar Languages, Varieties and Dialects*, pages 113–119, Kiyv, Ukraine. Association for Computational Linguistics.

In: Speech Recognition Technology ... ISBN: 978-1-68507-929-1
Editor: Vasile-Florian Păiş 

Chapter 6

# Linguistic Linked Open Data for Speech Processing

**Vasile-Florian Păiş[*] and Verginica Barbu Mititelu[†]**
Research Institute for Artificial Intelligence
"Mihai Drăgănescu", Romanian Academy,
Bucharest, Romania

**Abstract**

Linguistic Linked Open Data is becoming an important format for language resources, due to its power to ensure resources' interoperability and integration, which makes them more easily findable, accessible, interoperable and retrievable (i.e., FAIR). Romanian has fragmentary support with respect to the development of language resources and processing tools. Thus, in an effort to promote the existing ones, their conversion to Linked Data is a natural step. We focus here on resources for speech processing and present the RoLEX lexicon and the RTASC corpus that are relevant for this task: the former is the largest lexicon with phonetic transcription for Romanian words and their inflected forms, while the latter is a bimodal corpus relevant for training a robot's speech component for a specifically designed microworld. Both are converted to the Linguistic Linked Open Data format, linked to other existing resources for Romanian and made available as downloadable files and for query by means

[*]Corresponding Author's Email: vasile@racai.ro.
[†]Corresponding Author's Email: vergi@racai.ro.

of SPARQL language. Some scenarios for exploiting the power of Linked Data format of these resources are also described here.

**Keywords:** speech processing, phonetic lexicon, bimodal corpus, Linguistic Linked Open Data

# 1. Introduction

After more than seven decades of research in (written or spoken) language processing, numerous resources have been developed[1], mostly independently of each other, although the necessary number and linguistic content of resources even for languages such as English, which has important support for its technological development, is far from being reached. In addition to scarcity, another hindrance to resources availability and accessibility is represented by their diversity (Chiarcos and Pareja-Lora, 2020) in terms of: (i) the types of linguistic information contained, (ii) the complexity of the linguistic information represented in each resource, (iii) content representation, and (iv) data accessibility. Even when resources are available for a language, their format makes them impossible to use by existing tools and applications, and this deepens the gap between languages with respect to their representation in the language technology market.

One solution to efficiently use existing resources, even beyond the possibilities offered by their content, is making them interoperable (Ide and Pustejovsky, 2010) syntactically (i.e., being able "to process (read) exchanged data either directly or via trivial conversion") and semantically (i.e., being able "to interpret exchanged linguistic information in meaningful and consistent ways with reference to a common set of reference categories"). With the advent of the Semantic Web (Berners-Lee et al., 2001), the premises for ensuring such interoperability have been created: the data on the Web must be semantically structured, i.e., they must be made available in standard formats that can be understood, retrieved and processed by machines, they must be linked to each other and documented with metadata [2]. The Semantic Web uses technologies like RDF (Resource Description Framework, i.e. "a standard model for data interchange on the

[1] See https://live.european-language-grid.eu/resources for an up-to-date inventory of existing resources for the languages of Europe, mainly, but also of other languages.

[2] https://www.w3.org/2001/sw/wiki/Main_Page

Web"[3]) and ontologies (i.e., "formal, explicit specification of a shared conceptualization" (Studer et al., 1998)) for making the semantics of the data explicit.

Standards for representing resources and for their publication on the Web have been enforced within the Linked (Open) Data paradigm.

For Linguistic Linked Data (LLD), interoperability must be ensured at several levels (Ide and Pustejovsky, 2010):

- metadata: the same set of metadata labels, which correspond to "identically defined metadata categories", must be used;
- data categories: they must be standardized[4];
- publication: the resources must be published in a standardized format, with annotation in a common representation model, in acknowledged repositories, alongside their metadata and documentation;
- software sharing: resources must use the same data categories, to ensure compatibility with other resources and processing by the same tools.

We focus here on the representation of bimodal (speech and written text) resources in the Linguistic Linked Open Data paradigm. There are few such attempts for language resources, while for Romanian, this is the first such endeavour. In Section 2, we briefly describe the linked (open) data paradigm, its principles and advantages and then, in Section 3, we present the efforts of converting Romanian language resources to linked open data. In Section 4, we focus on resources for speech processing in linked open data format and then narrow the scope to Romanian ones, in Section 5, where we describe a lexicon and a corpus with respect to their content, structure, interlinking with other resources, exploitation and access.

[3]https://www.w3.org/RDF/

[4]http://datcatinfo.net/

## 2. Linguistic Linked Open Data

Linked data are "interlinked collections of datasets published on the Web" (Cimiano et al., 2020). They follow four principles [5] that ensure their:

- uniqueness: each element of a resource gets a unique Uniform Resource Identifier (URI);
- retrieval: HTTP URIs are used so that resources can be easily accessed by either a machine or a human user in an adequate format;
- interoperability: the resources are represented in a standardized way (Resource Description Framework, RDF (Klyne et al., 2004)), which allows for easy reuse and query by means of the same tools or language (SPARQL[6]); and
- interconnection with other resources: a network of language resources is created in which the components of a resource are linked to data categories (defined in specialized repositories) and (intra- or cross-linguistically) connected to components of (an)other resource(s) by means of relations that encode their equivalence, relatedness, etc.

These principles make resources more easily findable (each resource and each component of it are uniquely identified, while the standardized format of their content and metadata makes them reachable by search engines), accessible (given the standardized representation), interoperable (by reusing the same vocabularies to describe linguistic content) and reusable (by mechanisms of describing provenance, terms of use, licence type) (see the FAIR principles of data management) (Cimiano et al., 2020).

The dimension of the Linked Open Data paradigm is given by an associated cloud (LOD Cloud[7]), a diagram of resources generated periodically. One of the nine domains in the cloud is linguistics[8]. Registering metadata for resources in this cloud contributes to their FAIR characteristics.

[5] https://www.w3.org/DesignIssues/LinkedData.html

[6] https://www.w3.org/TR/rdf-sparql-query/

[7] https://lod-cloud.net/

[8] http://linguistic-lod.org/llod-cloud

# 3. Romanian Resources as Linguistic Linked Open Data

Resources for the Romanian language are recorded in the LOD Cloud due to community efforts of converting existing multilingual resources to LLOD format, on the one hand, and to efforts of the Research Institute for Artificial Intelligence to convert to this format the monolingual resources developed here, on the other hand. With respect to their types, the following are represented:

- corpora: Multext-East[9], the LegalNERo corpus[10] (Păiș et al., 2021b) manually annotated with named entities for the legal domain, the PARSEME-Ro corpus (Barbu Mititelu et al., 2021) manually annotated with verbal multiword expressions according to the PARSEME annotation guidelines[11], the Romanian Reference Treebank (RRT) (Barbu Mititelu et al., 2020), Robin Technical Acquisition Speech Corpus (RTASC) (see Section 5.2), the SiMoNERo treebank (Barbu Mititelu et al., 2021) manually annotated with medical named entities,

- lexicons and dictionaries: the Romanian WordNet (Barbu Mititelu et al., 2020), RoLEX (see Section 5.1), word embeddings and lemma and token frequencies extracted from CoRoLa (Barbu Mititelu et al., 2020),

- terminologies, thesauri and knowledge bases: EuroVoc[12].

These resources are either mono-modal (i.e., containing only text files) or bimodal (i.e., containing both text and audio files), the latter type characterizing only one Romanian resource, namely RTASC.

[9] http://nl.ijs.si/ME/Vault/V4/

[10] https://zenodo.org/record/4922385#.YbDAR1OxVhA

[11] https://parsemefr.lis-lab.fr/parseme-st-guidelines/1.2/?page=home

[12] https://op.europa.eu/en/web/eu-vocabularies/dataset/-/resource?uri=http://publications.europa.eu/resource/dataset/eurovoc

# 4. LLOD Resources for Speech Processing

Considering the available ontologies for multimedia annotation, Margenstern et al. (2013) review several specialized ontologies. The Core Ontology for Multimedia (COMM) (Arndt et al., 2009) was built by re-engineering the MPEG-7 standard for multimedia annotation and using DOLCE as its underlying foundational ontology. The Ontology for Media Resources 1.0[13] is both a core vocabulary (a set of properties describing media resources) and its mapping to a set of metadata formats currently describing media resources published on the Web. The set of properties of the Ontology for Media Resources 1.0 was selected with respect to the most commonly adopted set of elements from metadata formats currently in use to describe media resources. Multimedia Metadata Ontology (M3O) (Saathoff and Scherp, 2010) was developed within the weKnowIt project for annotating rich, structured multimedia content on the Web and unlocking its semantics by making it machine-readable and machine-understandable. Large-Scale Concept Ontology for Multimedia (LSCOM) (Naphade et al., 2006) defines a formal vocabulary that includes more than 2,000 concepts for the annotation and retrieval of broadcast news video.

From the point of view of speech data, we are interested primarily in associating the textual representation with the audio signal. This association can be aligned at different levels: document, sentence, word, and phoneme. Furthermore, characteristics associated with the audio data (such as speaker, recording device, sampling rate) should also be stored. This additional metadata could allow training speech recognition algorithms specific to certain setups. The Music Ontology[14] (Raimond et al., 2007), even though not directly oriented towards speech, provides main concepts and properties for describing music (i.e., artists, albums and tracks) on the Semantic Web. The Smart Musical Instruments (SMIs) Ontology[15] (Turchet et al., 2021) considers that SMIs are an emerging category of musical instruments that belong to the wider class of Musical Things within the Internet of Musical Things paradigm. It interacts with the Sensor, Observation, Sample, and Actuator (SOSA) ontology for the representation of

[13] https://www.w3.org/TR/mediaont-10/

[14] http://musicontology.com/specification/

[15] https://w3id.org/smi#

sensors and actuators. SOSA is a lightweight but self-contained core ontology within the larger Semantic Sensor Network (SSN)[16] ontology, used for describing sensors and their observations, the involved procedures, the studied features of interest, the samples used to do so, and the observed properties, as well as actuators.

The Studio Ontology Framework[17] (Fazekas and Sandler, 2011) was designed for describing and sharing detailed information about music production in the recording studio. The ontology may be used to describe real-world recording scenarios involving physical hardware or computer-based post-production. The framework contains some general, domain-independent elements, a set of core concepts and relationships to describe the studio domain, and some extensions covering more specific areas such as microphone techniques and multitrack production tools. One of the extensions for audio recording includes the Microphone Ontology for describing microphones and microphone techniques (Fazekas et al., 2011).

Advanced multimedia recordings may contain, apart from audio, image (either static images or video) and text content other forms of representations. (Mallik et al., 2011) recognizes that the preservation of intangible cultural heritage resources like language, art, music and dance, is more complex and requires a knowledge intensive approach. The authors propose an ontology-based approach for the preservation of intangible cultural heritage with a case study in the domain of Indian Classical Dance, by making use of the Multimedia Web Ontology Language (MOWL) (Mallik et al., 2013). Thus, the authors aim to encode, in addition to audio and video, things such as hand gestures, body movements and facial expressions of the dancer, which always express a natural language keyword or phrase in an Indian classical dance.

While working on a sound analysis system in a telemedicine project, Nguyen et al. (2006) try to detect situations of distress in a patients room based on sound analysis. For this purpose, the authors build a domain ontology of such situations by gathering abstract concepts of sounds and concepts, along with their properties and instances. Chebotko et al. (2004) developed an ontology-based linguistic multimedia annotator. Furthermore, the systems allow for searching and retrieval of multimedia documents based on ontology annotations.

[16]https://www.w3.org/TR/vocab-ssn/

[17]http://isophonics.org/content/studio-ontology

Multilingual terminologies and ontologies, such as WordNet (Fellbaum, 1998), IATE[18], EuroVoc[19] and SNOMED-CT[20], make it possible to query a database in one language and obtain results in other languages. This is possible by first mapping the query, expressed in the user's language, to the ontology, then performing the search using the ontological concepts, which were mapped in the resource's own language, and finally returning all the results. Additionally, by exploiting an ontology's structure, it becomes possible to search for concepts rather than just words. In this context, Tejedor et al. (2007) propose a framework for ontology-based retrieval of human speech, focusing on the complete recognition/retrieval cycle, from word spotting to semantic annotation, query processing, and search result presentation. Even though not directly focusing on speech data, a recent survey (Sikelis et al., 2021) focuses on key aspects of ontology-based knowledge extraction from various sources, such as text, databases, and human expertise, realized in the realm of feature selection. The authors note that selective and representative approaches span diverse application domains, such as document classification, opinion mining, manufacturing, recommendation systems, urban management and information security systems, and demonstrate the feasibility and applicability of such methods.

Kumar et al. (2021) combines ontology-based approaches with complex natural language processing methods, such as co-reference resolution and named entity recognition, to improve full-text search results related to travelling to different places. Yelibayeva et al. (2021) constructs an ontological model of nominative word combinations in the Kazakh language. The authors then propose using the model in semantic searches, question answering systems and in the development of software applications for obtaining knowledge, as well as for training and evaluation of knowledge on the syntax of the Kazakh language in e-learning approaches.

Manzoor et al. (2021) performs a survey regarding ontology-based knowledge representation in robotic systems. When considering human-robot interaction in particular (and any human-machine interaction in general), speech-based communication has become increasingly used. In this case, speech transcripts need to be mapped to the robot's knowledge base

[18] https://iate.europa.eu/home
[19] https://eur-lex.europa.eu/browse/eurovoc.html
[20] https://www.snomed.org/snomed-ct/sct-worldwide

by using an appropriate ontology. Furthermore, based on the reasoning taking place, the ontology data must be mapped into actions or text, which in turn can be used as input for a text-to-speech system. Sarthou et al. (2019) go even further and propose a long-term semantic memory for robotic agents. The authors introduce the ability to modify the knowledge base during execution, through dialogue or geometric reasoning, and keep these changes even after the robot is powered off. Hauck et al. (2011), while discussing the SOAR (Laird et al., 1987) cognitive architecture, mentions the usage of ontologies for knowledge exchange between autonomous agents. Thus, Onto2Soar translates the working memory of an SOAR agent into an ontology to allow exchange of declarative knowledge between several agents. Oltramari and Lebiere (2013) enhances the ACT-R (Anderson, 1983) cognitive architecture with relevant background knowledge embedded in the Hybrid Ontology for the Mind's Eye project (HOMinE), a semantic resource for actions. The integration of cognitive architectures and ontologies is further discussed by Oltramari and Lebiere (2011).

# 5. Romanian LLOD Resources for Speech Processing

In this section, we present the two Romanian resources relevant for speech processing, that have been converted to LLOD format. Due to the advantages provided by the LLOD format, it is a natural step to subject existing resources to such conversions. Furthermore, future new resources will most likely contain also an RDF representation. However, due to the formats being used by existing processing tools, it is not appropriate to create resources only in RDF "format".

## 5.1. The RoLEX Lexicon

RoLEX is a lexicon that was developed in the ReTeRom project[21] and includes morpho-syntactic information, lemma, syllabification, stress and phonetic transcription of words. Within the ReTeRom project, multiple technologies for the Romanian language were developed. These include text-to-speech synthesis with expressivity, speech recognition mod-

[21] https://www.racai.ro/p/reterom/index_en.html

els, technologies for processing written Romanian language and a thesaurus with audio and textual resources, annotated at different acoustic and linguistic levels. In this context, RoLEX was constructed based on the vocabulary extracted from the textual component of a speech corpus that contained data from the Romanian Wikipedia, news, interviews, talk-shows, spontaneous speech, fairy tales, and novels.

Syllabification, stress and phonetic transcription information is based, partially, on previous resources such as RoSyllabiDict (Barbu, 2008) and MaRePhor (Toma et al., 2017). The MaRePhor[22] vocabulary contains a total of 72,375 entries from the Romanian Scrabble Association's official list of words and the entries from an additional 15,517 words dictionary, developed according to the SpeechDat specifications. Although it is considered mostly a phonetic language (Calotă, 2001), the 31 letters in the Romanian alphabet are pronounced using 34 phonemes. Some letters have more than one pronunciation, some are pronounced using a combination of sounds and certain groups of letters are pronounced as only one sound. Both MaRePhor and now RoLEX adhere to the Speech Assessment Method Phonetic Alphabet (SAMPA)[23]. It is a machine-readable phonetic alphabet, developed in 1987-89 by an international group of phoneticians. In 1996 it was extended to include the Romanian language[24]. SAMPA consists of a mapping of symbols of the International Phonetic Alphabet onto the 7-bit printable ASCII characters.

New entries added to RoLEX (which were not available from previously created resources) were first processed using the tool of Stan et al. (2011). This tool was integrated into the TEPROLIN (Ion, 2018) web-service, an annotation pipeline resulting from the same ReTeRom project. Furthermore, the TEPROLIN pipeline was integrated in the RELATE platform (Păiș et al., 2019). Following automatic processing, manual correction of the RoLEX lexicon was performed, thus obtaining the largest validated resource of this type available for the Romanian language (330,866 entries).

We present some statistics for RoLEX in Table 1. The ten most frequent syllables in RoLEX are presented in Table 2. The frequency of each letter and of each phoneme in RoLEX are presented in Figures 1 and 2,

[22] https://speech.utcluj.ro/marephor/

[23] https://www.phon.ucl.ac.uk/home/sampa/

[24] https://www.phon.ucl.ac.uk/home/sampa/romanian.htm

**Table 1. Statistics for RoLEX**

| | Letters | Phonemes | Syllables |
|---|---|---|---|
| Total # in lexicon | 3,160,843 | 3,142,106 | 1,328,926 |
| # of distinct | 31 | 34 | 9,475 |
| Minimum # per word | 1 | 1 | 1 |
| Maximum # per word | 28 | 28 | 11 |
| Average # per word | 9.55 | 9.5 | 4.02 |
| Minimum length (in letters) | – | – | 1 |
| Maximum length (in letters) | – | – | 9 |
| Average length (in letters) | – | – | 2.38 |

respectively. The frequency of syllables of different lengths is presented in Figure 3.

**Table 2. The 10 most frequent syllables and their frequency in RoLEX**

| Syllable | Frequency in RoLEX |
|---|---|
| le | 32,764 |
| a | 30,983 |
| te | 29,399 |
| lor | 28,348 |
| se | 23,643 |
| ri | 23,259 |
| ne | 22,453 |
| re | 22,358 |
| ta | 21,438 |
| ti | 20,958 |

The first version of RoLEX was stored in a tab-separated format with six columns for each entry. The first column contains the word form, then there was its lemma, its morpho-syntactic description (MSD), syllabification, stress and phonetic transcription. During the conversion process to

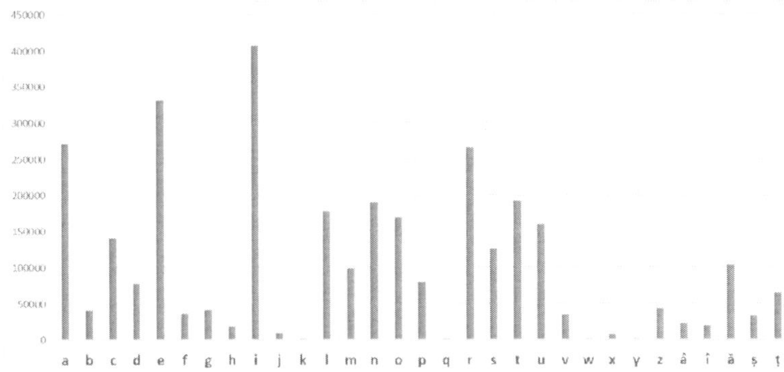


Figure 1. Frequency of each letter in RoLEX.

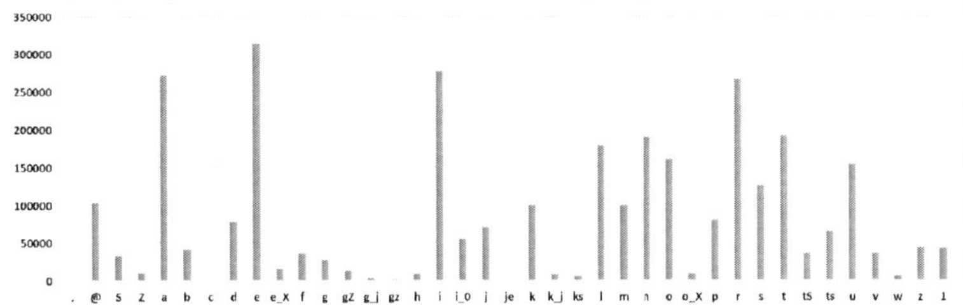


Figure 2. Frequency of each phoneme in RoLEX.

linguistic linked data format, additional references to the Romanian WordNet (Tufiș and Barbu Mititelu, 2014) were added. This makes both resources to become enriched: for each word in WordNet, phonetic information is provided: its stress, syllabic structure and pronunciation; each word in RoLEX obtains its semantics from the WordNet structure: in cases of homography (i.e., words spelt identically but pronounced differently) the semantic distinction between words also becomes visible due to this alignment. RoWN is aligned to Princeton WordNet via the Interlingual Index (ILI): each word in the WordNet is assigned the *ili* property that specifies to which ILI concept it maps. Mapping of different WordNets to ILI allows for cross-lingual lexico-semantic access.

The ontologies used within RoLEX are presented in Table 3. Each entry is instantiated using the LexicalEntry concept from the Lexicon Model for Ontologies (OntoLex). Different representations associated with an en-

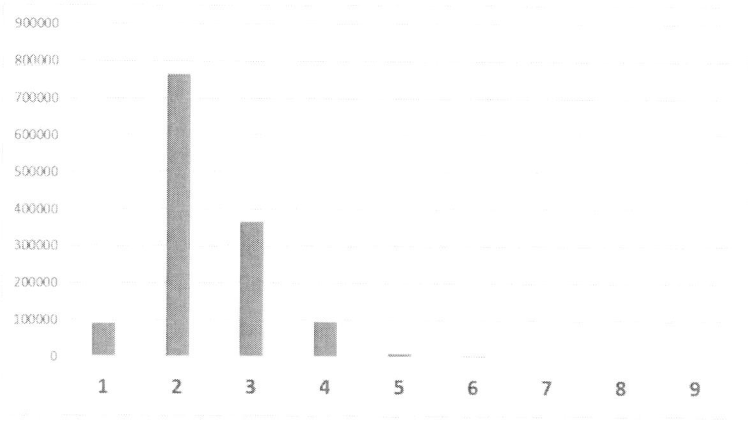


Figure 3. Frequency of syllables of different lengths in RoLEX.

try are in the form of *ontolex:Form* concepts. The *canonicalForm* attribute links the normal written form of a word with its entry and the *lexicalForm* attribute links other representations (syllabification, phonetic) to the main entry. Part-of-speech tags are primarily indicated using the CoNLL specification. When linking with the Romanian WordNet was possible, part-of-speech tags were also indicated using WordNet tags. Furthermore, in this case, WordNet synsets are indicated using the Interlingual Index (ILI).

Figure 4 shows a diagram of the classes used in the RoLEX lexicon, as well as example instances. Apart from the classes depicted in the diagram, other ontologies such as the Dublin Core Metadata Initiative (DCMI) Terms and Simple Knowledge Organization System (SKOS) are used to describe the resource itself, including the specification of associated language and licence. In Listing 1, we present three concepts associated with the word "copil" ("child").

Listing 1. Sample entries from the RoLEX lexicon

```
:lex_copil_n a ontolex:LexicalEntry;
        rdfs:label "copil_n"@ro;
        ontolex:canonicalForm :form_copil_n;
        wn:partOfSpeech wn:n;
        wn:ili ili:i88964 ;
        wn:ili ili:i88965 ;
        wn:ili ili:i39591 ;
        wn:ili ili:i91712 ;
        wn:ili ili:i93143 ;
```

**Table 3. Used vocabularies in RoLEX**

| Prefix | Name | URI |
|---|---|---|
| ontolex | Lexicon Model for Ontologies | http://www.w3.org/ns/lemon/ontolex |
| lime | LIngusitic MEtadata (LIME) | http://www.w3.org/ns/lemon/lime |
| conll | CoNLL tabular format | http://ufal.mff.cuni.cz/conll2009-st/task-description.html# |
| ili | Interlingual Index | http://ili.globalwordnet.org/ili/ |
| wn | WordNet | http://globalwordnet.github.io/schemas/wn |
| dc | DCMI Metadata Terms | http://purl.org/dc/elements/1.1/ |
| skos | Simple Knowledge Organization System | http://www.w3.org/2004/02/skos/core# |
| rdf | RDF | http://www.w3.org/1999/02/22-rdf-syntax-ns# |
| rdfs | RDF Schema | http://www.w3.org/2000/01/rdf-schema# |
| owl | OWL | http://www.w3.org/2002/07/owl# |

```
        wn:ili ili:i88966 ;
        wn:ili ili:i88417 ;
        ontolex:lexicalForm :form_copil_n_noun_ind_masc_plur;
        ontolex:lexicalForm :form_copil_n_noun_acc_nom_def_masc_plur;
        ontolex:lexicalForm :form_copil_n_noun_dat_gen_def_masc_plur;
        ontolex:lexicalForm :form_copil_n_noun_ind_masc_sing;
        ontolex:lexicalForm :form_copil_n_noun_dat_gen_def_masc_plur;
        ontolex:lexicalForm :form_copil_n_noun_acc_nom_def_masc_sing;
        ontolex:lexicalForm :form_copil_n_noun_voc_def_masc_sing;
        ontolex:lexicalForm :form_copil_n_noun_dat_gen_def_masc_sing .

:form_copil_n a ontolex:Form;
        ontolex:writtenRep "copil"@ro .

:form_copil_n_noun_ind_masc_plur a ontolex:Form;
        ontolex:writtenRep "copii"@ro;
        conll:POS "Ncmp-n";
        ontolex:writtenRep "co.pii"@syl;
        ontolex:writtenRep "cop'ii"@stress;
        ontolex:phoneticRep "k o p i j"@ro-RO-sampa .
```

The resulting linked data corpus representation contains 2,501,194 triples. It is available in RDF TTL[25] format from the RoLLOD website[26]. It was further indexed in an Apache Jena Fuseki[27] server integrated in the RELATE platform, thus allowing for direct interrogation of the SPARQL endpoint and integration in other applications without requiring the actual download of the corpus. Common use cases include searching for syl-

[25] https://www.w3.org/TR/turtle/
[26] https://www.racai.ro/p/llod/
[27] https://jena.apache.org/documentation/fuseki2/

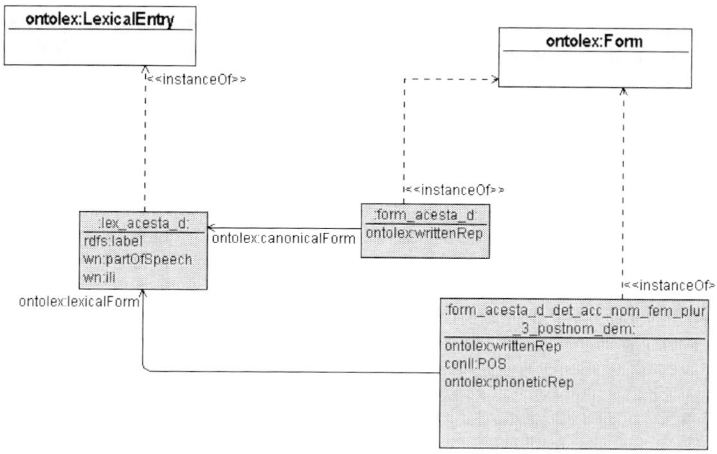


Figure 4. RoLEX classes diagram.

labification or phonetic transcriptions associated with a given word. Listing 2 gives an example search for the syllabification of the word "copil" ("child"). Listing 3 shows an example query for identifying the phonetic transcription associated with the same word "copil" ("child").

Listing 2. SPARQL query for syllabification of a specified word

```
PREFIX ontolex: <http://www.w3.org/ns/lemon/ontolex>
PREFIX : <https://www.racai.ro/p/llod/resources/rolex.ttl>

SELECT ?id ?form
WHERE {
  ?id a ontolex:Form .
  ?id ontolex:writtenRep "copil"@ro .
  ?id ontolex:writtenRep ?form .
  FILTER (lang(?form)="syl")
}
```

Listing 3. SPARQL query for phonetic transcription of a specified word

```
PREFIX ontolex: <http://www.w3.org/ns/lemon/ontolex>
PREFIX : <https://www.racai.ro/p/llod/resources/rolex.ttl>

SELECT ?id ?form
WHERE {
  ?id a ontolex:Form .
```

```
  ?id  ontolex:writtenRep  "copil"@ro  .
  ?id  ontolex:phoneticRep  ?form  .
}
```

## 5.2. The RTASC Corpus

The ROBIN Technical Acquisition Speech Corpus (RTASC)[28] (Păiş et al., 2021) was created in the ROBIN[29] project as a read speech corpus in the Romanian language. One of the objectives of the ROBIN-Dialog [30,31] component project was the creation of necessary Romanian language resources and processing tools for making the robot Pepper[32] able to communicate with users in tasks defined within several micro-worlds. An example micro-world is given by the interaction within the notebooks department of an electronics store. This micro-world comprises the physical space occupied by this department, the computers that are commercialized by the store and their characteristics on the basis of which customers decide what products they buy, their availability, the provisional date for their becoming available, the robot and the customers who interact with the robot for finding the notebook they want to purchase or for finding the right configuration for their needs. Acting as a shop assistant, the robot must be aware of the products the department commercializes, their availability, their characteristics, as well as the types of usage scenarios they are adequate for (e.g., notebooks for gaming, for design, programming, etc.).

In this context, human-robot interaction requires four steps: (1) speech recognition, converting the human speech into text; (2) primary text processing, including part-of-speech tagging, lemmatization and dependency parsing; (3) analysis of the user query and response formulation based on the internal knowledge base; and (4) text-to-speech translation of the formulated response. Avram et al. (2020b) and Avram et al. (2020a) describe a low-latency Automatic Speech Recognition (ASR) system, usable for robot communication. In this case, the focus is on obtaining a quick response from the system, thus allowing the other components of the pipeline to be

[28] https://doi.org/10.5281/zenodo.4626539
[29] http://aimas.cs.pub.ro/robin/en/
[30] http://aimas.cs.pub.ro/robin/en/robin-dialog/
[31] http://www.racai.ro/p/robin
[32] https://www.softbankrobotics.com/emea/en/pepper

executed without impacting the user's perception of the human-robot interaction time. Tufis et al. (2019) and Ion et al. (2020) described the pipelines used for text processing and the dialogue manager component. The ROBIN Dialogue Manager (RDM) is a Java-based dialogue manager that works with micro-worlds, designed to work on the Pepper robot, adapted to the Romanian language.

The RTASC corpus was used to enhance the performance of the ASR component in the domain-specific micro-world scenario and to evaluate the performance of the ASR component (Păiș et al., 2021a). It was recorded by a number of 6 native Romanian speakers of different genders (3 males and 3 females) and ages. For recording purposes, the RELATE[33] (Păiș et al., 2020) platform was extended to allow for audio files to be stored, recorded, listened, and, if needed, re-recorded. By making use of the already available Basic Language Resource Kit (BLARK) pipelines within the RELATE platform (Păiș, 2020), the text component of the corpus was automatically annotated with information such as lemma, part-of-speech tags, and dependency parsing. In addition to text and audio data, metadata were stored, containing corpus and speaker characteristics, including number of sentences, total duration, speaker's gender and age, number of recorded files by each speaker, and information about the recording device used. In order to anonymize the speaker related data, the name is not given and the age is stored only as intervals (for example "40-50" years).

The primary characteristics of the RTASC corpus are given in Table 4. More statistics are available in (Păiș et al., 2021a). Statistics were computed at all levels, including audio files, raw text and annotated text. Even though the text corpus is rather small, the number of hapax legomena (words appearing only once) is rather reduced (only 58 words). The most frequent part-of-speech tags present in the corpus are nouns and adjectives due to the micro-world scenario requiring the corpus to cover computer parts with different characteristics.

The corpus was further converted to linguistic linked data format, in order to open up more ways for its exploitation and to allow linking with other corpora. The vocabularies used in RTASC are given in Table 5. In order to cover all the information available in the corpus, we had to use multiple ontologies. The POWLA ontology contains concepts for describing

[33] https://relate.racai.ro

**Table 4. RTASC corpus characteristics**

| Characteristic | Value |
|---|---|
| Number of WAV files | 3,786 |
| Total duration | 6h25m03s |
| Average duration | 6.10s |
| Total size | 1.89Gb |
| Sample rate | 44.1KHz |
| Channels | 1 |
| Encoding | Signed Int16 PCM |
| Number of text files | 711 |
| Number of tokens | 11,927 |
| Unique tokens | 222 |
| Unique lemmas | 191 |

the corpus, individual documents and different representation layers associated with the documents (text, segmentation, annotations). The NIF ontology provides specialized concepts for different text segmentation levels, such as sentences and words. Token-based annotations follow the CoNLL-U[34] format, also used in the Universal Dependencies (UD) project. Audio specific information was represented using concepts from the Ontology for Media Resources 1.0. This was further combined with the Studio Ontology to account for recording conditions stored with the corpus. Finally, since speakers are human persons, we used the FOAF ontology to store certain attributes, such as the speaker's gender.

Figure 5 presents a diagram of the classes used in the RTASC corpus, as well as some example instances. Apart from the classes depicted in the diagram, other ontologies such as the Data Catalog (DCAT) 2 Vocabulary and the Dublin Core Metadata Initiative (DCMI) Terms are used to describe the corpus itself, including the specification of associated keywords, language and licence.

The resulting linked data corpus representation contains 284,683

[34] https://universaldependencies.org/format.html

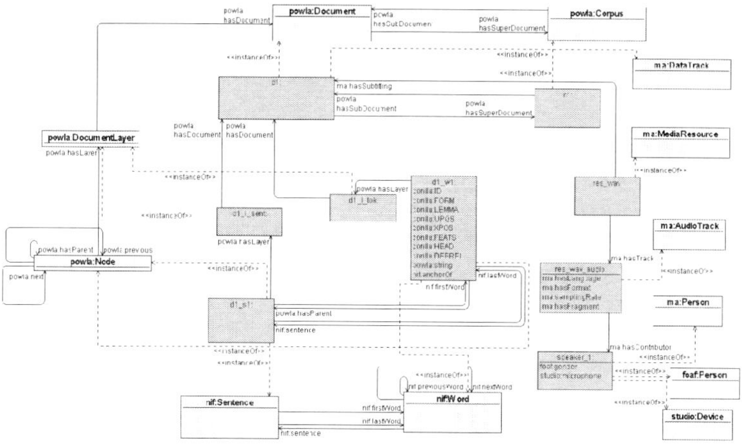


Figure 5. RTASC classes diagram.

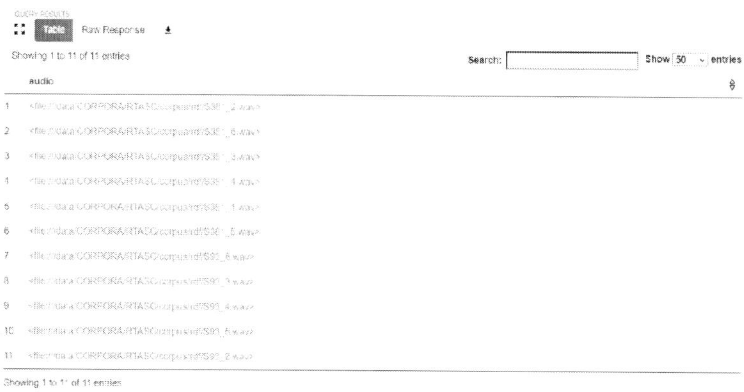


Figure 6. Query results from Listing 4.

triples. It is available in RDF TTL[35] format from the RoLLOD website[36]. It was also further indexed in an Apache Jena Fuseki server integrated in the RELATE platform, thus allowing for direct interrogation of the SPARQL endpoint and integration in other applications without requiring the actual download of the corpus.

[35]https://www.w3.org/TR/turtle/
[36]https://www.racai.ro/p/llod/

**Table 5. Used vocabularies in RTASC**

| Prefix | Name | URI |
|---|---|---|
| nif | NLP Interchange Format (NIF) | http://persistence.uni-leipzig.org/nlp2rdf/ontologies/nif-core# |
| powla | POWLA Ontology | http://purl.org/powla/powla.owl# |
| nerd | NERD Ontology | http://nerd.eurecom.fr/ontology# |
| conllu | CoNLL-U tabular format | https://universaldependencies.org/format.html# |
| foaf | FOAF | http://xmlns.com/foaf/0.1/ |
| ma | Ontology for Media Resources 1.0 | http://www.w3.org/ns/ma-ont# |
| studio | Studio Ontology | http://isophonics.net/content/studio-ontology |
| rdf | RDF | http://www.w3.org/1999/02/22-rdf-syntax-ns# |
| rdfs | RDF Schema | http://www.w3.org/2000/01/rdf-schema# |
| owl | OWL | http://www.w3.org/2002/07/owl# |
| dcat | DCAT 2 Vocabulary | http://www.w3.org/ns/dcat# |
| dct | DCMI Metadata Terms | http://purl.org/dc/terms/ |
| skos | SKOS Simple Knowledge Organization System | http://www.w3.org/2004/02/skos/core# |
| xsd | XSD | http://www.w3.org/2001/XMLSchema# |
| prov | PROV | http://www.w3.org/ns/prov# |
| pav | PAV - Provenance, Authoring and Versioning | http://pav-ontology.github.io/pav/ |

There are multiple ways to exploit the corpus as a linked data resource. Prior to the creation of the RTASC corpus, we experimented with interrogation of the speech component present in the Reference Corpus of Contemporary Romanian Language (CoRoLa) (Tufiș and Cristea, 2017; Barbu Mititelu et al., 2018; Tufiș et al., 2019). At that time, multiple query interfaces were available for the text part of the CoRoLa corpus (Cristea et al., 2019). The speech component of CoRoLa contains recordings aligned with text at different levels. Similar to RTASC there is a sentence-level alignment, but in addition to this, in CoRoLa there are also word-level alignments. A dedicated interface was created[37] (Boroș et al., 2018), allowing a human user to search for a word or an expression within the CoRoLa speech component. By employing the SPARQL language, the same aligned search can be performed directly in the RTASC corpus without requiring a special application. An example query is provided in Listing 4 for the word "autonomie" ("autonomy"). The results of this query are presented in Figure 6.

[37] http://relate.racai.ro/?path=corola/ocqp

Listing 4. SPARQL query for identification of audio files containing a specified word

```
prefix :        <https://www.racai.ro/p/llod/resources/
rtasc_v1.ttl>
prefix ma:      <http://www.w3.org/ns/ma-ont#>
prefix powla:   <http://purl.org/powla/powla.owl#>
prefix studio: <http://isophonics.net/content/
studio-ontology>
prefix conllu: <https://universaldependencies.org/
format.html#>

SELECT ?audio
WHERE {
  ?ida a ma:AudioTrack .
  ?ida ma:hasFragment ?audio .

  ?idr a ma:MediaResource .
  ?idr ma:hasTrack ?ida .
  ?idr ma:hasSubtitling ?id_doc .

  ?id_layer powla:hasDocument ?id_doc .

  ?id_tok powla:hasLayer ?id_layer .
  ?id_tok conllu:FORM "autonomie" .
}
LIMIT 25
```

# 6. Exploiting Multiple Resources for Advanced Usage Scenarios

Linked data representation has the advantage of allowing queries that span multiple datasets. Actually, queries can span multiple endpoints, which can be on the same physical server or distributed across the Internet. This is one of the reasons behind initiatives such as the Linked Open Data Cloud, which allows the discovery of resources from different institutions, the majority of which also allows direct queries of their SPARQL endpoints. Certain datasets contain direct links to other datasets, indicating a possible way to construct the queries (see above, in Section 5.1 the RoLEX lexicon containing links to the Romanian WordNet). However, even if direct links are not available, certain fields may be known to contain the same type of values that can be used to perform cross-dataset queries (for example the fields *conllu:FORM* in the RTASC corpus and *ontolex:writtenRep* in the RoLEX lexicon both contain word forms).

A W3C recommendation[38] defines SPARQL 1.1 Federated Query by introducing the *SERVICE* keyword as an extension to the SPARQL 1.1 Query Language[39]. This extension allows a query author to direct a portion of a query to a particular SPARQL endpoint. The results are returned to the federated query processor and are combined with the results from the rest of the query. The Apache Jena Fuseki server, which was mentioned throughout this chapter and was used to create SPARQL endpoints for the described Romanian resources, supports such federated queries. This means that a federated query, making use of the *SERVICE* keyword, can be launched at one of the existing SPARQL endpoints associated with one of the available resources and can further connect to other endpoints (on the same Fuseki server or external).

When running a federated query, it is possible that a remote endpoint would fail. This can happen for several reasons: the remote server is down, the endpoint may return an error or there is a timeout. Normally, under such circumstances the invoked query containing a *SERVICE* pattern fails as a whole. The W3C recommendation allows queries to explicitly allow failed *SERVICE* requests with the use of the additional *SILENT* keyword. This indicates that errors encountered while accessing a remote SPARQL endpoint should be ignored while processing the query. In this case, the failed *SERVICE* clause is treated as if it had a result of a single solution with no bindings. If needed, it is possible to combine multiple external requests in the same federated query, each with or without the *SILENT* keyword.

For the purposes of this section, we will focus on the described Romanian resources and present two use cases for federated queries. The first use case assumes that a user is interested in searching for a particular phoneme (or series of phonemes) and wants to identify speech files that contain it. Since phoneme transcription is not part of the RTASC corpus (see Section 5.2), the query must employ the RoLEX lexicon (see Section 5.1) to find

[38] https://www.w3.org/TR/sparql11-federated-query/
[39] https://www.w3.org/TR/sparql11-query/

Figure 7. Structure of a federated query combining RoLEX and RTASC.

words containing the requested phonemes and then use this list to query RTASC. We already provided in Listing 4 an example query for searching audio files containing a particular word and in Listing 3 an example query for the RoLEX lexicon (even though this query starts with a word and obtains the phonetic representation). Our considered scenario must employ a federated query combining the two queries from Listings 4 and 3.

Figure 7 presents a diagram of the proposed federated query. Since the two resources are hosted on the same Fuseki server, integrated in the RELATE platform, we could connect to any SPARQL endpoint on this server and carefully construct to query to use the other endpoint. However, since the query starts with a phonetic representation, using the SAMPA alphabet, as indicated in the diagram, it makes sense to start the query on the RoLEX endpoint and make use of the *SERVICE* keyword to connect to the other endpoint. Thus, the first part of the query constructs a list of words that will be used to query the RTASC endpoint. Finally, the list of audio files will be returned in the query result. The query result can be enhanced with additional information from RoLEX, such as the actual word that was identified in the specific audio file. Since we use a federated SPARQL query, no other programming is required, apart from the query itself. Listing 5 presents the federated query used to search for the phonemes "a k @", expressed in SAMPA notation.

Listing 5. Federated query combining RoLEX and RTASC allowing to identify audio files containing specific phonemes

```
prefix ontolex: <http://www.w3.org/ns/lemon/ontolex>
prefix rolex: <https://www.racai.ro/p/llod/resources/
rolex.ttl>
prefix rtasc: <https://www.racai.ro/p/llod/resources/
rtasc_v1.ttl>
prefix ma:      <http://www.w3.org/ns/ma-ont#>
prefix powla:  <http://purl.org/powla/powla.owl#>
prefix studio: <http://isophonics.net/content/
studio-ontology>
```

```
prefix conllu: <https://universaldependencies.org/
format.html#>

SELECT ?formPhonetic ?formString ?audio
WHERE {
  { SELECT DISTINCT ?formString ?formPhonetic WHERE {
  ?id a ontolex:Form .
  ?id ontolex:phoneticRep ?formPhonetic .
  FILTER(REGEX(?formPhonetic,"a k @","i")) .

  ?id ontolex:writtenRep ?formWritten .
  FILTER (lang(?formWritten)="ro") .
  BIND (str(?formWritten) as ?formString) .
    }}

  SERVICE <https://relate.racai.ro/datasets/rtasc/sparql> {
    ?id_tok conllu:FORM ?formString .
    ?id_tok powla:hasLayer ?id_layer .
    ?id_layer powla:hasDocument ?id_doc .

    ?idr a ma:MediaResource .
    ?idr ma:hasSubtitling ?id_doc .
    ?idr ma:hasTrack ?ida .

    ?ida a ma:AudioTrack .
    ?ida ma:hasFragment ?audio .

  }
}
LIMIT 1000
```

Ontology-based retrieval of human speech is a challenging endeavour. Tejedor et al. (2007) propose a semi-automatic approach to annotating audio files based on concept-keyword mapping. (Narasimman, 2014) propose a voice-enabled ontology-based search engine to aid blind people. To overcome the requirement for annotating audio files with concepts, the interlinking of linked data resources can be exploited. The RTASC corpus contains the text documents associated with audio files, but there are no concepts marked at this point. The RoLEX lexicon contains different word forms, some of them referencing the Romanian WordNet by making use of the Inter-lingual Index (ILI). Finally, the Romanian WordNet contains hypernymous relations between different concepts.

One way of tackling the concept-based search is to start by interrogat-

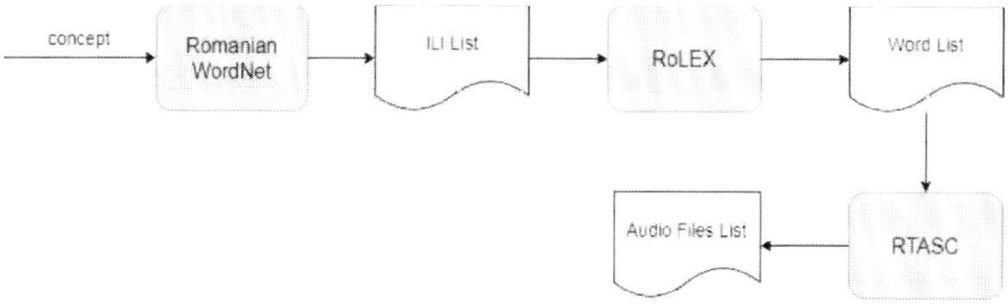


Figure 8. Structure of a federated query combining Romanian WordNet, RoLEX and RTASC, allowing concept-based retrieval of speech files.

ing the Romanian WordNet for the given concept. Then, additional concepts can be retrieved by using the hypernymy relations. The associated ILI identifiers can then be used to look up the corresponding lexicon entries in RoLEX. Finally, a query with all the identified word forms can be performed in RTASC, thus retrieving the associated audio files. Listing 5 provides a way of linking RoLEX and RTASC. The new federated query will have to also involve the Romanian WordNet as a first step and then make use of the ILI identifiers instead of the *phoneticRep* which was used in Listing 5. A diagram of the desired flow of data is presented in Figure 8.

Similar to the previous query, multiple endpoints must be reached to gather all the required information. In this case, a total of 3 endpoints are required. From the SPARQL language point of view, it doesn't truly matter to which one of the endpoints the query is first sent. The other two additional endpoints must be specified using the *SERVICE* keyword. However, similar to the previous approach, since the first query involves the RoWN, we propose starting the request on the associated endpoint. Thus, with regard to the query, RoLEX and RTASC become remote endpoints. In our proposed approach, the request starts by identifying concepts having as hypernym the desired WordNet concept. The list of ILIs is retrieved and passed to the RoLEX endpoint. For each ILI the list of written forms is gathered from the lexicon. Finally, the word list is sent to the RTASC endpoint and the audio files containing any of the words are identified. This final list is returned to the user as the query result. It contains for each entry the ILI, the actual word and the associated audio file. An example implementation is given in Listing 6. For brevity, we omitted the *prefix* descriptions that were the same as those present in other listings.

Listing 6. Federated query combining Romanian WordNet with RoLEX and RTASC allowing concept-based retrieval of speech files

```
SELECT ?ili ?formString ?audio
WHERE {
  { SELECT DISTINCT ?ili1 WHERE {
    ?idConcept ontolex:writtenRep "calculator"@ro .
    ?idLex a ontolex:LexicalEntry .
    ?idLex ontolex:canonicalForm ?idConcept .
    ?idLex ontolex:Sense ?sense .
    ?sense a ontolex:LexicalSense .
    ?sense ontolex:reference ?ref .
    ?ref a ontolex:LexicalConcept .
    ?ref wn:ili ?ili .
    ?x vartrans:source ?ref .
    ?x vartrans:category wn:hypernym .
    ?x vartrans:target ?ref1 .
    ?senser1 ontolex:reference ?ref1 .
    ?ref1 wn:ili ?ili1 .
    ?idr1 ontolex:Sense ?senser1 .
    ?idr1w ontolex:writtenRep ?w .
    ?idr1 ontolex:canonicalForm ?idr1w .
    }}

  SERVICE <https://relate.racai.ro/datasets/rolex/sparql> {
    ?idRolex wn:ili ?ili1 .
    ?idRolex ontolex:lexicalForm ?idRolexForm .
    ?idRolexForm ontolex:writtenRep ?formWritten .
    FILTER (lang(?formWritten)="ro") .
    BIND (str(?formWritten) as ?formString) .
  }

  SERVICE <https://relate.racai.ro/datasets/rtasc/sparql> {
    ?id_tok conllu:FORM ?formString .
    ?id_tok powla:hasLayer ?id_layer .
    ?id_layer powla:hasDocument ?id_doc .

    ?idr a ma:MediaResource .
    ?idr ma:hasSubtitling ?id_doc .
    ?idr ma:hasTrack ?ida .

    ?ida a ma:AudioTrack .
    ?ida ma:hasFragment ?audio .
  }
}
```

## Conclusion

Linguistic linked data, even though more used with textual resources, can also be successfully exploited for speech applications. In this chapter, we described two resources containing information relevant for speech processing, in the Romanian language, making use of linked data format. We have shown that the resources themselves can be useful for a number of applications, such as identifying phonemes associated with words and retrieving speech resources based on specific keywords or metadata characteristics. Nevertheless, the true power of linked data is unleashed when combining multiple datasets. We have shown in Section 6 examples of advanced scenarios where federated queries, employing multiple SPARQL endpoints, are able to solve very challenging problems. In the first case, we were able to look up audio files containing very specific phonemes. For the second use-case, we combined three resources, the Romanian Wordnet, the RoLEX lexicon and the RTASC corpus, enabling a concept-based search of audio resources.

For Romanian the Linguistic Linked Data era is only at its dawn: resources, for both the written and the spoken language, with the former more numerous though, have been developed, although the focus is still not on linked data, especially given that existing tools do not support this format and RDF vocabularies are still unsatisfactory with respect to the possibility of representing different types of linguistic information. Nonetheless, the advantages of this type of data representation, as presented here, will definitely contribute to new conversions to it, new intra- and inter-lingual linkings, thus adding up to the value of the resources.

## References

Anderson, J. R. (1983). *The architecture of cognition*. Harvard University Press.

Arndt, R., Troncy, R., Staab, S., and Hardman, L. (2009). *COMM: A Core Ontology for MultimediaAnnotation*, pages 403–421. Springer Berlin Heidelberg, Berlin, Heidelberg.

Avram, A.-M., Păiș, V., and Tufiș, D. (2020a). Romanian speech recognition experiments from the robin project. In *The 15th International*

*Conference on Linguistic Resources and Tools for Natural Language Processing*, pages 103–114.

Avram, A.-M., Păiș, V., and Tufiș, D. (2020b). Towards a Romanian end-to-end automatic speech recognition based on DeepSpeech2. *Proceedings of the Romanian Academy Series A*, 21:395–402.

Barbu, A.-M. (2008). Romanian lexical data bases: Inflected and syllabic forms dictionaries. In *Proceedings of the Sixth International Conference on Language Resources and Evaluation (LREC'08)*, pages 1937–1941, Marrakech, Morocco. European Language Resources Association (ELRA).

Barbu Mititelu, V., Irimia, E., Păiș, V., Avram, A.-M., Mitrofan, M., and Curea, E. (2020). Romanian resources in LLOD format. In *Proceedings of the 15th International Conference Linguistic Resources and Tools for Natural Language Processing*, pages 29–40, Iași, Romania.

Barbu Mititelu, V., Irimia, E., Păiș, V., Mitrofan, M., Avram, A.-M., and Curea, E. (2021). Linked open data resources for Romanian. In *Proceedings of the 16th International Conference Linguistic Resources and Tools for Natural Language Processing*, pages 29–40, Iași, Romania.

Barbu Mititelu, V., Tufiș, D., and Irimia, E. (2018). The reference corpus of the contemporary romanian language (CoRoLa). In *Proceedings of the Eleventh International Conference on Language Resources and Evaluation (LREC 2018)*, pages 1178–1185.

Berners-Lee, T., Hendler, J., and Ora, L. (2001). The semantic web. *Scientific American*.

Boroș, T., Dumitrescu, Ș. D., and Păiș, V. (2018). Tools and resources for romanian text-to-speech and speech-to-text applications. In *Proceedings of the International Conference on Human-Computer Interaction (RoCHI)*, pages 46–53.

Calotă, I. (2001). *Mică enciclopedie a românei corecte*. Niculescu Publishing House.

Chebotko, A., Deng, Y., Lu, S., Fotouhi, F., Aristar, A., Brugman, H., Klassmann, A., Sloetjes, H., Russel, A., and Wittenburg, P. (2004). Ontoelan: an ontology-based linguistic multimedia annotator. In *IEEE Sixth International Symposium on Multimedia Software Engineering*, pages 329–336.

Chiarcos, C. and Pareja-Lora, A. (2020). *Open DataLinked DataLinked Open DataLinguistic Linked Open Data (LLOD): A General Introduction*, pages 1–17. The MIT Press.

Cimiano, P., Chiarcos, C., McCrae, J. P., and Gracia, J. (2020). *Linguistic Linked Data. Representation, Generation and Applications*. Springer.

Cristea, D., Diewald, N., Haja, G., Mărănduc, C., Barbu Mititelu, V., and Onofrei, M. (2019). How to find a shining needle in the haystack. Querying CoRoLa: solutions and perspectives. *RRL*, 64(3):279–292.

Fazekas, G. and Sandler, M. B. (2011). The studio ontology framework. In *12th International Society for Music Information Retrieval Conference (ISMIR)*, pages 471–476.

Fazekas, G., Wilmering, T., and Sandler, M. (2011). A knowledge representation framework for context-dependent audio processing. In *Audio Engineering Society Conference: 42nd International Conference: Semantic Audio*.

Fellbaum, C. (1998). *WordNet: An Electronic Lexical Database*. MIT Press, Cambridge, MA.

Hauck, E., Ewert, D., Gramatke, A., and Henning, K. (2011). Software architecture, knowledge compiler and ontology design for cognitive technical systems suitable for controlling assembly tasks. In Jeschke, S., Isenhardt, I., and Henning, K., editors, *Automation, Communication and Cybernetics in Science and Engineering 2009/2010*, pages 383–391, Berlin, Heidelberg. Springer Berlin Heidelberg.

Ide, N. and Pustejovsky, J. (2010). What does interoperability mean, anyway? toward an operational definition of interoperability for language technology. In *Proceedings of the 2nd International Conference on Global Interoperability for Language Resources (ICGL 2010)*.

Ion, R. (2018). TEPROLIN: An extensible, online text preprocessing platform for Romanian. In *The 13th International Conference on Linguistic Resources and Tools for Natural Language Processing - CONSILR*, pages 69–76.

Ion, R., Badea, V. G., Cioroiu, G., Barbu Mititelu, V., Irimia, E., Mitrofan, M., and Tufiş, D. (2020). A dialog manager for micro-worlds. *Studies in Informatics and Control*, 29(4):411–420.

Klyne, G., Carroll, J., and McBride, B. (2004). Resource Description Framework (RDF): Concepts and Abstract Syntax.

Kumar, K., Haider, M. T. U., and Ahsan, S. S. (2021). Ontology-based full-text searching using named entity recognition. In Hura, G. S., Singh, A. K., and Siong Hoe, L., editors, *Advances in Communication and Computational Technology*, pages 211–222, Singapore. Springer Singapore.

Laird, J. E., Newell, A., and Rosenbloom, P. S. (1987). Soar: An architecture for general intelligence. *Artificial intelligence*, 33(1):1–64.

Mallik, A., Chaudhury, S., and Ghosh, H. (2011). Nrityakosha: Preserving the intangible heritage of indian classical dance. *J. Comput. Cult. Herit.*, 4(3):1–25.

Mallik, A., Ghosh, H., Chaudhury, S., and Harit, G. (2013). Mowl: An ontology representation language for web-based multimedia applications. *ACM Trans. Multimedia Comput. Commun. Appl.*, 10(1):1–21.

Manzoor, S., Rocha, Y. G., Joo, S.-H., Bae, S.-H., Kim, E.-J., Joo, K.-J., and Kuc, T.-Y. (2021). Ontology-based knowledge representation in robotic systems: A survey oriented toward applications. *Applied Sciences*, 11(10).

Margenstern, M., Psarris, K., and Mandic, D., editors (2013). *Ontologies for Multimedia Annotation: An overview*. WSEAS Press. Proceedings of the 4th European Conference of Computer Science.

Naphade, M., Smith, J., Tesic, J., Chang, S.-F., Hsu, W., Kennedy, L., Hauptmann, A., and Curtis, J. (2006). Large-scale concept ontology for multimedia. *IEEE MultiMedia*, 13(3):86–91.

Narasimman, K. (2014). Voice enabled ontology based search engine on semantic web for blind. *International Journal of Computer Science & Engineering Technology*, 5:341–344.

Nguyen, C. P., Pham, N. Y., and Castelli, E. (2006). First steps to an audio ontology-based classifier for telemedicine. In Li, X., Zaïane, O. R., and Li, Z., editors, *Advanced Data Mining and Applications*, pages 845–855, Berlin, Heidelberg. Springer Berlin Heidelberg.

Oltramari, A. and Lebiere, C. (2011). Mechanisms meet content: Integrating cognitive architectures and ontologies. *AAAI Fall Symposium - Technical Report*, pages 257–264.

Oltramari, A. and Lebiere, C. (2013). *Knowledge in Action: Integrating Cognitive Architectures and Ontologies*, pages 135–154. Springer Berlin Heidelberg, Berlin, Heidelberg.

Păiş, V., Ion, R., Barbu Mititelu, V., Irimia, E., Mitrofan, M., and Avram, A. (2021). ROBIN Technical Acquisition Speech Corpus.

Păiș, V. (2020). Multiple annotation pipelines inside the RELATE platform. In *The 15th International Conference on Linguistic Resources and Tools for Natural Language Processing*, pages 65–75.

Păiș, V., Ion, R., Avram, A.-M., Irimia, E., Mititelu, V. B., and Mitrofan, M. (2021a). Human-machine interaction speech corpus from the robin project. In *2021 International Conference on Speech Technology and Human-Computer Dialogue (SpeD)*, pages 91–96.

Păiș, V., Ion, R., and Tufiș, D. (2020). A processing platform relating data and tools for Romanian language. In *Proceedings of the 1st International Workshop on Language Technology Platforms*, pages 81–88, Marseille, France. European Language Resources Association.

Păiș, V., Mitrofan, M., Gasan, C. L., Coneschi, V., and Ianov, A. (2021b). Named entity recognition in the Romanian legal domain. In *Proceedings of the Natural Legal Language Processing Workshop 2021*, pages 9–18, Punta Cana, Dominican Republic. Association for Computational Linguistics.

Păiș, V., Tufiș, D., and Ion, R. (2019). Integration of Romanian NLP Tools into the RELATE platform. In *International Conference on Linguistic Resources and Tools for Natural Language Processing*, pages 181–192, Iași, Romania.

Raimond, Y., Abdallah, S., Sandler, M., and Giasson, F. (2007). The music ontology. In *Proceedings of the 8th International Conference on Music Information Retrieval, ISMIR 2007*.

Saathoff, C. and Scherp, A. (2010). Unlocking the semantics of multimedia presentations in the web with the multimedia metadata ontology. In *Proceedings of the 19th International Conference on World Wide Web*, WWW '10, pages 831–840, New York, NY, USA. Association for Computing Machinery.

Sarthou, G., Clodic, A., and Alami, R. (2019). Ontologenius: A long-term semantic memory for robotic agents. In *2019 28th IEEE International Conference on Robot and Human Interactive Communication (RO-MAN)*, pages 1–8.

Sikelis, K., Tsekouras, G. E., and Kotis, K. (2021). Ontology-based feature selection: A survey. *Future Internet*, 13(6).

Stan, A., Yamagishi, J., King, S., and Aylett, M. (2011). The romanian speech synthesis (rss) corpus: Building a high quality hmm-based speech synthesis system using a high sampling rate. *Speech Communication*, 53(3):442–450.

Studer, R., Benjamins, V., and Fensel, D. (1998). Knowledge engineering: principles and methods. *Data & Knowledge Engineering*, 25:161–197.

Tejedor, J., Garcia, R., Fernandez, M., Lopez-Colino, F. J., Perdrix, F., Macias, J. A., Gil, R. M., Oliva, M., Moya, D., Colas, J., and Castells, P. (2007). Ontology-based retrieval of human speech. In *18th International Workshop on Database and Expert Systems Applications (DEXA 2007)*, pages 485–489.

Toma, Ş.-A., Stan, A., Pura, M.-L., and Bârsan, T. (2017). MaRePhoR - an open access machine-readable phonetic dictionary for Romanian. In *2017 International Conference on Speech Technology and Human-Computer Dialogue (SpeD)*, pages 1–6. IEEE.

Tufiș, D. and Barbu Mititelu, V. (2014). *The Lexical Ontology for Romanian*, volume 48 of *Text, Speech and Language Technology*, pages 491–504. Springer.

Tufiș, D., Barbu Mititelu, V., Irimia, E., Păiș, V., Ion, R., Diewald, N., Mitrofan, M., and Mihaela, O. (2019). Little Strokes Fell Great Oaks. Creating CoRoLa, the Reference Corpus of Contemporary Romanian. *Revue Roumaine de Linguistique*, 64(3):227–240.

Tufiș, D. and Cristea, D. (2017). An outlook over CoRoLa: The reference corpus of contemporary written and spoken corpus. In *Proceedings of SpeD conference, (invited talk)*, Bucharest, Romania.

Tufis, D., Barbu Mititelu, V., Irimia, E., Mitrofan, M., Ion, R., and Cioroiu, G. (2019). Making Pepper Understand and Respond in Romanian. In *2019 22nd International Conference on Control Systems and Computer Science (CSCS)*, pages 682–688.

Turchet, L., Bouquet, P., Molinari, A., and Fazekas, G. (2021). The smart musical instruments ontology. *Journal of Web Semantics*, page 100687.

Yelibayeva, G., Sharipbay, A., Bekmanova, G., and Omarbekova, A. (2021). Ontology-based extraction of kazakh language word combinations in natural language processing. In *International Conference on Data Science, E-Learning and Information Systems 2021*, DATA'21, pages 58–59, New York, NY, USA. Association for Computing Machinery.

In: Speech Recognition Technology ... ISBN: 978-1-68507-929-1
Editor: Vasile-Florian Păiş 

Chapter 7

# Transformer-Based Romanian Text-to-Speech System Using Boolean Masking for Improved Prosody

**George-Alexandru Vlad[1,*], Gabriel Bercaru[2,†], Costin-Gabriel Chiru[2,‡] and Traian Rebedea[2,§]**
[1]SoftTehnica, Bucharest, Romania
[2]University Politehnica of Bucharest, Romania

**Abstract**

A speech-based Human-Computer Interface usually consists of two main components, symmetrical to each other from the user-experience point of view: a module capable of understanding the user spoken language, transcribing the sound wave to text (STT - Speech-To-Text) and a second module that transforms written text to human-like speech (TTS - Text-To-Speech). At the most basic level, TTS can be posed as an autoregressive transduction problem, in which a sequence of tokens is analysed to produce a sequence of acoustic features. However, practical approaches do not rely directly on tokens and acoustic features, but rather on phonemes and much lower dimensional sound wave representations, such as spectrograms. For some TTS models described in the literature, these

[*]Corresponding Author's Email: georgealexandruvlad@gmail.com.
[†]Author's Email: gabriel.bercaru10@gmail.com.
[‡]Author's Email: costin.chiru@upb.ro.
[§]Author's Email: traian.rebedea@upb.ro.

requirements mean that end-to-end training is no longer possible; consequently, additional modules are inserted into the TTS pipeline, such as a text-to-phoneme converter, an aligner which ensures that some phonemes are extended in order to match with the transcript, and finally a vocoder which "translates" a spectrogram into an audible sound wave. However, the backbone of the pipeline still performs a sequence-to-sequence task; recently, Transformer-based architectures have achieved state-of-the-art results in sequence modeling problems, including TTS. The experiments described in this chapter present a Transformer-based TTS pipeline trained on examples belonging to two pre-existing Romanian speech corpora: SWARA and RSS. Moreover, since both of these datasets lack high-quality male voice recordings, we create a novel male voice dataset, following the same structure as RSS. While both of the first two corpora are multi-speaker, we experiment with Transformer-based TTS variants for both single-speaker and multi-speaker scenarios. The multi-speaker version offers the possibility to control the speaker identity by providing an encoding of the speaker identity to the encoder module during inference. To align the phonemes with the audio clip, we experiment with two approaches: employing a neural model to learn to perform the alignment or making use of a statistical alignment tool (MFA). For the spectrogram-to-sound wave conversion, we used a pretrained HiFiGAN vocoder available online. Subjective human evaluation shows improvements in comparison to previous TTS approaches for Romanian (e.g. Tacotron 2 and WaveNet) in terms of pronunciation, prosody, and audio quality. In addition to the well-known Transformer ability to capture long-term dependencies, another advantage of using this architecture for TTS systems is that the model is no longer autoregressive (FastSpeech 2), meaning that the output spectogram does not have to be sequentially generated.

**Keywords:** speech synthesis, text-to-speech, transformers, boolean masking, Romanian speech

# 1. Introduction

Speech synthesis, or text-to-speech (TTS) is currently indispensable to any speech-based human-computer interface, in order to provide the user with the sense of a natural, human-like interaction. TTS applications are very common in a number of domains, such as personal assistants or voice-based chatbots (Abdul-Kader and Woods, 2015), which incorporate a processing pipeline consisting of an Automatic Speech Recognition module (ASR), an internal logic stage (which generates a textual reply, based on the textual user query) and finally a TTS stage, which converts the textual reply into audible speech. Moreover, TTS systems have been successfully used to produce artificial training data for ASR (Laptev et al., 2020) or Automatic Speech Validation (ASV) systems (Kinnunen et al., 2017; Reimao and Tzerpos, 2019). Since audio data is less frequent compared to textual data, obtaining a rich corpus of audio-textual data for training ASR models might prove difficult, unless TTS is considered. In contrast to offline data augmentation, some systems are leveraging the complementary nature of TTS and ASR tasks by combining auto-encoders to reconstruct the original data (i.e., speech and texts) with TTS $\rightarrow$ ASR and ASR $\rightarrow$ TTS modules, in a closed-loop setup (Tjandra et al., 2020; Ren et al., 2019b). Even though recently, there have been proposed a number of textless architectures (such as chatbots which operate solely at speech level - Lakhotia et al., 2021; Kharitonov et al. 2021), which should eliminate the necessity of working with an intermediary textual representation, TTS still represents an important building block for the training sets used by such models.

Initially, text-to-speech conversion was achieved through concatenative or Hidden Markov Model (HMM) based approaches (Hunt and Black, 1996; Qian et al., 2006; Yamagishi et al., 2009); however, recently emerged deep learning solutions have proven superior performance with regard to a number of key aspects, such as generated voice tone, prosody and overall naturalness (Wang et al., 2017; Shen et al., 2018; Li et al., 2019).

Most deep learning approaches for TTS split the task of generating speech from text into two distinct phases: the text is first converted to a compact representation of possible acoustic features and this intermediary representation is, in turn, analysed to generate an intelligible sound wave denoting the generated speech.

Two of the most important factors for the success of any such deep learning speech generation model are the quality of the input data and the duration of the speech generation process. To date, the Romanian language lacks an adequate speech dataset for male speakers. We compensate for this disadvantage by recording speech and creating a complex dataset following existing high-quality recordings available for female voices in Romanian (Stan et al., 2011). Even though other publicly available Romanian speech datasets contain male voices, the number of such examples is low and the quality is not good enough for adequate speech synthesis using neural models.

To achieve high speech generation speed, we employ a novel architecture, inspired by the Transformer (Vaswani et al., 2017) models used in natural language processing. Previous deep learning speech generation models for the Romanian language (Dumitrache and Rebedea, 2020) have not used the Transformer architecture. They have mostly made use of recurrent neural networks, which introduced latencies not only into the training process, but also at inference time. As this chapter will show, the transformer-based speech generation system achieves low inference time, which makes it suitable for real-time speech applications.

Thus, our research described in this chapter proposes three main contributions:

1. A new Romanian male single-speaker dataset, named *RSS-Alex*. The dataset was created and publicly released to encourage further text-to-speech research on Romanian language.

2. A non-autoregressive transformer-based model for Romanian combining elements from FastSpeech (Ren et al., 2019a) and FastSpeech 2 (Ren et al., 2021) architectures. The quality of the model is assessed by human evaluators and the reported scores show that the generated speech has a very high quality, especially when trained on the Romanian male dataset released with this chapter.

3. A robust solution to the addition of graphical markers, such as suprasegmentals, which play a decisive role in the overall prosody and word spelling but should not have a corresponding mel-spectrogram counterpart when taken individually.

In contrast to Transformer-based models, such as FastSpeech (Ren et al., 2019a) and FastSpeech 2 (Ren et al., 2021), which generate mel-spectrogram features for each input token, we opted to select the inputs requiring a mel-spectrogram representation by introducing a Boolean masking component between the decoder and mel-spectrogram projection layer. This method ensures that the contribution of any input token is leveraged by the attention mechanism from the encoder and decoder without being constrained in generating a mel-spectrogram segment for it.

We conjecture that the Boolean masking technique may be extended to other special characters that might be introduced in the input text (through an additional preprocessing step) to give better directions on various features of the output audio (speaker identity, speaker tone, elements of prosody etc.).

The rest of the document is structured as follows: *Section* 2 provides an overview of existing neural speech generation models and components for both English and Romanian languages. *Section* 3 describes in detail the existing datasets that were used in our research and how the Romanian male speech RSS-Alex dataset was created. *Section* 4 presents the proposed TTS architecture and some modifications brought to an existing state-of-the-art Transformer-based text-to-speech implementation. *Section* 5 shows the experiments performed and the experimental setups for all our models, while *Section* 6 provides a comparative analysis of the results obtained by our models. Finally, a conclusion of the work and possible future steps are enumerated in *Section* 6 and *Section* 6, respectively.

# 2. Related Work

As the main focus of this chapter is neural speech synthesis, this section provides a description of the most important existing deep learning models used for this task in both English and Romanian languages. At the most basic level, deep learning approaches are mostly incremental: one step of the pipeline analyses the input text and produces a spectrogram representation, while the second step generates audio based on the spectrogram. The following subsections will go into detail with respect to this high-level structure.

## 2.1. Deep Neural Models for Speech Synthesis

Tacotron (Wang et al., 2017) is a neural network that takes as input the audio transcripts at the character level and outputs the raw mel-spectograms, which will be decoded in audio by employing a vocoder. The Tacotron architecture consists of an encoder, a sequence-to-sequence decoder with attention and a postprocessing network to generate mel-spectograms. The authors used the Griffin-Lim vocoder (Griffin and Lim, 1984) as a trade-off between architectural simplicity and the quality of the synthesized audio, obtaining a mean opinion score (MOS) of 3.82 out of 5. The test set comprised 100 US English sentences unseen during model training. As the authors mention, training data came from an internal North American English dataset, comprising 24.6 hours of speech recorded by a professional female speaker (Wang et al., 2017).

A large improvement in audio quality has been achieved with the second iteration of Tacotron, Tacotron 2 (Shen et al., 2018), obtaining a mean opinion score of 4.53 out of 5, which is almost on par with the 4.58 score of professionally recorded speech. While it preserves a similar high-level structure (i.e., encoder, decoder, postprocessing net), in Tacotron 2 the architecture is simplified by using gated recurrent unit (GRU) layers (Chung et al., 2014) instead of the convolutional bank highway GRU (CBHG) module (Wang et al., 2017). Moreover, to reduce the artifacts of decoding the mel-spectrogram into time-domain waveforms, a modified WaveNet vocoder (van den Oord et al., 2016) has been used as a replacement for the Griffin-Lim algorithm.

Although Tacotron 2 achieved state-of-the-art results, the architecture still suffers from two main drawbacks associated with the choice of using recurrent neural networks: longer training and inference times due to processing the input states sequentially and the incapacity to model long-term dependencies. Transformer-TTS (Li et al., 2019) comes as a solution to the aforementioned issues by replacing the recurrent layers with Transformer blocks (Vaswani et al., 2017) capable of attending the whole input sequence in parallel, taking advantage of the high level operation parallelisation of modern computing hardware, such as GPUs and TPUs. The model consists of a prenet encoder that takes as input phoneme embeddings, a transformer encoder, an autoregressive transformer decoder, and a postnet stack of 5 CNN layers to generate the mel-spectrograms.

While the Transformer-TTS architecture represents a better choice with respect to computational speed compared to Tacotron 2, the use of an autoregressive decoder still represents a limitation in unlocking the full computational potential modern processing devices (GPU, TPU) are capable of. FastSpeech (Ren et al., 2019a) obtains a speed-up of 270x in mel-spectrogram generation and 38x faster speech synthesis in an end-to-end fashion (i.e., when adding the vocoder) by replacing the autoregressive decoder with non-autoregressive transformer-based blocks. To enable mel-spectrogram decoding in parallel, the model imposes hard alignments between phonemes and mel-spectrogram dimensions by employing a duration predictor. The aforementioned component allows for speech controllability by lengthening or shortening phoneme duration, which might improve the prosody of the generated voice.

FastSpeech 2 (Ren et al., 2021) further improves the controllability of generated speech by introducing variance adaptor blocks for energy and pitch. Here, the teacher-student paradigm for the phoneme's duration prediction is removed and replaced with the Montreal Forced Aligner (McAuliffe et al., 2017), as the duration extracted by the latter is considered more reliable, less prone to alignment errors, and easier to produce. FastSpeech 2 achieves a MOS value of 3.83 and its end-to-end variant FastSpeech 2s, which directly generates outputs in the wave domain instead of using a vocoder, obtains a MOS value of 3.71. Considering the distinct evaluators and the fact that FastSpeech 2 was trained and evaluated on a subset of LjSpeech (while Tacotron 2 used an internal dataset) the mean opinion scores cannot be directly compared to assert the better architecture. To obtain a fair comparison, the authors of the FastSpeech 2 model also present the scores obtained by the Tacotron 2 model trained and evaluated on the same training/test subsets. Both versions, FastSpeech 2 and FastSpeech 2s, outperform the Tacotron 2 MOS of 3.70.

The model introduced in this chapter is similar in structure to FastSpeech (Ren et al., 2019a), with the addition of a FastSpeech 2 (Ren et al., 2021) feature (pitch variance adaptor). Moreover, we also use the Montreal Forced Aligner (McAuliffe et al., 2017), instead of the autoregressive aligner.

Nonetheless, an equally important part in generating human-like (Romanian) speech is the vocoder module. In the literature, two of the most frequently used approaches are the Griffin-Lim algorithm (Griffin and Lim, 1984) and a neural based approach, WaveNet (van den Oord et al., 2016). The Griffin-Lim algorithm (Griffin and Lim, 1984) is an iterative algorithm that relies solely on the analysis of a given spectrogram. Considering a partially decoded signal (i.e., sound wave) up until the $t$'th timestep, the amplitude for timestep $t+1$ is obtained by performing a short-time Fourier transform (STFT) on the already decoded signal plus finding a signal whose STFT is closest to the obtained STFT by optimizing the least square error between the two values.

WaveNet (van den Oord et al., 2016) draws inspiration from other probabilistic and autoregressive models applied in computer vision (such as PixelRNN (Oord et al., 2016)), which can model complex distributions over high-dimensional data (for instance, how a pixel color intensity is conditioned on previously generated pixels). However, applying a similar architecture for even higher dimensional data, such as a speech wave (which might be tens of thousands of samples per second of audio) becomes unfeasible. The novelty element introduced in the proposed architecture is the dilated causal convolution, which can exponentially increase the receptive field over the generated signal, directly proportional to the number of such layers. For example, stacking several dilation layers, each time doubling the dilation measure would produce a receptive field of 1024 using only 10 layers. The authors mention that a receptive field size of 1024 could also be achieved with a single layer, $1 \times 1024$ convolution; however this would not be as efficient and would not capture nonlinearities in the data as well as in the first case.

The proposed WaveNet architecture also makes use of a custom decoding scheme to produce output values for the intensity of each audio segment. Since audio clips are usually stored as 16 bit integer intensity values, the output layer should model the output probabilities as a categorical distribution of 65,536 possible values. To reduce the possible output size, binning similar intensity values could be used. However linear quantization would not produce the best results for audio data and the authors instead use the $\mu$-law quantization.

For the experimental part, the authors adapt the WaveNet architecture (van den Oord et al., 2016) for various tasks, such as text-to-speech (in which they report state of the art results using the North American English and Mandarin Chinese TTS data sets), multi-speaker speech generation and speech recognition and audio modeling (where the results are fairly good).

However, despite all the advantages of the WaveNet architecture, the downside is that the model is still autoregressive, which means that generating a waveform for a test sequence has to occur sequentially. This might introduce undesired delays for long sequences. Therefore, instead of using it as the vocoder for our experiments, we opted out for another solution called HiFi-GAN (Kong et al., 2020), which is a computationally efficient generative adversarial network (GAN) based approach. Unlike a standard GAN architecture, the discriminator is composed of multiple small subdiscriminators, each attending and labeling a section of the input data as either 'real' or 'fake'. While high speed audio generation can be definitely achieved with a 'standard' version of the proposed system, the memory footprint is also an important metric to consider (especially when making use of the vocoder model for mobile applications). The authors mention that a much smaller version of the HiFi-GAN network (only 920,000 parameters) can still achieve good results and increase the relative decoding speed (compared to state-of-the-art vocoding systems) by a factor of approximately 13.44 on a CPU and 1.18 on a GPU.

## 2.2. Speech Synthesis for the Romanian Language

For the Romanian language, the work done by (Dumitrache and Rebedea, 2020) provides state-of-the-art results in terms of generated speech naturalness. Previous systems designed for Romanian speech generation are either HMM or Deep Neural Network (DNN) based and they make use of various mel-spectrogram decoding methods (Griffin-Lim algorithm, neural vocoders); however, auditing samples generated with them might prove that the voice is still unnatural, considering multiple criteria (voice tone or prosody, for example).

The system proposed by (Dumitrache and Rebedea, 2020) comprises a hierarchical architecture consisting of a neural speech-spectrogram encoder, a decoder and a neural vocoder. An open-source implementation of Tacotron 2 is modified to include Romanian special diacritics and the corresponding phonemes in the model characters list. For spectrogram to speech conversion, the WaveRNN network produced the most natural sounding audio. The final model achieves the best MOS value for Romanian speech generation (4.197).

(Săracu and Stan, 2021) showed that a model pretrained on Romanian Tacotron 2 can be finetuned on other speakers using as little data as one utterance of few seconds of recorded speech. The system was pretrained on SWARA 2.0, which is an extension of the multi-speaker SWARA dataset (Stan et al., 2017), without conditioning the speech generation on the speaker identity. The system was evaluated in three data availability setups: a random speech utterance, 3-4 speech utterances selected to contain all the Romanian graphemes, and 35-37 utterances (at most 5 minutes of recorded speech).

Another work tackling speech synthesis for Romanian is the one conducted by (Boroș et al., 2018). They describe a statistical parametric speech synthesis system (Speech Synthesis for Lightweight Applications - SSLA), which is especially designed for mobile applications, given the small memory footprint. Speech parameters such as phoneme duration, voice tone, or energy are modeled at the frame level with the help of a decision tree. The authors note that the spectral envelope is converted into audio using either an MLSA filter (Mel-Log Spectral Approximation - (Imai et al., 1983)) or a different method called STRAIGHT (Speech Transformation and Representation using Adaptive Interpolation of weiGHTed spectrum - (Kawahara et al., 1999)). Another design choice with respect to the mobile environment is to use MLSA, since it is less computationally expensive at the cost of providing inferior audio quality compared to STRAIGHT. To develop the model, the authors created a custom Romanian speech corpus comprising filtered Romanian Wikipedia texts and transcripts from a book. While the Wikipedia extracts are selected to maximize phonetic diversity and coverage, the book transcript has been chosen because of the persuasive prosodic features, which should be replicated by the speaker while reading the transcripts. The article does not provide a quantitative analysis on the performance of the speech synthesis component; however, the authors make their system available as an online service[1] for subjective human analysis.

# 3. Datasets for the Romanian Language

For any successful deep learning system, data availability and data quality are crucial. As we will outline in the following subsections, public, high-quality data for Romanian language speech are quite scarce. This motivates us to create our own dataset and make it publicly available.

## 3.1. Existing Datasets

The RSS corpus (Stan et al., 2011) represents the largest single speaker text-to-speech dataset available for the Romanian language, containing $4,000$ utterances recorded by a native Romanian female speaker in a professional setup. Texts have been gathered from a large variety of sources:

[1] https://slp.racai.ro/index.php/ssla/ (last accessed on January 5th, 2022)

newspaper articles, novels, short stories written by the Romanian novelist Ion Creangă, and a corpus of sentences used for intelligibility tests. After curation, 3,716 transcript-audio pairs were available for training and testing.

At the moment of conducting our research, to the best of our knowledge, good quality male voice recordings for developing text-to-speech systems for Romanian are available only in multi-speaker datasets, such as SWARA (Stan et al., 2017) and RSC (Cucu et al., 2014). There is also another male voice dataset as described by (Boroș et al., 2018), which has a total length of approximately 6 hours and 3 minutes; however it is not publicly available. SWARA contains audio recordings for 16 speakers, 8 female speakers and 8 male speakers based on a subset of transcripts from the RSS corpus that varies for each of the speakers. The number of recordings for a single male speaker is limited to at most 1,500 utterances, representing less than half the data available in RSS for the female voice. RSC is the largest multi-speaker dataset available for Romanian, containing recordings for 157 speakers, but lacks the audio quality of the RSS corpus as the recordings have been performed by speakers with their personal audio equipment. Thus the audio recordings in the RSC are considerably noisier than those available in the RSS.

### 3.2. Introducing a New Male Voice Dataset - RSS-Alex

Due to their large number of parameters, modern neural network-based systems for speech synthesis heavily rely on data availability to achieve good performance. Thus, the scarcity of single-speaker male voice recordings for Romanian represents a major impediment in fully exploiting the potential of some architectural choices. To overcome this limitation, we create a new single-speaker male voice dataset using the voice of the main author. We recorded 3,716 audio files based on all the texts available in the curated version of the RSS dataset. Thus, the created male dataset has the same size as the female dataset from RSS, being the largest (publicly available) single-speaker male speech dataset in Romania. The recording was performed at the sample level, following the segmentation from the RSS. Each text segment is represented by either a single sentence or a small fragment of multiple sentences. The following recording workflow was chosen to ensure the best recording quality:

1. The speaker reads out loud the target segment to become familiar with the textual content of a particular segment, to minimize speech errors and determine the required prosody based on the punctuation marks.

2. The speaker reads out loud the target segment a second time while the voice is recorded.

3. The resulting audio recording is empirically evaluated against word skipping and mispronunciations, and that the recording follows prosody, with emphasizing speech pauses imposed by punctuation marks.

4. If the conditions for quality from point 3 are not met for a particular recording, the process is repeated from step 2 until a satisfactory result is achieved.

For the speaker, performing the previously described routine might prove tedious for long periods of time. To maintain the same level of quality of recorded audio, the reading was performed in episodes of reading a maximum of 50-100 segments with breaks between episodes. We approximate that the recording process took 40 hours, not considering the breaks between readings. The resulting dataset contains 4.81 hours of raw recorded speech.

The speaker's voice was recorded using a Samson C01U USB studio condenser microphone. All recordings were made using 1 channel at a sample rate of 48 kHz and a bit depth of 16 bit. Due to the lack of better professional devices to record, the resulting audio files contain minor background white noise. This noise is fully removed in a post-processing step to ensure audio high-quality, comparable with the recordings in the RSS dataset. For denoising the audio files we use the *reduce_noise* function from the *noisereduce*[2] Python package with the following parametric configuration: *stationary*, *n_std_thresh_stationary*, and *n_fft* are set to *True*, 0.1 and 2048, respectively. We keep the rest of the function's parameters to their default values. Moreover, by employing an automated process long silences have been trimmed to a maximum threshold dimension to reduce the length of unnecessary large speech pauses, regardless of whether they

[2]https://github.com/timsainb/noisereduce (last accessed on January 5th, 2022)

appear inside the spoken segment or at the beginning/end of the recordings. Thus, we ensure speech pauses imposed by punctuation markers, such as commas, have a lower length variance and are easier to learn by a text-to-speech model. After trimming long silences, the resulting dataset contains 4.02 hours of speech.

# 4. FastSpeech TTS with Boolean Masking

Our experimental setup is based on the Transformer-TTS[3] repository. The architecture's implementation could be regarded as a FastSpeech model with the addition of the pitch variance adaptor as described in the FastSpeech 2 architecture. The model is structured as follows: an embedding layer, a non-autoregressive encoder and decoder, variance predictors for phoneme duration and pitch, and a final fully connected layer to project the hidden states returned by the decoder in mel-spectrogram dimensions. The encoder and decoder implementation follows the structural changes proposed in the FastSpeech article (Ren et al., 2019a), where the two fully connected layers in the Transformer architecture are replaced with two 1D convolutional layers to better attend to nearby context. Duration and pitch predictors share the same architectural structure as described in FastSpeech with the mention that durations are not predicted on a logarithmic scale, but as real values using a ReLU activation on the last dense layer. The duration predictor plays a key role in mel-spectrogram generation by up-sampling the encodings of the phonemes to their corresponding number of mel-spectrogram dimensions.

In contrast to autoregressive decoders such as Tacotron 2 or Transformer-TTS, the non-autoregressive transformer-based decoder requires ground-truth phoneme durations at training time. FastSpeech uses a teacher-student paradigm by employing the autoregressive Transformer-TTS architecture to predict the alignment between phonemes (including punctuation) and the number of corresponding mel-spectrograms. The extracted durations are used as target values to train the length regulator and, at the same time, as hard-alignments for encodings' upsampling to match the mel-spectrogram dimension. FastSpeech's authors state that speech silences can be enlarged by adding space characters to texts (Ren et al.,

[3]https://github.com/as-ideas/TransformerTTS (last accessed on December 20th, 2021)

2019a). We argue that the main use of space characters is to represent graphical boundaries for words, facilitating the reading process, with no meaningful impact on the overall prosody. Spoken speech often flows uninterrupted, with no noticeable pauses between words to be detected empirically by listeners or visible on the waveform of a voice recording. We would like to shift the silence controllability from space character addition to the usage of proper punctuation markers responsible for this goal. Unfortunately, in the case of a comma followed by a space character, for which there exists silence in audio, we cannot directly constrain the aligner model (i.e., autoregressive Transformer-TTS model) to correlate the speech break with the comma character. In fact, the silence controllability presented in FastSpeech proves that it is unlikely for the model trained by gradient descent to arrive at such decisions on its own.

To increase phoneme alignment accuracy and simplify the overall training pipeline, the autoregressive teacher model is removed and replaced by the Montreal Forced Aligner (McAuliffe et al., 2017). The extracted durations will be used in the duration predictor layer as the ground-truth number of mel-spectrogram dimensions corresponding to each phoneme. To exploit the good results of FastSpeech 2, we integrate MFA in our setup. The result of the MFA alignment is represented by TextGrid files containing audio boundaries as time intervals for words and phonemes. Because the TTS model generates mel-spectrograms instead of raw waveform, the time intervals for phonemes have to be translated in the corresponding number of mel-spectrogram dimensions. When both the sample rate and hop-length are known for waveform to mel-spectrum space transformation, the conversion from time intervals to the number of mel-spectrograms can be trivially computed as in Equation 1.

$$\begin{aligned} frame\_rate &= sample\_rate \div hop\_length \\ mel\_dims &= time\_interval * frame\_rate \end{aligned} \tag{1}$$

One of the data preprocessing steps undergone by MFA consists of punctuation removal. The silences in speech, graphically represented in written texts as commas or full stop markers, are attributed to a silence token. Moreover, question marks represent another graphic indication that vastly impacts the overall intonation of speech. We would like our model to differentiate between such markers, as they imply distinct prosody for the generated speech. To achieve this goal, we map commas (‘,’) and full stop

('.') markers with the corresponding speech silence durations, or we artificially introduce durations of 1 to ensure their presence in the decoding step, as a duration of 0 would represent the corresponding phoneme encoding will not be passed to decoder. These additional durations will create an offset between the generated mel-spectrogam and the target mel-spectrogram extracted from ground-truth audio. To restore the alignment we create a Boolean mask with ones and zeros specifying for which phonemes the mel-spectrogram representations from the decoder should be selected.

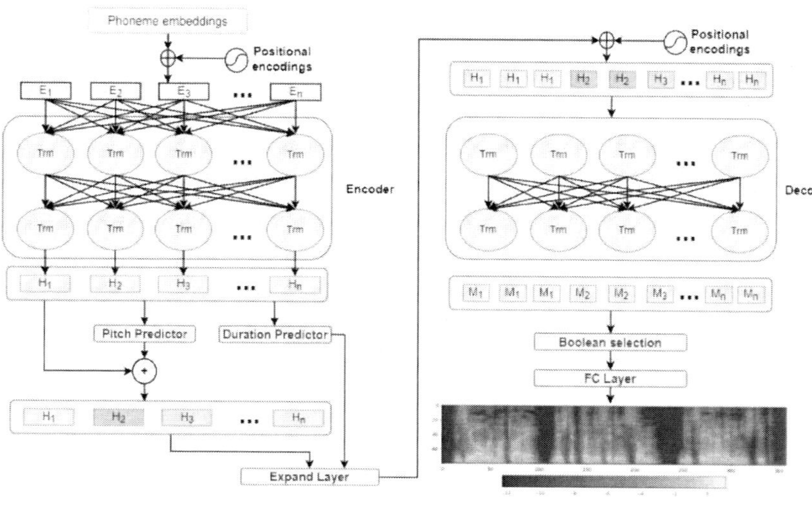


Figure 1. Non-autoregressive transformer-based speech synthesis model with Boolean masking for improved prosody.

During training, we expand the mask using the ground-truth durations, as is the case with phoneme representations to match their corresponding number of mel-spectogram dimensions. Only the decoder outputs corresponding to values of one from the Boolean mask are selected to ensure the artificially added durations do not contribute to the final generated mel-spectrogram and that the alignment is kept. The masking and selective technique is well suited for any graphical characters that contribute to the prosody of the generated audio, but do not have a correspondence in sound on their own. We argue that examples of such characters are spaces between words and suprasegmentals. Suprasegmentals play a decisive role in attaining a good, natural prosody, but they work only in association with vowels or consonants, influencing the tone, stress or word juncture of other phonemes. By attributing a duration of one, we ensure their presence in the decoder, enabling the attention mechanism to leverage their influence on the mel-spectrogram representations. As they do not correspond to sounds when taken independently, we remove their representations from the decoder output, leaving only those encodings that should be translated into mel-spectrogram dimensions and later in sound by the vocoder. We drew inspiration from BERT (Devlin et al., 2019) for Named Entity Recognition task, which employs Boolean masking selection to make class predictions only over the encoder representations of the first sub-token resulting from the WordPiece (Wu et al., 2016) segmentation of the input sequence.

The non-autoregressive TTS model being fully parallelizable, we opted to further speed-up the training process by utilizing TPUs (Jouppi et al., 2017). We modified the original implementation[4] to utilize only tensor operations supported on TPU hardware. The layer used for expanding the phoneme representations returned by the encoder to mel-spectrogram dimensions has been replaced with a gather operation. Previously, the layer received the array of durations $d = [d_1, d_2, ..., d_n]$, where $d_i$ represents the number of times phoneme encoding $i$ should be repeated to match its corresponding number of mel-spectrogam dimensions. The input of this layer has been replaced with an array $i_{gather} = [i_1, i_1, i_1, i_2, i_2, ..., i_n]$, where $i_i$ represents the phoneme's index in the input phoneme sequence, and the number of times the $i^{th}$ index appears in the array is given by $d_i$. Furthermore, we still maintain the duration array $d$ as input to the model as it is used to compute the duration loss between the predicted and ground-truth durations.

A high-level overview of the non-autoregressive architecture with masking over the decoder outputs is represented in Figure 1. The implementation, with the exception of the Boolean masking layer and pitch variance predictor, follows the FastSpeech design.

[4]https://github.com/as-ideas/TransformerTTS (last accessed on December 23rd, 2021)

## 5. Experiments

We aim to experiment with two configurations for both the largest single-speaker datasets available for Romanian, RSS (female voice) and the newly created male voice dataset. In the first configuration we employ the autoregressive Transformer-TTS to extract the durations which will be later used as ground-truth phoneme and mel-spectrogram alignments for the customized FastSpeech model. In the second experiment, we extract the target durations with the MFA tool[5] and perform the alignment steps described in *Section 4*.

As it has been proven to positively impact the training and results of neural speech synthesis models (Zhang et al., 2019), we use phonemes as input to the embedding layer. To obtain the phonetic transcriptions from texts, we used eSpeak-NG[6], an open-source text-to-speech software with support for more than 100 languages, including Romanian. As a lightweight solution with low latency for text-to-phoneme transliteration, eSpeak-NG can be easily integrated in the TTS system pipeline as a preprocessing step. For the first experiment, we segment the phonetic transcription at the character level following the implementation already existing in the Transformer-TTS repository. For the second experiment, we opt to keep the phonetic notation as returned by eSpeak-NG for a subset of frequent Romanian phonemes (*ts*, *dʒ*, *tʃ*, *ʲʲ*) to mitigate the responsibility of the attention mechanism to infer correct mel-spectrogram features, other multicharacter phonetic notations being split into their constituent characters as in the first experiment. This approach of splitting multicharacter phonemes into their components, not only leads to a smaller phonetic vocabulary, but also contributes to better alignments for phonemes with fewer occurrences, modelling rarer sounds through transition probabilities being preferred by the MFA tool[7]. We also include the suprasegmentals returned by eSpeak-NG as they play a critical role in word spelling and overall prosody.

For the first experiment, the autoregressive teacher model is trained to infer durations for each input character, including spaces and prosody-

[5]https://montreal-forced-aligner.readthedocs.io/en/latest/ (last accessed on December 21st, 2021)

[6]https://github.com/espeak-ng/espeak-ng (last accessed on December 21st, 2021)

[7]https://montreal-forced-aligner.readthedocs.io/en/latest/user_guide/formats/dictionary.html#multilingual-ipa (last accessed on December 23rd, 2021)

**Table 1. Training and optimizer hyperparameters configuration for the two experiments**

| Hyperparameters | Experiment 1 | Experiment 2 |
|---|---|---|
| Start learning rate | 1e-4 | 1e-4 |
| End learning rate | 5e-5 | 1e-5 |
| Decay steps | 150k | 100k |
| Training steps | 200k | 120k |
| Warmup proportion | 2e-2 | 2e-2 |
| Weight decay | 1e-3 | 1e-3 |

related markers such as suprasegmentals. For the second experiment, such additional characters are removed along with the punctuation before MFA training. To ensure their presence in both the encoder and decoder, we introduce them in the duration array with a value of 1 and mask their presence in the final fully connected layer by setting the corresponding mask value to 0. We leave the attention mechanism to leverage their contribution to other phonemes, as the suprasegmental characters taken independently do not have a corresponding sound to be included in the generated mel-spectrogram.

We use the Adam optimizer (Kingma and Ba, 2015) with a learning rate of 1e-4, a weight decay of 1e-3, a warmup proportion of 0.2 of the total number of training steps and polynomial decay of the learning rate. The full training hyperparameters and optimizer configurations for each experiment are described in Table 1.

Moreover, we keep the same model's hyperparameters as described in Appendix A of the FastSpeech paper (Ren et al., 2019a). We use a global batch size of 128, batches of 16 examples being equally distributed on each of the 8 cores of a TPU v2. TPU training was performed inside Google Colab sessions.

Because the TTS architecture of FastSpeech is based on non-autoregressive transformer blocks, we opted to run our experiments on TPUs for improved training time. Training the model for 200k steps takes approximately 16.7 hours on TPU as opposed to 67.7 hours on GPU (Tesla T4 GPU available on Google Colab), which accounts for a speed-up of 4x. As a side remark, in the MFA-masking setup we are able to synthesize intelligible and reasonably clean speech after only 20k training iterations for both (male and female) voices, as opposed to the model using the durations extracted by the neural aligner, for which the speech generated after 30k steps still suffers from slight audio artifacts.

## 6. Results

Using all the models described in the previous section, we generated audio samples for texts belonging to Romanian literature texts and news to assess the performance of these models. We aimed to create a distinct test set that exhibits high variability in terms of audio lengths, pronunciation complexity and prosodic elements. In total, we gathered 30 texts belonging to three popular Romanian novels published in the 19th and 20th centuries (*Moara cu noroc* by Ioan Slavici, *Iona* by Marin Sorescu, and *Enigma Otiliei* by George Clinescu) and to a popular online news website. The first two novels were selected because they were also used for the evaluation phase in the work done by (Dumitrache and Rebedea, 2020). To evaluate the robustness of our TTS architecture to longer and shorter sequences alike, the evaluation texts range from a maximum of 54 words to a minimum of only 8, with an average of 20.5 words per example. Because speech prosody represented one of our target goals, our selection of texts incorporates multiple occurrences of commas, 1.8 on average and a maximum of 6. Moreover, to ensure that our system performs well on texts containing more than one phrase or sentence, we added a sequence of 3 short sentences in the evaluation set, with each sentence ending in full stop.

The resulting audio recordings with synthesized speech by the proposed models have been subject to human evaluation. We asked 14 native Romanian speakers to rate each audio clip with a score from 1 to 5, based on the naturalness of the audio (1 - very unnatural to 5 - very natural). The computed MOS values for the 4 different models (male or female, neural or MFA aligner) are available in Table 3. All evaluators annotated all 30 generated speech samples for each of the 4 models presented in the table, resulting in a total of 120 MOS ratings per evaluator. Table 2 contains a subset of the texts used for evaluation along with their English translation.

Although we also trained a multi-speaker version of our modified Transformer-TTS architecture, we did not include these results in the evaluation phase, as the resulting multi-speaker models have been found to ig-

**Table 2. Six out of the 30 texts used for MOS and CMOS qualitative evaluation**

| Romanian text | English translated text |
|---|---|
| Aceti muni au fost, din cele mai vechi timpuri, loc de retragere i de adpost al populaiei pe timpul invaziilor strine. | These mountains have been, since the ancient times, a place of retreat and shelter for the population during the foreign invasions. |
| Nemaiateptnd rspunsul, Stnic ncepu s caute prin dulap, trntind uile. | Without waiting for the answer, Stnic began to search the closet, slamming the doors. |
| Adevrul este c Stnic avea sim familial i c familia lui mprtea acest sentiment. | The truth is that Stnic had a family sense and that his family shared this feeling. |
| M-am gndit bine, lucrul sta l-a face cu drag inim. | I thought it through, I would do this thing with an open heart. |
| nainte de invenia i adoptarea tiparului, toate crile erau copiate de mn, de aceea ele erau scumpe i rare. | Before the invention and the adoption of the printer, all the books were copied by hand, that's why they were expensive and rare. |
| Astzi am fost mputernicit de ctre Comitetul Executiv s negociez i s semnez contractul cu urmtorul selecioner al echipei naionale. | Today I have been authorized by the Executive Committee to negotiate and sign the contract with the next coach of the national team. |

nore prosody. This behaviour is most likely generated by the lack of punctuation in the SWARA dataset used for training the multi-speaker models. Because the SWARA contains only a subset of transcript files from the RSS corpus, we opted to pair SWARA audio files with the transcripts from RSS which contain punctuation markers such as full stop, comma and question mark. We have conducted the experiments using the first experimental setup (i.e., employing the neural aligner). The synthesized speech suffers from audio artifacts, the noise being prevalent at the end of generated speech, in the case of longer audio sequences. We hypothesize that the poor audio quality is caused by the transcript subset used in SWARA,

**Table 3. MOS values obtained for each of the four models. Evaluation was conducted by assigning a score between 1 and 5 (with an increment of 1) for each audio clip and was performed by 14 native Romanian speakers**

| Model Implementation | MOS value |
|---|---|
| Female voice + aligner | 3.840 |
| Female voice + MFA | 4.133 |
| Male voice + aligner | 3.919 |
| Male voice + MFA | 4.319 |

which contains only lines with short texts, and the insufficient number of examples per speaker. Although the RSS contains a few punctuation markers, the hyphen, which is a frequently used character in Romanian texts, is removed and the words are linked together. Sometimes, the resulting construction represents the correct form of a distinct word in the Romanian vocabulary (e.g., *la - coward*, compared to *l-a - I would (verb) it/him*). This might slightly affect the prosody learned by the text-to-speech model. In future work we would like to solve the missing punctuation issue by employing punctuation restoration techniques (Păiş and Tufiş, 2021).

From the results presented in Table 3, we can observe that the models using MFA aligner to predict phoneme durations perform significantly better than their neural aligner counterparts. This confirms our intuition that MFA provides a better alignment and that our proposed model with Boolean masking improves prosody and, thus, the overall quality of the generated speech. Training a neural aligner module solely based on scarce datasets, such as those available for Romanian language speech, was not expected to perform better than MFA. Additionally, the generated male voice outperforms the female equivalent. This was indeed expected since while recording the male voice dataset, additional care was taken with respect to prosodic elements in the speech.

To better understand the performance of the two male voice models, we also evaluated them in comparison, reporting the comparative mean opinion score (CMOS) values. The scores obtained by the two male voice models are presented in Table 4.

**Table 4. CMOS values for each of the two male voice models. Evaluation was conducted by assigning an integer score between -2 and 2 (with an increment of 1) for each audio clip and was performed by 15 native Romanian speakers**

| Model Implementation 1 | Model Implementation 2 | CMOS value |
|---|---|---|
| Male voice + aligner | Male voice + MFA | 0.4606 |

According to the voting options, the CMOS value is restricted to be between -2 and 2, the first meaning that the first model and generated speech clearly outperform the second one and the latter having the opposite interpretation. From the results in Table 4 we observe that the evaluators considered that the second implementation (Male voice + MFA) sounds more natural overall, compared to the first implementation. These results are in par with those exposed by the MOS analysis, and the difference of almost half of the CMOS point shows that the proposed RSS-Alex dataset and neural model with MFA and Boolean masking produces a significantly better quality audio than using the standard neural aligner.

We do not report loss value evolution during training or validation, as we have found (similar to other text-to-speech related works, such as Dumitrache and Rebedea, 2020) that decreasing loss does not necessarily produce better audio overall. Particularly, we noticed that training the model for longer (without masking) would decrease both training and validation loss values, however it would also introduce background noise and other artifacts in the generated audio.

Compared to previous Tacotron 2 based approaches, the proposed model is better in terms of preventing audio repetitions. The scores obtained by the proposed model (using MFA) for female voice are in par with the ones reported by (Dumitrache and Rebedea, 2020) for the Tacotron 2 - WaveRNN approach (4.197), even though we did not conduct a direct evaluation with audio samples generated by the model described in their work. And in turn, our male voice model (using MFA) outperforms both, as shown in the MOS analysis in 3.

Lastly, a selection of the audios used for evaluation is publicly available online[8].

## Conclusion

Text-to-speech systems are continuously improving, and the latest architectures achieve more natural speech while, at the same time, lowering the training and inference times. For low-resource languages, such as Romanian, data scarcity might prove to be a bottleneck for synthesizing natural, high-quality speech with modern, data-hungry systems. In this chapter, we attempted to alleviate the data availability limitation for Romanian by releasing a new single-speaker male-voiced dataset. We hope that our contribution will lay the grounds for better future TTS system evaluations and improvements for the Romanian language.

We conducted two experiments employing a customized version of the FastSpeech model and evaluated the results on the newly created male speaker dataset and RSS female speaker dataset in a single-speaker setup. With the second configuration of our model, using the durations extracted by MFA and the mel-spectrogram masking technique, we achieved natural, punctuation sensitive speech from texts with a MOS of 4.319 and 4.133 for male and female datasets, respectively. Moreover, we modified the system's implementation to be compliant with the set of operations supported by TPU. By training our model on TPU we obtained a 4x training time speed-up over the GPU runs, making the experimentation under different configurations more accessible.

By employing a Boolean selection layer after the decoder, we offer a solution for including additional characters relevant for prosody but without a specific mel-spectrogram counterpart. Using the masking procedure we enable character addition for phonetic stress which impacts prosody and word spelling but should not have a mel-spectrogram representation on their own. By this means, we ensure that both the encoder and the decoder are attending each character from the input text, leveraging their importance in the resulting mel-spectrogram.

[8] https://ro-tts-eval.net/index-presentation.php (last accessed on December 20th, 2021)

## Future Work

In terms of future work, we intend to evaluate our model in a multi-speaker setup by adding a variance predictor for speaker identity following the approach described in FastSpeech 2. Moreover, we plan to study and replace the quadratic attention from the transformer-based encoder and decoder with linear time complexity attention (Choromanski et al., 2021; Wang et al., 2020) to further speed-up training and inference.

## Acknowledgments

This research was funded by the Romanian Ministry of European Investments and Projects through the Competitiveness Operational Program (POC) project "HOLOTRAIN" (grant no. 29/221, SMIS code: 129077).

## References

Abdul-Kader, S. A. and Woods, J. C. (2015). Survey on chatbot design techniques in speech conversation systems. *International Journal of Advanced Computer Science and Applications*, 6(7).

Boroș, T., Dumitrescu, Ș. D., and Păiș, V. (2018). Tools and resources for romanian text-to-speech and speech-to-text applications. In *Proceedings of the International Conference on Human-Computer Interaction (RoCHI)*, pages 46–53.

Choromanski, K. M., Likhosherstov, V., Dohan, D., Song, X., Gane, A., Sarlos, T., Hawkins, P., Davis, J. Q., Mohiuddin, A., Kaiser, L., Belanger, D. B., Colwell, L. J., and Weller, A. (2021). Rethinking attention with performers. In *International Conference on Learning Representations*.

Chung, J., Gulcehre, C., Cho, K., and Bengio, Y. (2014). Empirical evaluation of gated recurrent neural networks on sequence modeling. In *NIPS 2014 Workshop on Deep Learning*.

Cucu, H., Buzo, A., Petrică, L., Burileanu, D., and Burileanu, C. (2014). Recent improvements of the speed romanian lvcsr system. In *2014*

*10th International Conference on Communications (COMM)*, pages 1–4. IEEE.

Devlin, J., Chang, M.-W., Lee, K., and Toutanova, K. (2019). Bert: Pre-training of deep bidirectional transformers for language understanding. In *Proceedings of the 2019 Conference of the North American Chapter of the Association for Computational Linguistics: Human Language Technologies, Volume 1 (Long and Short Papers)*, pages 4171–4186. Association for Computational Linguistics.

Dumitrache, M. and Rebedea, T. (2020). Exploring end-to-end neural text-to-speech synthesis for romanian. In *15th edition of The International Conference on Linguistic Resources and Tools for Natural Language Processing ConsILR-2020*, page 93.

Griffin, D. and Lim, J. (1984). Signal estimation from modified short-time fourier transform. *IEEE Transactions on acoustics, speech, and signal processing*, 32(2):236–243.

Hunt, A. J. and Black, A. W. (1996). Unit selection in a concatenative speech synthesis system using a large speech database. In *1996 IEEE International Conference on Acoustics, Speech, and Signal Processing Conference Proceedings*, volume 1, pages 373–376. IEEE.

Imai, S., Sumita, K., and Furuichi, C. (1983). Mel log spectrum approximation (mlsa) filter for speech synthesis. *Electronics and Communications in Japan (Part I: Communications)*, 66(2):10–18.

Jouppi, N. P., Young, C., Patil, N., Patterson, D., Agrawal, G., Bajwa, R., Bates, S., Bhatia, S., Boden, N., Borchers, A., et al. (2017). In-datacenter performance analysis of a tensor processing unit. In *Proceedings of the 44th annual international symposium on computer architecture*, pages 1–12.

Kawahara, H., Masuda-Katsuse, I., and De Cheveigne, A. (1999). Restructuring speech representations using a pitch-adaptive time–frequency smoothing and an instantaneous-frequency-based f0 extraction: Possible role of a repetitive structure in sounds. *Speech communication*, 27(3-4):187–207.

Kharitonov, E., Lee, A., Polyak, A., Adi, Y., Copet, J., Lakhotia, K., Nguyen, T.-A., Rivire, M., Mohamed, A., Dupoux, E., and Hsu, W.-N. (2021). Text-free prosody-aware generative spoken language modeling.

Kingma, D. P. and Ba, J. (2015). Adam: A method for stochastic optimization. In *ICLR (Poster)*.

Kinnunen, T., Sahidullah, M., Delgado, H., Todisco, M., Evans, N. W. D., Yamagishi, J., and Lee, K. (2017). The asvspoof 2017 challenge: Assessing the limits of replay spoofing attack detection. In *INTERSPEECH*, pages 2–6. ISCA.

Kong, J., Kim, J., and Bae, J. (2020). Hifi-gan: Generative adversarial networks for efficient and high fidelity speech synthesis. In *NeurIPS*.

Lakhotia, K., Kharitonov, E., Hsu, W.-N., Adi, Y., Polyak, A., Bolte, B., Nguyen, T.-A., Copet, J., Baevski, A., Mohamed, A., et al. (2021). Generative spoken language modeling from raw audio.

Laptev, A., Korostik, R., Svischev, A., Andrusenko, A., Medennikov, I., and Rybin, S. (2020). You do not need more data: Improving end-to-end speech recognition by text-to-speech data augmentation. In *2020 13th International Congress on Image and Signal Processing, BioMedical Engineering and Informatics (CISP-BMEI)*, pages 439–444. IEEE.

Li, N., Liu, S., Liu, Y., Zhao, S., and Liu, M. (2019). Neural speech synthesis with transformer network. In *Proceedings of the AAAI Conference on Artificial Intelligence*, volume 33, pages 6706–6713.

McAuliffe, M., Socolof, M., Mihuc, S., Wagner, M., and Sonderegger, M. (2017). Montreal forced aligner: Trainable text-speech alignment using kaldi. In *Interspeech*, volume 2017, pages 498–502.

Oord, A. v. d., Kalchbrenner, N., and Kavukcuoglu, K. (2016). Pixel recurrent neural networks. In *International Conference on Machine Learning*, pages 1747–1756. PMLR.

Păiş, V. and Tufiş, D. (2021). Capitalization and punctuation restoration: a survey. *Artificial Intelligence Review*, pages 1–42.

Qian, Y., Soong, F., Chen, Y., and Chu, M. (2006). An hmm-based mandarin chinese text-to-speech system. In *International Symposium on Chinese Spoken Language Processing*, pages 223–232. Springer.

Reimao, R. and Tzerpos, V. (2019). For: A dataset for synthetic speech detection. In *2019 International Conference on Speech Technology and Human-Computer Dialogue (SpeD)*, pages 1–10. IEEE.

Ren, Y., Hu, C., Tan, X., Qin, T., Zhao, S., Zhao, Z., and Liu, T. (2021). Fastspeech 2: Fast and high-quality end-to-end text to speech. In *ICLR*. OpenReview.net.

Ren, Y., Ruan, Y., Tan, X., Qin, T., Zhao, S., Zhao, Z., and Liu, T. (2019a). Fastspeech: Fast, robust and controllable text to speech. In *NeurIPS*, pages 3165–3174.

Ren, Y., Tan, X., Qin, T., Zhao, S., Zhao, Z., and Liu, T.-Y. (2019b). Almost unsupervised text to speech and automatic speech recognition. In *International Conference on Machine Learning*, pages 5410–5419. PMLR.

Săracu, G. and Stan, A. (2021). An analysis of the data efficiency in tacotron2 speech synthesis system. In *2021 International Conference on Speech Technology and Human-Computer Dialogue (SpeD)*, pages 172–176. IEEE.

Shen, J., Pang, R., Weiss, R. J., Schuster, M., Jaitly, N., Yang, Z., Chen, Z., Zhang, Y., Wang, Y., Skerrv-Ryan, R., et al. (2018). Natural tts synthesis by conditioning wavenet on mel spectrogram predictions. In *2018 IEEE International Conference on Acoustics, Speech and Signal Processing (ICASSP)*, pages 4779–4783. IEEE.

Stan, A., Dinescu, F., Ţiple, C., Meza, Ş., Orza, B., Chirilă, M., and Giurgiu, M. (2017). The swara speech corpus: A large parallel romanian read speech dataset. In *2017 International Conference on Speech Technology and Human-Computer Dialogue (SpeD)*, pages 1–6. IEEE.

Stan, A., Yamagishi, J., King, S., and Aylett, M. (2011). The romanian speech synthesis (rss) corpus: Building a high quality hmm-based speech synthesis system using a high sampling rate. *Speech Communication*, 53(3):442–450.

Tjandra, A., Sakti, S., and Nakamura, S. (2020). Machine speech chain. *IEEE/ACM Transactions on Audio, Speech, and Language Processing*, 28:976–989.

van den Oord, A., Dieleman, S., Zen, H., Simonyan, K., Vinyals, O., Graves, A., Kalchbrenner, N., Senior, A. W., and Kavukcuoglu, K. (2016). WaveNet: A generative model for raw audio. In *SSW*, page 125. ISCA.

Vaswani, A., Shazeer, N., Parmar, N., Uszkoreit, J., Jones, L., Gomez, A. N., Kaiser, Ł., and Polosukhin, I. (2017). Attention is all you need. In *Advances in neural information processing systems*, pages 5998–6008.

Wang, S., Li, B. Z., Khabsa, M., Fang, H., and Ma, H. (2020). Linformer: Self-attention with linear complexity.

Wang, Y., Skerry-Ryan, R. J., Stanton, D., Wu, Y., Weiss, R. J., Jaitly, N., Yang, Z., Xiao, Y., Chen, Z., Bengio, S., Le, Q. V., Agiomyrgiannakis, Y., Clark, R., and Saurous, R. A. (2017). Tacotron: Towards end-to-end speech synthesis. In *INTERSPEECH*, pages 4006–4010. ISCA.

Wu, Y., Schuster, M., Chen, Z., Le, Q. V., Norouzi, M., Macherey, W., Krikun, M., Cao, Y., Gao, Q., Macherey, K., et al. (2016). Google's neural machine translation system: Bridging the gap between human and machine translation.

Yamagishi, J., Nose, T., Zen, H., Ling, Z.-H., Toda, T., Tokuda, K., King, S., and Renals, S. (2009). Robust speaker-adaptive hmm-based text-to-speech synthesis. *IEEE Transactions on Audio, Speech, and Language Processing*, 17(6):1208–1230.

Zhang, Y., Weiss, R. J., Zen, H., Wu, Y., Chen, Z., Skerry-Ryan, R., Jia, Y., Rosenberg, A., and Ramabhadran, B. (2019). Learning to speak fluently in a foreign language: Multilingual speech synthesis and cross-language voice cloning.

# About the Editor

**Vasile Păiş** received his BS from the Politehnica University of Bucharest, the Faculty of Automatic Control and Computers, then his PhD in computer science from the School of Advanced Studies of the Romanian Academy. He is currently a scientific researcher in the field of artificial intelligence, working at the Research Institute for Artificial Intelligence "Mihai Drăgănescu" of the Romanian Academy. He has been involved in many national and international research projects. His scientific papers were published in international journals and conference proceedings. His research interests include natural language understanding, language technology platforms and advanced neural network architectures.

Email: vasile@racai.ro

# About the Contributors

**Dan Tufiş** received his BS and PhD from the University Politehnica of Bucharest, the Faculty of Automatic Control and Computers. He is currently a full member of the Romanian Academy and the Director of the Research Institute for Artificial Intelligence "Mihai Drăgănescu" of the Romanian Academy, since 2003. He received various distinctions and prizes for his research throughout his career and is currently Doctor Honoris Causa of the University Agora of Oradea and Honorary professor of the University "A.I. Cuza" of Iaşi. He is a member of the Editorial Boards of several international journals. His research interests include natural language processing, machine translation, knowledge representation, semantic web.

**Mihai Dascalu** is a full professor at UPB, responsible for the courses of Object Oriented Programming, Semantic Web Applications, and Data Mining and Data Warehousing. He was head of class in 2009 (e.g., GPA 10/10; ranked 1st across specialization and university) at University Politehnica of Bucharest and holds a double PhD with the highest distinctions in Computer Science and Educational Sciences, with his thesis published as book in Springer, Studies in Computational Intelligence. He has extensive experience in national and international research projects with more than 200 published papers, including 30+ articles at top-tier conferences (AAAI, CogSci, AIED, ITS, CSCL), 80+ papers indexed ISI at renowned international conferences (ICALT, EC-TEL, ICWL, ISPDC, AIMSA), and 10 Q1 journal papers.

**Traian Rebedea** is Associate Professor at University Politehnica of Bucharest, with a PhD thesis defended in 2013 on using natural language processing techniques for analyzing CSCL conversations to offer detailed feedback to learners engaged in multi-party discussions. In the last couple of years, Dr. Traian Rebedea was involved in several applied projects involving information extraction, NLP and machine learning with applications in opinion mining, information extraction from public data about companies and persons, conversational agents and question-answering systems. Published over 50 papers in top venues in NLP and CSCL, coordinated two research projects in collaboration with companies, as well as an innovation grant for startups offered by the European Commission through the Open Data Incubator.

**Costin-Gabriel Chiru** is an Associate Professor at University Politehnica of Bucharest. His PhD Thesis, defended in 2011, was focused on using Natural Language Processing for the analysis of the discourse structure in online conversations. Over time, he participated in several national and international research projects and his research was disseminated through papers published in national and international conference proceedings and journals, including top-tier conferences (CSCL, ITS, ICNIP, ICTAI,) and journals (Computers in Human Behavior, Creativity Research Journal). Currently, Costin is interested in projects involving Machine Learning, Natural Language Processing and Time Series Analysis.

**Verginica Barbu Mititelu** received her BA in philology, her MA in Theoretical Linguistics and her PhD (Summa cum laude) in linguistics from the University of Bucharest. Since 2003 she has been affiliated with the Romanian Academy Research Institute for Artificial Intelligence in Bucharest, where she has been involved in many projects, national and international, in which language resources, tools for language processing or natural language-based applications were created. In the last few years, she has been focusing on the Linked Open Data paradigm for language resources development, publication and reuse.

**Radu Ion** joined the Romanian Academy Research Institute for Artificial Intelligence (RACAI) in 2001. He received his BSc in software engineering from Politehnica University of Bucharest in 2001, MSc in theoretical linguistics from University of Bucharest in 2003 and PhD in computer science from Romanian Academy in 2007. He is currently a senior research fellow at RACAI and his main research interests revolve around deep neural networks and deep learning for natural languages. Dr. Ion has published more than 100 papers in peer-reviewed journals and conferences and he is frequently invited to serve in program committees of many important conferences of the NLP field. Dr. Ion is currently a member of the editorial board of the Proceedings of the Romanian Academy Series A, the Information Science section.

**Maria Carp (Mitrofan)** received her PhD degree in computer science from the School of Advanced Studies of the Romanian Academy, in 2020. She is currently a researcher at the Research Institute for Artificial Intelligence "Mihai Drăgănescu" of the Romanian Academy. Her research interests include natural language processing, machine learning and neural nets.

**Andrei-Marius Avram** received a BS degree in computer engineering from Military Technical Academy of Bucharest "Ferdinand I" and an MS degree in Artificial Intelligence from University Politehnica of Bucharest. He is currently a research assistant at the Research Institute for Artificial Intelligence "Mihai Drăgănescu", Romanian Academy. His research interests include machine learning, natural language processing, information retrieval and speech recognition.

**Dan Ungureanu** is a second year PhD student at University Politehnica of Bucharest studying under Professor Mihai Dascalu. His general interests are in the area of speech processing and natural language processing. His current research is focused on speech recognition systems and their applications. Before that, he finished his Bachelor's Degree in Computer Science and Engineering and Master's Degree in Parallel and Distributed Computer Systems at UPB. His Master's thesis topic was "Natural Language Interactions with Internet-of-Things Devices" and involved development of Automatic Speech Recognition and Speech Synthesis systems.

**George-Alexandru Vlad** is a machine learning engineer with hands-on experience in deep learning architectures for natural language processing. In 2021 he completed his master's degree studies in artificial intelligence at the University Politehnica of Bucharest on automated systems for propaganda and hate speech detection from multimodal sources. He participated in several AI challenges developing highly competitive solutions. Winner of the IBM's Great Minds Internship 2020, he joined IBM's research laboratory in Zurich for 5 months as part of the AI department working with top leading scientists and engineers on named entity recognition tasks.

**Gabriel Bercaru** is a PhD student and machine learning engineer with a strong interest towards deep learning architectures. His main focus is on the field of natural language processing and understanding, specifically on developing conversational agents. He finished his Master's studies in artificial intelligence at University Politehnica of Bucharest in 2021, with his dissertation on reinforcement learning applications for task-oriented dialogue. He started his PhD in natural language processing at University Politehnica of Bucharest in 2021; his research is targeted towards modeling the multimodal interaction between a user and a chatbot in a 3D simulated environment. Previously, he worked as a software development engineer at AWS.

# Index

## F



## G



## H



## I



## K



## L



## M



## N

## O



## P



## Q



## R

## S



## T



## U



## V



## W



## X